Building Modern Data Applications Using Databricks Lakehouse

Develop, optimize, and monitor data pipelines on Databricks

Will Girten

Building Modern Data Applications Using Databricks Lakehouse

Group Product Manager: Apeksha Shetty

Publishing Product Managers: Arindam Majumder and Nilesh Kowadkar

Book Project Manager: Shambhavi Mishra

Senior Content Development Editor: Shreya Moharir

Technical Editor: Seemanjay Ameriya

Copy Editor: Safis Editing

Proofreader: Shreya Moharir

Indexer: Manju Arasan

Production Designer: Prashant Ghare

Senior DevRel Marketing Coordinator: Nivedita Singh

First published: October 2024

Production reference: 1181024

Published by Packt Publishing Ltd.
Grosvenor House
11 St Paul's Square
Birmingham
B3 1RB, UK

ISBN 978-1-80107-323-3

www.packtpub.com

To my beautiful and caring wife, Ashley, and our smiley son, Silvio Apollo, thank you for your unwavering support and encouragement.

– Will Girten

Contributors

About the author

Will Girten is a lead specialist solutions architect who joined Databricks in early 2019. With over a decade of experience in data and AI, Will has worked in various business verticals, from healthcare to government and financial services. Will's primary focus has been helping enterprises implement data warehousing strategies for the lakehouse and performance-tuning BI dashboards, reports, and queries. Will is a certified Databricks Data Engineering Professional and Databricks Machine Learning Professional. He holds a Bachelor of Science in computer engineering from the University of Delaware.

I want to give a special thank you to one of my greatest supporters, mentors, and friends, YongSheng Huang.

About the reviewer

Oleksandra Bovkun is a senior solutions architect at Databricks. She helps customers adopt the Databricks Platform to implement a variety of use cases, follow best practices for implementing data products, and extract the maximum value from their data. During her career, she has participated in multiple data engineering and MLOps projects, including data platform setups, large-scale performance optimizations, and on-prem to cloud migrations. She previously had data engineering and software development roles for consultancies and product companies. She aims to support companies in their data and AI journey to maximize business value using data and AI solutions. She is a regular presenter at conferences, meetups, and user groups in Benelux and Europe.

Table of Contents

2

Applying Data Transformations Using Delta Live Tables   27

3

Managing Data Quality Using Delta Live Tables   49

4

Scaling DLT Pipelines   69

Part 2: Securing the Lakehouse Using the Unity Catalog

5

Mastering Data Governance in the Lakehouse with Unity Catalog   91

6

Managing Data Locations in Unity Catalog   115

7

Viewing Data Lineage Using Unity Catalog   133

Part 3: Continuous Integration, Continuous Deployment, and Continuous Monitoring

8

Deploying, Maintaining, and Administrating DLT Pipelines Using Terraform   155

9

Leveraging Databricks Asset Bundles to Streamline Data Pipeline Deployment   177

10

Monitoring Data Pipelines in Production   195

Preface

As datasets have exploded in size with the introduction of cheap cloud storage and processing data in near real time has become an industry standard, many organizations have turned to the lakehouse architecture, which combines the fast BI speeds of a traditional data warehouse with the scalable ETL processing of big data in the cloud. The Databricks Data Intelligence Platform – built upon several open source technologies, including Apache Spark, Delta Lake, MLflow, and Unity Catalog – eliminates friction points and accelerates the design and deployment of modern data applications built for the lakehouse.

In this book, you'll start with an overview of the Delta Lake format, cover core concepts of the Databricks Data Intelligence Platform, and master building data pipelines using the Delta Live Tables framework. We'll dive into applying data transformations, how to implement the Databricks medallion architecture, and how to continuously monitor the quality of data landing in your lakehouse. You'll learn how to react to incoming data using the Databricks Auto Loader feature and automate real-time data processing using Databricks workflows. You'll learn how to use CI/CD tools such as **Terraform** and **Databricks Asset Bundles** (**DABs**) to deploy data pipeline changes automatically across deployment environments, as well as monitor, control, and optimize cloud costs along the way. By the end of this book, you will have mastered building a production-ready, modern data application using the Databricks Data Intelligence Platform.

With Databricks recently named a Leader in the 2024 Gartner Magic Quadrant for Data Science and Machine Learning Platforms, the demand for mastering a skillset in the Databricks Data Intelligence Platform is only expected to grow in the coming years.

Who this book is for

This book is for data engineers, data scientists, and data stewards tasked with enterprise data processing for their organizations. This book will simplify learning advanced data engineering techniques on Databricks, making implementing a cutting-edge lakehouse accessible to individuals with varying technical expertise. However, beginner-level knowledge of Apache Spark and Python is needed to make the most out of the code examples in this book.

What this book covers

Chapter 1, An Introduction to Delta Live Tables, discusses building near-real-time data pipelines using the Delta Live Tables framework. It covers the fundamentals of pipeline design as well as the core concepts of the Delta Lake format. The chapter concludes with a simple example of building a Delta Live Table pipeline from start to finish.

Chapter 2, Applying Data Transformations Using Delta Live Tables, explores data transformations using Delta Live Tables, guiding you through the process of cleaning, refining, and enriching data to meet specific business requirements. You will learn how to use Delta Live Tables to ingest data from a variety of input sources, register datasets in Unity Catalog, and effectively apply changes to downstream tables.

Chapter 3, Managing Data Quality Using Delta Live Tables, introduces several techniques for enforcing data quality requirements on newly arriving data. You will learn how to define data quality constraints using Expectations in the Delta Live Tables framework, as well as monitor the data quality of a pipeline in near real time.

Chapter 4, Scaling DLT Pipelines, explains how to scale a **Delta Live Tables** (**DLT**) pipeline to handle the unpredictable demands of a typical production environment. You will take a deep dive into configuring pipeline settings using the DLT UI and Databricks Pipeline REST API. You will also gain a better understanding of the daily DLT maintenance tasks that are run in the background and how to optimize table layouts to improve performance.

Chapter 5, Mastering Data Governance in the Lakehouse with Unity Catalog, provides a comprehensive guide to enhancing data governance and compliance of your lakehouse using Unity Catalog. You will learn how to enable Unity Catalog on a Databricks workspace, enable data discovery using metadata tags, and implement fine-grained row and column-level access control of datasets.

Chapter 6, Managing Data Locations in Unity Catalog, explores how to effectively manage storage locations using Unity Catalog. You will learn how to govern data access across various roles and departments within an organization while ensuring security and auditability with the Databricks Data Intelligence Platform.

Chapter 7, Viewing Data Lineage using Unity Catalog, discusses tracing data origins, visualizing data transformations, and identifying upstream and downstream dependencies by tracing data lineage in Unity Catalog. By the end of the chapter, You will be equipped with the skills needed to validate that data is coming from trusted sources.

Chapter 8, Deploying, Maintaining, and Administrating DLT Pipelines Using Terraform, covers deploying DLT pipelines using the Databricks Terraform provider. You will learn how to set up a local development environment and automate a continuous build and deployment pipeline, along with best practices and future considerations.

Chapter 9, Leveraging Databricks Asset Bundles to Streamline Data Pipeline Deployment, explores how DABs can be used to streamline the deployment of data analytics projects and improve cross-team collaboration. You will gain an understanding of the practical use of DABs through several hands-on examples.

Chapter 10, Monitoring Data Pipelines in Production, delves into the crucial task of monitoring data pipelines in Databricks. You will learn various mechanisms for tracking pipeline health, performance, and data quality within the Databricks Data Intelligence Platform.

To get the most out of this book

While not a mandatory requirement, to get the most out of this book, it's recommended that you have beginner-level knowledge of Python and Apache Spark, and at least some knowledge of navigating around the Databricks Data Intelligence Platform. It's also recommended to have the following dependencies installed locally in order to follow along with the hands-on exercises and code examples throughout the book:

Software/hardware covered in the book	Operating system requirements
Python 3.6+	Windows, macOS, or Linux
Databricks CLI 0.205+	

Furthermore, it's recommended that you have a Databricks account and workspace to log in, import notebooks, create clusters, and create new data pipelines. If you do not have a Databricks account, you can sign up for a free trial on the Databricks website `https://www.databricks.com/try-databricks`.

If you are using the digital version of this book, we advise you to type the code yourself or access the code from the book's GitHub repository (a link is available in the next section). Doing so will help you avoid any potential errors related to the copying and pasting of code.

Download the example code files

You can download the example code files for this book from GitHub at `https://github.com/PacktPublishing/Building-Modern-Data-Applications-Using-Databricks-Lakehouse`. If there's an update to the code, it will be updated in the GitHub repository.

We also have other code bundles from our rich catalog of books and videos available at `https://github.com/PacktPublishing/`. Check them out!

Conventions used

There are a number of text conventions used throughout this book.

`Code in text`: Indicates code words in text, database table names, folder names, filenames, file extensions, pathnames, dummy URLs, user input, and Twitter handles. Here is an example: "The result of the data generator notebook should be three tables in total: `youtube_channels`, `youtube_channel_artists`, and `combined_table`."

A block of code is set as follows:

```
@dlt.table(
    name="random_trip_data_raw",
    comment="The raw taxi trip data ingested from a landing zone.",
    table_properties={
        "quality": "bronze"
    }
)
```

When we wish to draw your attention to a particular part of a code block, the relevant lines or items are set in bold:

```
@dlt.table(
    name="random_trip_data_raw",
    comment="The raw taxi trip data ingested from a landing zone.",
    table_properties={
        "quality": "bronze",
        "pipelines.autoOptimize.managed": "false"
    }
)
```

Any command-line input or output is written as follows:

```
$ databricks bundle validate
```

Bold: Indicates a new term, an important word, or words that you see onscreen. For instance, words in menus or dialog boxes appear in **bold**. Here is an example: "Click the **Run all** button at the top right of the Databricks workspace to execute all the notebook cells, verifying that all cells execute successfully."

> **Tips or important notes**
> Appear like this.

Get in touch

Feedback from our readers is always welcome.

General feedback: If you have questions about any aspect of this book, email us at `customercare@packtpub.com` and mention the book title in the subject of your message.

Errata: Although we have taken every care to ensure the accuracy of our content, mistakes do happen. If you have found a mistake in this book, we would be grateful if you would report this to us. Please visit `www.packtpub.com/support/errata` and fill in the form.

Piracy: If you come across any illegal copies of our works in any form on the internet, we would be grateful if you would provide us with the location address or website name. Please contact us at `copyright@packtpub.com` with a link to the material.

If you are interested in becoming an author: If there is a topic that you have expertise in and you are interested in either writing or contributing to a book, please visit `authors.packtpub.com`.

Share Your Thoughts

Once you've read *Building Modern Data Applications Using Databricks Lakehouse*, we'd love to hear your thoughts! Scan the QR code below to go straight to the Amazon review page for this book and share your feedback.

`https://packt.link/r/1-801-07323-6`

Your review is important to us and the tech community and will help us make sure we're delivering excellent quality content.

Download a free PDF copy of this book

Thanks for purchasing this book!

Do you like to read on the go but are unable to carry your print books everywhere?

Is your eBook purchase not compatible with the device of your choice?

Don't worry, now with every Packt book you get a DRM-free PDF version of that book at no cost.

Read anywhere, any place, on any device. Search, copy, and paste code from your favorite technical books directly into your application.

The perks don't stop there, you can get exclusive access to discounts, newsletters, and great free content in your inbox daily

Follow these simple steps to get the benefits:

1. Scan the QR code or visit the link below

https://packt.link/free-ebook/978-1-80107-323-3

2. Submit your proof of purchase

3. That's it! We'll send your free PDF and other benefits to your email directly

Part 1: Near-Real-Time Data Pipelines for the Lakehouse

In this first part of the book, we'll introduce the core concepts of the **Delta Live Tables (DLT)** framework. We'll cover how to ingest data from a variety of input sources and apply the latest changes to downstream tables. We'll also explore how to enforce requirements on incoming data so that your data teams can be alerted of potential data quality issues that might contaminate your lakehouse.

This part contains the following chapters:

- *Chapter 1, An Introduction to Delta Live Tables*
- *Chapter 2, Applying Data Transformations Using Delta Live Tables*
- *Chapter 3, Managing Data Quality Using Delta Live Tables*
- *Chapter 4, Scaling DLT Pipelines*

1

An Introduction to Delta Live Tables

In this chapter, we will examine how the data industry has evolved over the last several decades. We'll also look at why real-time data processing has significant ties to how a business can react to the latest signals in data. We'll address why trying to build your own streaming solution from scratch may not be sustainable, and why the maintenance does not easily scale over time. By the end of the chapter, you should completely understand the types of problems the **Delta Live Tables (DLT)** framework solves and the value the framework brings to data engineering teams.

In this chapter, we're going to cover the following main topics:

- The emergence of the lakehouse

- The importance of real-time data in the lakehouse

- The maintenance predicament of a streaming application

- What is the Delta Live Tables framework?

- How are Delta Live Tables related to Delta Lake?

- An introduction to Delta Live Tables concepts

- A quick Delta Lake primer

- A hands-on example – creating your first Delta Live Tables pipeline

Technical requirements

It's recommended to have access to a Databricks premium workspace to follow along with the code examples at the end of the chapter. It's also recommended to have Databricks workspace permissions to create an all-purpose cluster and a DLT pipeline using a cluster policy. Users will create and attach a notebook to a cluster and execute the notebook cells. All code samples can be downloaded from this chapter's GitHub repository, located at `https://github.com/PacktPublishing/Building-Modern-Data-Applications-Using-Databricks-Lakehouse/tree/main/chapter01`. This chapter will create and run a new DLT pipeline using the Core product edition. As a result, the pipeline is estimated to consume around 5–10 **Databricks Units** (**DBUs**).

The emergence of the lakehouse

During the early 1980s, the data warehouse was a great tool for processing structured data. Combined with the right indexing methods, data warehouses allowed us to serve **business intelligence** (**BI**) reports at blazing speeds. However, after the turn of the century, data warehouses could not keep up with newer data formats such as JSON, as well as new data modalities such as audio and video. Simply put, data warehouses struggled to process semi-structured and unstructured data that most businesses used. Additionally, data warehouses struggled to scale to millions or billions of rows, common in the new information era of the early 2000s. Overnight, batch data processing jobs soon ran into BI reports scheduled to refresh during the early morning business hours.

At the same time, cloud computing became a popular choice among organizations because it provided enterprises with an elastic computing capacity that could quickly grow or shrink, based on the current computing demand, without having to deal with the upfront costs of provisioning and installing additional hardware on-premises.

Modern **extract, transform, and load** (**ETL**) processing engines such as Apache Hadoop and Apache Spark™ addressed the performance problem of processing big data ETL pipelines, ushering in a new concept, a **data lake**. Conversely, data lakes were terrible for serving BI reports and oftentimes offered degrading performance experiences for many concurrent user sessions. Furthermore, data lakes had poor data governance. They were prone to sloppy data wrangling patterns, leading to many expensive copies of the same datasets that frequently diverged from the source of truth. As a result, these data lakes quickly earned the nickname of *data swamps*. The big data industry needed a change. The lakehouse pattern was this change and aimed to combine the best of both worlds – fast BI reports and fast ETL processing of structured, semi-structured, and unstructured data in the cloud.

The Lambda architectural pattern

In the early 2010s, data streaming took a foothold in the data industry, and many enterprises needed a way to support both batch ETL processing and append-only streams of data. Furthermore, data architectures with many concurrent ETL processes needed to simultaneously read and change the underlying data. It was not uncommon for organizations to experience frequent conflicting write failures that led to data corruption and even data loss. As a result, in many early data architectures, a two-pronged Lambda architecture was built to provide a layer of isolation between these processes.

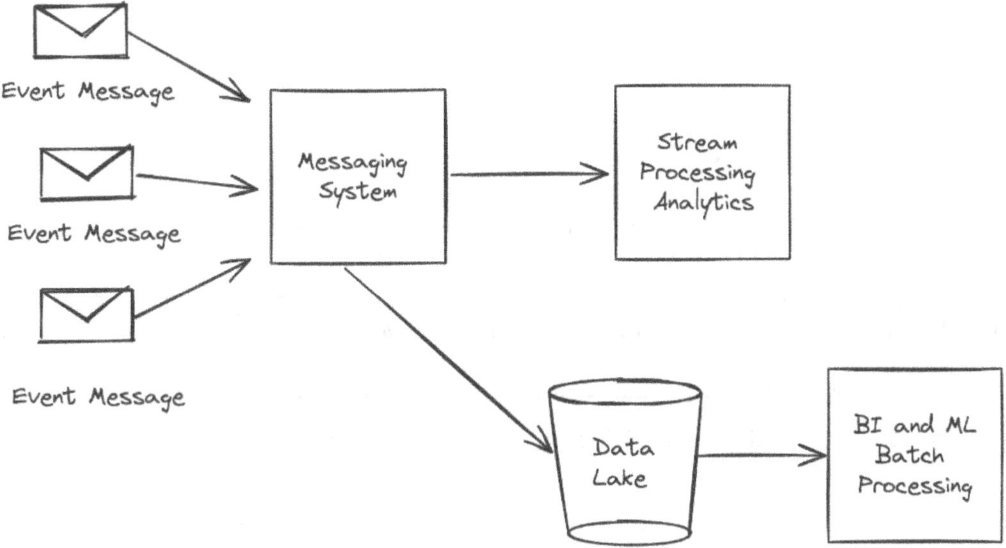

Figure 1.1 – A Lambda architecture was oftentimes created to support both real-time streaming workloads and batch processes such as BI reports

Using the Lambda architecture, downstream processes such as BI reports or **Machine Learning (ML)** model training could execute calculations on a snapshot of data, while streaming processes could apply near real-time data changes in isolation. However, these Lambda architectures duplicated data to support concurrent batch and streaming workloads, leading to inconsistent data changes that needed to be reconciled at the end of each business day.

Introducing the medallion architecture

In an effort to clean up data lakes and prevent bad data practices, data lake architects needed a data processing pattern that would meet the high demands of modern-day ETL processing. In addition, organizations needed a simplified architecture for batch and streaming workloads, easy data rollbacks, good data auditing, and strong data isolation, while scaling to process terabytes or even petabytes of data daily.

As a result, a design pattern within the lakehouse emerged, commonly referred to as the medallion architecture. This data processing pattern physically isolates data processing and improves data quality by applying business-level transformations in successive data hops, also called **data layers**.

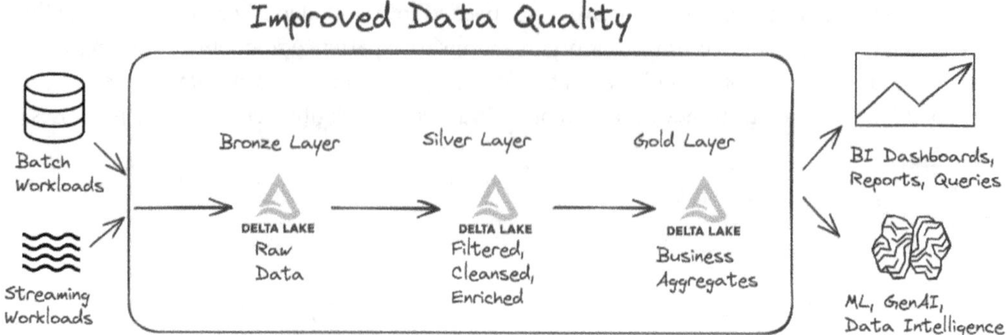

Figure 1.2 – The lakehouse medallion architecture

A typical design pattern for organizing data within a lakehouse (as shown in *Figure 1.2*) includes three distinct data layers – a bronze layer, a silver layer, and finally, a gold layer:

- The bronze layer serves as a landing zone for raw, unprocessed data.

- Filtered, cleaned, and augmented data with a defined structure and enforced schema will be stored in the silver layer.

- Lastly, a refined, or gold layer, will deliver pristine, business-level aggregations ready to be consumed by downstream BI and ML systems.

Moreover, this simplified data architecture unifies batch and streaming workloads, by storing datasets in a big data format that supports concurrent batch and streaming data operations.

The Databricks lakehouse

The Databricks lakehouse combines the processing power of a new high-performance processing engine, called the Photon Engine, with the augmentation of Apache Spark. Combined with open data formats for data storage, and support for a wide range of data types, including structured, semi-structured, and unstructured data, the Photon engine can process a wide variety of workloads using a single, consistent snapshot of the data in cheap and resilient cloud storage. In addition, the Databricks lakehouse simplifies data architecture by unifying batch and streaming processing with a single API – the Spark DataFrame API. Lastly, the Databricks lakehouse was built with data governance and data security in mind, allowing organizations to centrally define data access patterns and consistently apply them across their businesses.

In this book, we'll cover three major features that the Databricks lakehouse is anchored in:

- The Delta Lake format
- The Photon Engine
- Unity Catalog

While Delta Lake can be used to process both batch and streaming workloads concurrently, most data teams choose to implement their ETL pipelines using a batch execution model, mainly for simplicity's sake. Let's look at why that might be the case.

The maintenance predicament of a streaming application

Spark Structured Streaming provides near-real-time stream processing with fault tolerance, and exactly-once processing guarantees through the use of a DataFrame API that is near-identical to batch processing in Spark. As a result of a common DataFrame API, data engineering teams can convert existing batch Spark workloads to streaming with minimal effort. However, as the volume of data increases and the number of ingestion sources and data pipelines naturally grows over time, data engineering teams face the burden of augmenting existing data pipelines to keep up with new data transformations or changing business logic. In addition, Spark Streaming comes with additional configuration maintenance such as updating checkpoint locations, managing watermarks and triggers, and even backfilling tables when a significant data change or data correction occurs. Advanced data engineering teams may even be expected to build data validation and system monitoring capabilities, adding even more custom pipeline features to maintain. Over time, data pipeline complexity will grow, and data engineering teams will spend most of their time maintaining the operation of data pipelines in production and less time gleaning insights from their enterprise data. It's evident that a framework is needed that allows data engineers to quickly declare data transformations, manage data quality, and rapidly deploy changes to production where they can monitor pipeline operations from a UI or other notification systems.

What is the DLT framework?

DLT is a declarative framework that aims to simplify the development and maintenance operations of a data pipeline by abstracting away a lot of the boilerplate complexities. For example, rather than declaring how to transform, enrich, and validate data, data engineers can declare what transformations to apply to newly arriving data. Furthermore, DLT provides support to enforce data quality, preventing a data lake from becoming a data swamp. DLT gives data teams the ability to choose how to handle poor-quality data, whether that means printing a warning message to the system logs, dropping invalid data, or failing a data pipeline run altogether. Lastly, DLT automatically handles the mundane data engineering tasks of maintaining optimized data file sizes of the underlying tables, as well as cleaning up obsolete data files that are no longer present in the Delta transaction log (`Optimize` and `Vacuum` operations are covered later in the *A quick Delta Lake primer* section).

DLT aims to ease the maintenance and operational burden on data engineering teams so that they can focus their time on uncovering business value from the data stored in their lakehouse, rather than spending time managing operational complexities.

How is DLT related to Delta Lake?

The DLT framework relies heavily on the Delta Lake format to incrementally process data at every step of the way. For example, streaming tables and materialized views defined in a DLT pipeline are backed by a Delta table. Features that make Delta Lake an ideal storage format for a streaming pipeline include support for **Atomicity, Consistency, Isolation, and Durability (ACID)** transactions so that concurrent data modifications such as inserts, updates, and deletions can be incrementally applied to a streaming table. Plus, Delta Lake features scalable metadata handling, allowing Delta Lake to easily scale to petabytes and beyond. If there is incorrect data computation, Delta Lake offers time travel – the ability to restore a copy of a table to a previous snapshot. Lastly, Delta Lake inherently tracks audit information in each table's transaction log. Provenance information such as what type of operation modified the table, by what cluster, by which user, and at what precise timestamp are all captured alongside the data files. Let's look at how DLT leverages Delta tables to quickly and efficiently define data pipelines that can scale over time.

Introducing DLT concepts

The DLT framework automatically manages task orchestration, cluster creation, and exception handling, allowing data engineers to focus on defining transformations, data enrichment, and data validation logic. Data engineers will define a data pipeline using one or more dataset types. Under the hood, the DLT system will determine how to keep these datasets up to date. A data pipeline using the DLT framework is made up of the streaming tables, materialized views, and views dataset types, which we'll discuss in detail in the following sections. We'll also briefly discuss how to visualize the pipeline, view its triggering method, and look at the entire pipeline data flow from a bird's-eye view. We'll also briefly understand the different types of Databricks compute and runtime, and Unity Catalog. Let's go ahead and get started.

Streaming tables

Streaming tables leverage the benefits of Delta Lake and Spark Structured Streaming to incrementally process new data as it arrives. This dataset type is useful when data must be ingested, transformed, or enriched at a high throughput and low latency. Streaming tables were designed specifically for data sources that append new data only and do not include data modification, such as updates or deletes. As a result, this type of dataset can scale to large data volumes, since it can incrementally apply data transformations as soon as new data arrives and does not need to recompute the entire table history during a pipeline update.

Materialized views

Materialized views leverage Delta Lake to compute the latest changes to a dataset and materialize the results in cloud storage. This dataset type is great when the data source includes data modifications such as updates and deletions, or a data aggregation must be performed. Under the hood, the DLT framework will perform the calculations to recompute the latest data changes to the dataset, using the full table's history. The output of this calculation is stored in cloud storage so that future queries can reference the pre-computed results, as opposed to re-performing the full calculations each time the table is queried. As a result, this type of dataset will incur additional storage and compute costs each time the materialized view is updated. Furthermore, materialized views can be published to Unity Catalog, so the results can be queried outside of the DLT data pipeline. This is great when you need to share the output of a query across multiple data pipelines.

Views

Views also recompute the latest results of a particular query but do not materialize the results to cloud storage, which helps save on storage costs. This dataset type is great when you want to quickly check the intermediate result of data transformations in a data pipeline or apply other ad hoc data validations. Furthermore, the results of this dataset type cannot be published to Unity Catalog and are only available within the context of the data pipeline.

The following table summarizes the differences between the different dataset types in the DLT framework and when it's appropriate to use one dataset type versus the other:

Dataset type	When to use it
Streaming table	Ingestion workloads, when you need to continuously append new data to a target table with high throughput and low latency.
Materialized view	Data operations that include data modifications, such as updates and deletions, or you need to perform aggregations on the full table history.
View	When you need to query intermediate data without publishing the results to Unity Catalog (e.g., perform data quality checks on intermediate transformations)

Table 1.1 – Each dataset type in DLT serves a different purpose

Pipeline

A DLT pipeline is the logical data processing graph of one or more streaming tables, materialized views, or views. The DLT framework will take dataset declarations, using either the Python API or SQL API, and infer the dependencies between each dataset. Once a pipeline update runs, the DLT framework will update the datasets in the correct order using a dependency graph, called a **dataflow graph**.

Pipeline triggers

A pipeline will be executed based on some triggering event. DLT offers three types of triggers – manual, scheduled, and continuous triggers. Once triggered, the pipeline will initialize and execute the dataflow graph, updating each of the dataset states.

Workflow

Databricks workflows is a managed orchestration feature of the **Databricks Data Intelligence Platform** that allows data engineers to chain together one or more dependent data processing tasks. For more complex data processing use cases, it may be necessary to build a data pipeline using multiple, nested DLT pipelines. For those use cases, Databricks workflows can simplify the orchestration of these data processing tasks.

Types of Databricks compute

There are four types of computational resources available to Databricks users from the Databricks Data Intelligence Platform.

Job computes

A job compute is an ephemeral collection of **virtual machines** (**VMs**) with the **Databricks Runtime** (**DBR**) installed that are dynamically provisioned for the duration of a scheduled job. Once the job is complete, the VMs are immediately released back to the cloud provider. Since job clusters do not utilize the UI components of the Databricks Data Intelligence Platform (e.g., notebooks and the query editor), job clusters assess a lower **Databricks Unit** (**DBU**) for the entirety of their execution.

All-purpose computes

An all-purpose compute is a collection of ephemeral VMs with the DBR installed that is dynamically provisioned by a user, directly from the Databricks UI via a button click, or via the Databricks REST API (using the `/api/2.0/clusters/create` endpoint, for example), and they remain running until a user, or an expiring auto-termination timer, terminates the cluster. Upon termination, the VMs are returned to the cloud provider, and Databricks stops assessing additional DBUs.

Instance pools

Instance pools are a feature in Databricks that helps reduce the time it takes to provision additional VMs and install the DBR. Instance pools will pre-provision VMs from the cloud provider and hold them in a logical container, similar to a valet keeping your car running in a valet parking lot.

For some cloud providers, it can take 15 minutes or more to provision an additional VM, leading to longer troubleshooting cycles or ad hoc development tasks, such as log inspection or rerunning failed notebook cells during the development of new features.

Additionally, instance pools improve efficiency when many jobs are scheduled to execute closely together or with overlapping schedules. For example, as one job finishes, rather than releasing the VMs back to the cloud provider, the job cluster can place the VMs into the instance pool to be reused by the next job.

Before returning the VMs to the instance pool, the Databricks container installed on the VM is destroyed, and a new container is installed on the VM containing the DBR when the next scheduled job requests the VM.

> **Important note**
>
> Databricks will not assess additional DBUs while VM(s) are up and running. However, the cloud provider will continue to charge for as long as the VMs are held in the instance pools.

To help control costs, instance pools provide an autoscaling feature that allows the size of the pool to grow and shrink, in response to demand. For example, the instance pool might grow to 10 VMs during peak hours but shrink back to 1 or 2 during lulls in the processing demand.

Databricks SQL warehouses

The last type of computational resource featured in the Databricks Data Intelligence Platform is **Databricks SQL (DBSQL)** warehouses. DBSQL warehouses are designed to run SQL workloads such as queries, reports, and dashboards. Furthermore, DBSQL warehouses are pre-configured computational resources designed to limit the configuration that a data analyst or SQL analyst would need to optimize for ad hoc data exploration and query execution. DBSQL warehouses are preconfigured with the latest DBRs, leverage the Databricks Photon engine, and have advanced Spark configuration settings preconfigured to optimize performance. A DBSQL warehouse also includes additional performance features such as results caching and disk caching, which can accelerate workloads by moving data closer to the hardware performing the query calculations. Combined with the processing speed of the Photon engine, the DBSQL warehouse achieves cloud warehouse speeds that Apache Spark once struggled to meet.

Databricks Runtime

The Databricks Runtime is a set of libraries pre-installed on the driver and worker nodes of a cluster during cluster initialization. These libraries include popular Java, R, and Python libraries to assist end users with ad hoc data wrangling or other development tasks. The libraries include core components that interface with the Databricks backend services to support rich platform features, such as collaborative notebooks, workflows, and cluster metrics. Furthermore, DBR includes other performance features such as data file caching (known as disk caching), the Databricks Photon engine for accelerated Spark processing, and other computational speed-ups. DBR comes in two varieties, Standard and ML, which are tailored to assist with the workloads anticipated to be run, based on the end user persona. For example, DBR for ML would have popular Python libraries such as TensorFlow and scikit-learn pre-installed to assist end users with the training of ML models, feature engineering, and other ML development tasks.

Unity Catalog

As the name suggests, Unity Catalog is a centralized governance store that is intended to span multiple Databricks workspaces. Rather than repeatedly defining the data governance policies for users and groups within each Databricks workspace, Unity Catalog allows data administrators to define access policies once in a centralized location. As a result, Unity Catalog acts as a single source of truth for data governance.

In addition to data access policies, Unity Catalog also features data auditing, data lineage, data discovery, and data sharing capabilities, which will be covered in *Chapters 5*, *6*, and *7*.

Unity Catalog is tightly integrated into the Databricks lakehouse, making it easy to build near-real-time data pipelines with strong data security in mind, using an open lakehouse storage format such as Delta Lake.

A quick Delta Lake primer

Delta Lake is a big data file protocol built around a multi-version transaction log that provides features such as ACID transactions, schema enforcement, time travel, data file management, and other performance features on top of existing data files in a lakehouse.

Originally, big data architectures had many concurrent processes that both read and modified data, leading to data corruption and even data loss. As previously mentioned, a two-pronged Lambda architecture was created, providing a layer of isolation between processes that applied streaming updates to data and downstream processes that needed a consistent snapshot of the data, such as BI workloads that generated daily reports or refreshed dashboards. However, these Lambda architectures duplicated data to support these batch and streaming workloads, leading to inconsistent data changes that needed to be reconciled at the end of each business day.

Fortunately, the Delta Lake format provides a common storage layer for a lakehouse across disparate workloads and unifies both batch and streaming workloads. As such, a Delta table serves as the foundation for a Delta Live Table. Under the hood, a Delta Live Table is backed by a Delta table that is added to a dataflow graph, and whose state is updated by the DLT system whenever a DLT pipeline update is executed.

The architecture of a Delta table

The Delta transaction log is a key piece of the architecture for this big data format. Each Delta table contains a transaction log, which is a directory name, `_delta_log`, located at a table's root directory. The transaction log is a multi-version system of records that keeps track of the table's state over a linear period of time.

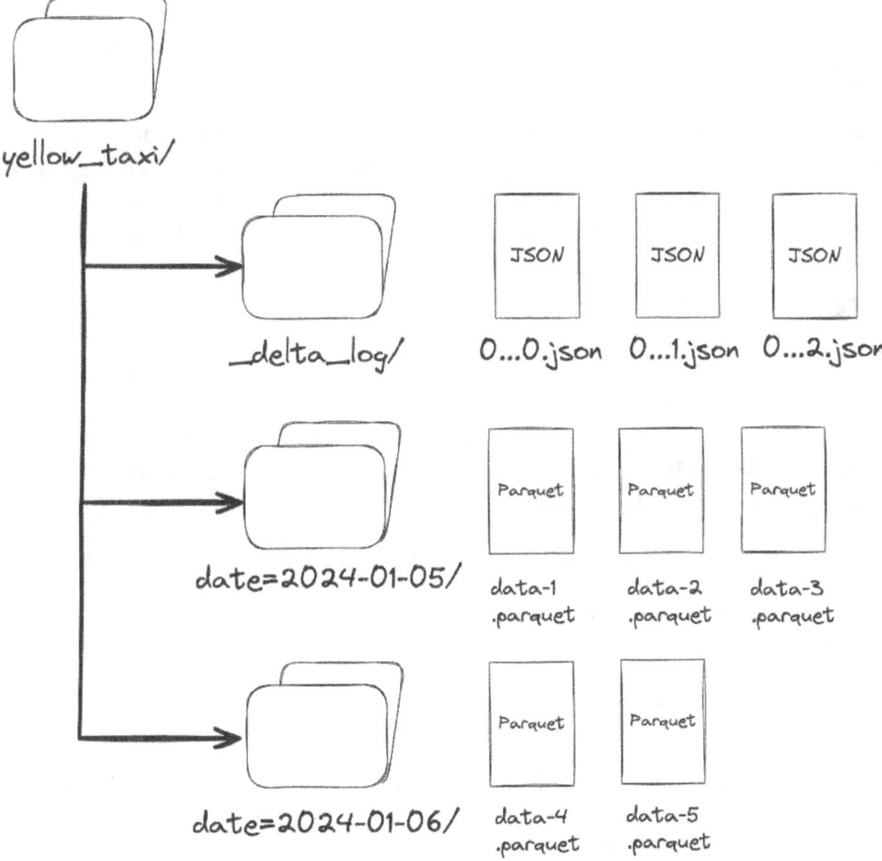

Figure 1.3 – The Delta transaction log sits alongside the partition directories and data files in a separate directory titled _delta_log

The transaction log informs the Delta Lake engine which data files to read to answer a particular query.

Within each transaction log directory, there will be one or more files stored in the JSON format, as well as other metadata information to help quickly and efficiently calculate the Delta table's state (covered in the following section).

As new data is appended, updated, or even deleted from a Delta table, these changes are recorded, or committed, to this directory as metadata information, stored as atomic JSON files. The JSON files are named using an ordered integer, starting with `00...0.json` and incrementing by one after each successful transaction commit.

If a Delta table is partitioned, there will be one or more subdirectories containing the partitioning column information within the table's root directory. Hive-style table partitioning is a very common performance technique that can speed up a query by collocating similar data within the same directory. The data is collocated by a particular column's value (e.g., `"date=2024-01-05"`). Optionally, there can be even more subdirectories nested within these partition directories, depending upon how many columns a table is partitioned by.

Within these partition subdirectories are one or more data files, stored using the Apache Parquet format. Apache Parquet is a popular columnar storage format, with efficient data compression and encoding schemes that yield fast data storage and retrieval for big data workloads. As a result, this open format was chosen as a foundation to store the data files that make up a Delta table.

The contents of a transaction commit

As mentioned earlier, the transaction log is the single source of truth for a Delta table. Each committed transaction (the JSON file under the `_delta_log` directory) will contain metadata information about the operation, or action, being applied to a particular Delta table. These JSON files can be viewed as a set of actions. Although there can be many concurrent transactions, the history of transaction commits is replayed in a linear order by table readers, and the result is the latest state of the Delta table.

Each JSON file could contain any of the following actions, as outlined by the Delta Lake protocol:

- **Change metadata**: This type of action is used to update the name, schema, or partitioning information of a table.

- **Add file**: Perhaps the most frequent action applied, this action adds a new data file to a table along with statistical information about the first 32 columns of a Delta table.

- **Remove file**: This action will logically delete a particular data file. Note that the physical data file will remain in cloud storage even after this transaction is committed (there's more about this topic in the *Tombstoned data files* section).

- **Add Change Data Capture (CDC) information**: This action is used to add a CDC file that will contain all the data that has changed as a result of a particular table transaction.

- **Transaction identifiers**: This action is used for Structured Streaming workloads and will contain the unique identifier for a particular stream, as well as the epoch identifier for the most recently committed Structured Streaming micro-batch.

- **Protocol evolution**: Provides backward compatibility and ensures that old Delta Lake table readers can read the metadata information within the transaction log.

- **Commit provenance information**: This type of action will contain information about the process of committing a particular data transaction to a table. This will include information including the timestamp, the operation type, cluster identifier, and user information.

- **Domain metadata**: This type of action sets the configuration for a particular domain. There are two types of domain metadata – system domain and user-controlled domain.

- **Sidecar file information**: This type of action will commit a separate metadata file to the transaction log, which contains summary information about the checkpoint file that was created (checkpoints are covered in the following section).

Supporting concurrent table reads and writes

There are two types of concurrency control methods in storage systems – pessimistic concurrency control and optimistic concurrency control. A pessimistic concurrency control will attempt to thwart possible table conflicts by locking an entire table until an ongoing transaction has been completed. Conversely, optimistic concurrency control does not lock a table and will permit potential transaction conflicts to happen.

The authors of the Delta Lake protocol chose to implement the Delta Lake format using optimistic concurrency control. The reason why this design choice was made is that most big data workloads will append new data to an existing table, as opposed to modifying existing data.

As an example, let's look at how Delta Lake will deal with a concurrent write conflict between two table writers – Table Writer A and Table Writer B:

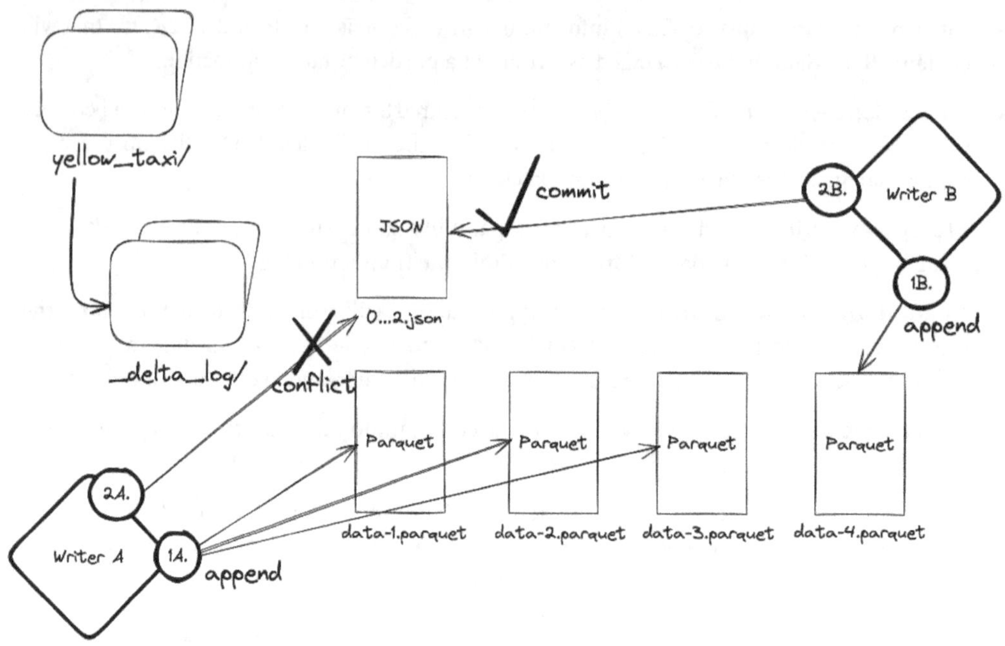

Figure 1.4 – Delta Lake implements an optimistic concurrency scheme to handle concurrent write conflicts

Imagine that the two table writers modify the same data files and attempt to commit the data changes that conflict with one another. Let's look at how Delta Lake handles this type of scenario.

1. Writer A will first record the starting version identifier of the transaction that it will attempt to commit to the transaction log.

2. Writer A will then write all the data files for the transaction that it would like to commit.

3. Next, Writer A will attempt to commit the transaction to the Delta transaction log.

4. At the same time, Writer B has already committed their transaction using the same table version identifier.

5. Writer A detects Writer B's commit and replays the commit information to determine whether any of the underlying data files have changed (e.g., the data has been updated).

6. If no data has changed (for example, both Writer A and Writer B commit append-only operations to the transaction log), then Writer A will increment the version identifier by 1 and attempt to recommit the transaction to the transaction log.

7. If the data has changed, then Writer A will need to recompute the transaction from scratch, increment the version identifier, and attempt to recommit the transaction.

Tombstoned data files

When an update is applied to a Delta table that requires the data within a file to be updated, a new file using the `AddFile` operation will be created. Similarly, the file containing the out-of-date data will be logically deleted, using a `RemoveFile` operation. Then, both actions will be committed to the transaction log.

By default, Delta Lake will retain the table metadata (transaction log data) for 30 days before being automatically removed from cloud storage. When a particular data file is removed from the Delta transaction log, this is often referred to as a **tombstoned file**.

To help control cloud storage costs, these tombstoned files, or files that no longer make up the latest Delta table state and are no longer referenced in the transaction log, can be removed from cloud storage altogether. A separate Delta Lake file management utility, called the `Vacuum` command, can be run as a separate process to identify all the tombstoned data files and remove them.

Furthermore, the `Vacuum` command is configurable, and the length of time to remove the table files can be specified as an optional input parameter. For example, the following code snippet will execute the `Vacuum` command on the Delta table, `yellow_taxi`, removing data files from the last 14 days of table history:

```
%sql
-- Vacuums the Delta table `yellow_taxi`
-- and retains 14 days of table history
VACUUM yellow_taxi RETAIN 336 HOURS
```

As we'll see in the upcoming chapter, this process is automatically run and managed for DLT pipelines.

Calculating Delta table state

As alluded to in the previous section, Delta Lake will automatically compact metadata in a transaction log. As you can imagine, in big data workloads with thousands or even millions of transactions each day, a Delta table can rapidly grow in size. Similarly, the commit information in the transaction log will also grow comparatively.

For every 10th commit, Delta Lake will create a checkpoint file, using the Apache Parquet format, that contains the latest table state information.

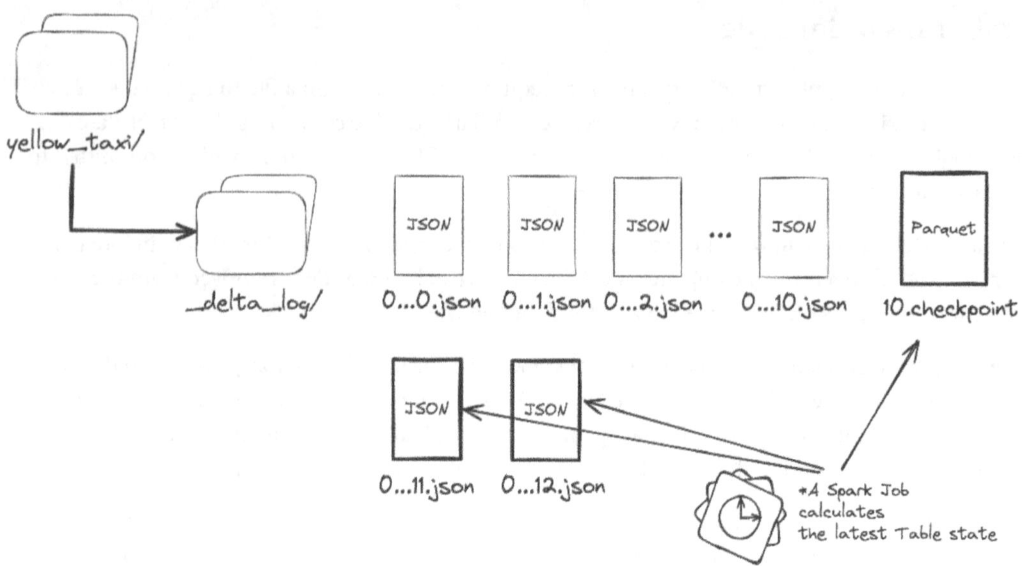

Figure 1.5 – For every 10th commit, Delta Lake will write a checkpoint file

Under the hood, a Delta Lake reader creates a separate Apache Spark Job to efficiently read the Delta table's commit logs. For example, to calculate the latest table state, a Delta Lake reader will begin by reading the latest checkpoint file and applying the transaction commits that may have occurred after the file was created.

Storing the table state information in checkpoint files alongside the data files in cloud storage was another pivotal design choice for the Delta Lake format. By using this method, calculating a table's state could scale much better than other methods, such as using the Hive Metastore to serve table metadata information. Traditional big data metastores, such as the Hive Metastore, struggle to scale when many large, heavily active tables are queried concurrently and the table metadata information needs to be retrieved to answer queries.

To further speed up queries, Delta Lake readers will also cache the table state in local memory; that way, table readers can calculate which data files will answer a particular table query much faster.

Time travel

Another file management utility in Delta Lake is the time travel feature that allows end users to query a table's state from a previous version. Time travel offers two methods to specify table state – using the table version number assigned in the transaction log or by using a timestamp.

Users can query a previous Delta table's state directly using the SQL syntax:

```sql
%sql
SELECT *
  FROM yellow_taxi
  TIMESTAMP AS OF '2023-12-31'
```

Similarly, Python users on the Databricks Data Intelligence Platform can use the Python API:

```py
%py
display(
    (spark.read
        .format("delta")
        .option("timestampAsOf", "2023-12-31")
        .load("s3a://my-data-lake/yellow_taxi/"))
)
```

It's important to note that, by default, the `Vacuum` utility will remove all data files from a particular Delta table, from the last seven days of table versions.

As a result, if the `Vacuum` command is run and a user attempts to query table history beyond the last seven days, the end user will receive a runtime exception, specifying that the data referenced in the transaction log no longer exists.

Furthermore, Delta Lake's time travel feature was designed to correct recent data issues, so it should not be used for long-term data storage requirements, such as implementing an auditing system with a history spanning years.

Tracking table changes using change data feed

Delta Lake's **Change Data Feed** (**CDF**) feature tracks row-level changes that have been made to a Delta table, as well as metadata about those changes. For example, CDF will capture information about the operation type, the timestamp confirming that the change was made, and other provenance information such as cluster identification and user information.

For update operations, CDF will capture a snapshot of the row before an update, as well as a snapshot of the row after the update has been applied.

ID	pickup_loc	pickup_timestamp	_change_type	_commit_version	_commit_timestamp
12	Brooklyn	2023-12-31 20:15:01	update_preimage	213	2024-01-01 06:05:01
12	Manhattan	2023-12-31 20:15:01	update_postimage	213	2024-01-01 06:05:01
334	Bronx	2023-12-29 21:33:59	insert	214	2024-01-01 06:23:51:

Figure 1.6 – CDF captures the operation type, commit version, and timestamp

This feature is not enabled by default but can be configured by updating a Delta table's properties. For example, CDF can be enabled on an existing table by altering the table, using a SQL ALTER statement:

```sql
%sql
ALTER TABLE yellow_taxi
SET TBLPROPERTIES (delta.enableChangeDataFeed = true)
```

Similarly, CDF can also be enabled when a table is created by including the table property as a part of the CREATE TABLE statement:

```sql
%sql
CREATE TABLE IF NOT EXISTS yellow_taxi
TBLPROPERTIES (delta.enableChangeDataFeed = true)
```

As we'll see in the next chapter, this feature is important in how DLT can efficiently apply changes from a source table to downstream datasets and implement **slowly changing dimensions (SCDs)**.

A hands-on example – creating your first Delta Live Tables pipeline

In this section, we'll use a NYC taxi sample dataset to declare a data pipeline, using the DLT framework, and apply a basic transformation to enrich the data.

> **Important note**
>
> To get the most value out of this section, it's recommended to have Databricks workspace permissions to create an all-purpose cluster and a DLT pipeline, using a cluster policy. In this section, you will attach a notebook to a cluster, execute notebook cells, as well as create and run a new DLT pipeline.

Let's start by creating a new all-purpose cluster. Navigate to the Databricks Compute UI by selecting the **Compute** button from the sidebar navigation on the left side.

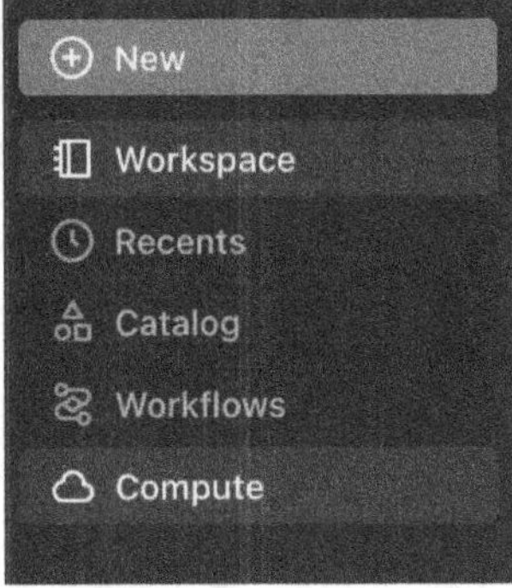

Figure 1.7 – Navigate to the Compute UI from the left-hand sidebar

Click the button titled **Create compute** at the top right. Next, provide a name for the cluster. For this exercise, the cluster can be a small, single-node cluster. Click the **Single node** radio button for the cluster type. Select the latest DBR in the runtime dropdown. Accept the defaults and click the **Create compute** button once again.

Now that we have a cluster up and running, we can begin the development of our very first data pipeline.

Let's first start by creating a new Databricks notebook under your workspace home directory. Create a new notebook by clicking the **Workspace** button on the left sidebar, clicking on the **Add** dropdown, and selecting **Notebook**. Give the notebook a meaningful name, such as My First DLT Pipeline. This new notebook is where we will declare the datasets and dependencies that will make up our Delta Live Table pipeline.

All Databricks workspaces come with a set of sample datasets, located at /databricks-datasets in the Databricks FileSystem. You can browse the list of available datasets by listing the directory contents, using the Databricks FileSystem utility:

```
%py
display(
    dbutils.fs.ls('/databricks-datasets')
)
```

Next, we need to import the dlt Python module. The dlt module contains function decorators that will instruct the DLT system on how to build our data pipeline, the dependencies, and an internal data processing graph, called a dataflow graph.

Add the following line to a new notebook cell:

```
import dlt
```

DLT is built on top of PySpark, so we can leverage Spark DataFrames to define how to ingest data from cloud storage and how to apply data transformations. Let's start by defining a function that will use Spark to read the NYC taxi sample dataset from the `/databricks-datasets` directory:

```python
def yellow_taxi_raw():
    path = "/databricks-datasets/nyctaxi/tripdata/yellow"
    return (spark.readStream
        .schema(schema)
        .format("csv")
        .option("header", True)
        .load(path))
```

In this example, we've declared a simple function with a meaningful name, and when invoked, the function will use Spark to read the raw data stored in the yellow taxi dataset and return it as a streaming DataFrame.

Now, we need to tell the DLT framework that we should use this declared function as a part of a data pipeline. We can do this by adding the `@dlt.table()` function decorator. This function decorator will create a Delta Live Table from the function and add it to the pipeline's dataflow graph. Let's also add some descriptive text to the optional `comment` parameter of this function decorator:

```python
@dlt.table(
    comment="The raw NYC taxi cab trip dataset located in `/
databricks-datasets/`"
)
def yellow_taxi_raw():
    path = "/databricks-datasets/nyctaxi/tripdata/yellow"
    return (spark.readStream
        .schema(schema)
        .format("csv")
        .option("header", True)
        .load(path))
```

After executing the notebook cell, the Databricks Data Intelligence Platform will detect a DLT table, print the output schema, and prompt you to create a new DLT pipeline.

`yellow_taxi_raw` is defined as a **Delta Live Tables** dataset with schema:

Name	Type
vendor_id	string
pickup_datetime	timestamp
dropoff_datetime	timestamp
passenger_count	int
trip_distance	float
pickup_longitude	float
pickup_latitude	float
rate_code	int
store_and_fwd_flag	int
dropoff_longitude	float
dropoff_lattitude	float
payment_type	string
fare_amount	float
surcharge	float
mta_tax	float
tip_amount	float
tolls_amount	float
total_amount	float

To populate your table you must either:

○ Run an existing pipeline using the **Delta Live Tables** menu

○ Create a new pipeline: Create Pipeline

Figure 1.8 – Databricks will parse the DLT table declaration and print the output schema

Let's click the **Create Pipeline** button to generate a new DLT pipeline. Give the data pipeline a meaningful name, such as `Yellow Taxi Cab Pipeline`. Select **Core** as the product edition and **Triggered** as the pipeline execution mode.

Create pipeline Provide feedback

General

* Pipeline name

Yellow Taxi Cab Pipeline

☐ Serverless ⓘ

Product edition

Core

Help me choose

Pipeline mode ⓘ

● Triggered ○ Continuous

Figure 1.9 – Create a new DLT pipeline using the Core product edition

Next, under the **Target Location** settings, select the Unity Catalog radio button, and specify the target catalog and schema where you would like to store the dataset. Under the **Compute** settings, set **Min workers** to 1 and **Max workers** to 1. Then, accept the defaults by clicking the **Create** button. Finally, click the **Start** button to execute the data pipeline. You will be taken to a visual representation of the dataflow graph.

Figure 1.10 – The dataflow graph will contain the streaming table we declared in our notebook

As you can see, our dataflow graph consists of a single streaming table, which is a new dataset that will ingest raw NYC taxi trip data from the `/databricks-datasets/` location on the Databricks FileSystem. While a trivial example, this example shows the declarative nature of DLT framework, as well as how quickly we can declare a data pipeline using the familiar PySpark API. Furthermore, you should now have a feel for how we can monitor and view the latest state of our data pipeline from the DLT UI.

Summary

In this chapter, we examined how and why the data industry has settled on a lakehouse architecture, which aims to merge the scalability of ETL processing and the fast data warehousing speeds for BI workloads under a single, unified architecture. We learned how real-time data processing is essential to uncovering value from the latest data as soon as it arrives, but real-time data pipelines can halt the productivity of data engineering teams as complexity grows over time. Finally, we learned the core concepts of the Delta Live Tables framework and how, with just a few lines of PySpark code and function decorators, we can quickly declare a real-time data pipeline that is capable of incrementally processing data with high throughput and low latency.

In the next chapter, we'll take a deep dive into the advanced settings of Delta Live Tables pipelines and how the framework will optimize the underlying datasets for us. Then, we'll look at more advanced data transformations, using a real-world use case to develop a data pipeline.

2

Applying Data Transformations Using Delta Live Tables

In this chapter, we'll dive straight into how **Delta Live Tables** (**DLT**) makes ingesting data from a variety of input sources simple and straightforward, whether it's files landing in cloud storage or connecting to an external storage system, such as a **relational database management system** (**RDBMS**). Then, we'll take a look at how we can efficiently and accurately apply changes from our input data sources to downstream datasets, using the APPLY CHANGES command. Lastly, we'll conclude the chapter with a deep dive into the advanced data pipeline settings.

To summarize, in this chapter, we're going to cover the following main topics:

- Ingesting data from input sources
- Applying changes to downstream tables
- Publishing datasets to Unity Catalog
- Data pipeline settings
- Hands-on exercise – applying SCD Type 2 changes

Technical requirements

To follow along in this chapter, it's recommended to have Databricks workspace permissions to create an all-purpose cluster and a DLT pipeline, using a cluster policy. It's also recommended to have Unity Catalog permissions to create and use catalogs, schemas, and tables. All code samples can be downloaded from the chapter's GitHub repository, located at `https://github.com/PacktPublishing/Building-Modern-Data-Applications-Using-Databricks-Lakehouse/tree/main/chapter02`. This chapter will create and run several new notebooks and a DLT pipeline using the **Core** product edition. As a result, the pipelines are estimated to consume around 10–15 **Databricks Units** (**DBUs**).

Ingesting data from input sources

DLT makes ingesting data from a variety of input sources simple. For example, DLT can efficiently process new files landing in a cloud storage location throughout the day, ingest structured data by connecting to an external storage system, such as a relational database, or read static reference tables that can be cached into memory. Let's look at how we can use DLT to incrementally ingest new data that arrives in a cloud storage location.

Ingesting data using Databricks Auto Loader

One of the key features of the Databricks Data Intelligence Platform is a feature called **Auto Loader**, which is a simple yet powerful ingestion mechanism for efficiently reading input files from cloud storage. Auto Loader can be referenced in a DataFrame definition by using the `cloudFiles` data source. For example, the following code snippet will use the Databricks Auto Loader feature to ingest newly arriving JSON files from a storage container:

```
df = (spark.readStream
    .format("cloudFiles")
    .option("cloudFiles.format", "json")
    .option("cloudFiles.schemaLocation", schema_path)
    .load(raw_data_path))
```

Auto Loader can scale to process billions of files in cloud storage efficiently. Databricks Auto Loader supports ingesting files stored in the CSV, JSON, XML, Apache Parquet, Apache Avro, and Apache Orc file formats, as well as text and binary files. Furthermore, one thing that you may have noticed in the preceding code snippet is that a schema definition was not specified for the input stream but, rather, a target schema location. That is because Auto Loader will automatically infer the data source schema and keep track of the changes to the schema definition in a separate storage location. Behind the scenes, Auto Loader will sample up to the first 1,000 cloud file objects to infer the schema structure for a cloud file source. For semi-structured formats such as JSON, where the schema can change over time, this can alleviate a huge burden on data engineering teams by them not having to maintain an up-to-date definition of the latest schema definition.

Scalability challenge in structured streaming

Traditionally, data pipelines that used Spark Structured Streaming to ingest new files, where files were appended to a cloud storage location, struggled to scale as data volumes grew into GB or even TB. As new files were written to the cloud storage container, Structured Streaming would perform a directory listing. For large datasets, (i.e., datasets comprised of millions of files or more), the directory listing process alone would take a lengthy amount of time. In addition, the cloud provider would assess API fees for these directory listing calls, adding to the overall cloud provider fees. For files that have already been processed, this directory listing was both expensive and inefficient.

Databricks Auto Loader supports two types of cloud file detection modes – notification mode and legacy directory listing mode. In notification mode, Auto Loader bypasses this expensive directory listing process entirely by automatically deploying a more scalable architecture under the hood. With just a few lines of Python code, Databricks pre-provisions backend cloud services that will automatically keep track of new files that have landed in cloud storage, as well as files that have already been processed.

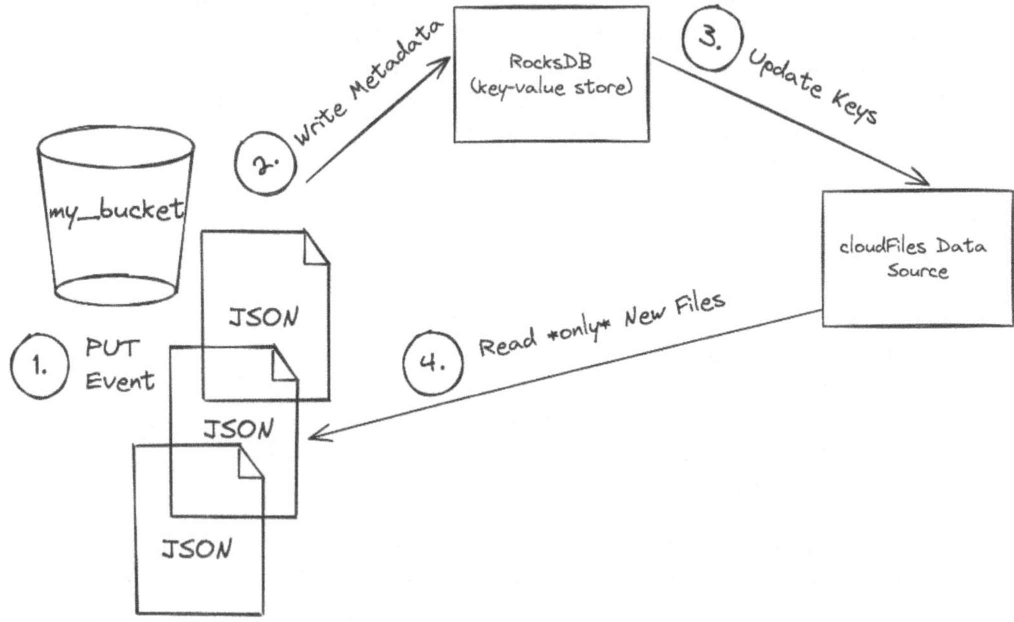

Figure 2.1 – In notification mode, Databricks Auto Loader uses an event stream to keep track of new, unprocessed files in cloud storage

Let's walk through an example of how the Auto Loader feature, configured in notification mode, will efficiently process newly arriving cloud file objects together:

1. The process begins with the Databricks Auto Loader listening to a particular cloud storage path for new file object creation events, also referred to as PUT events, named after the HTTP verb used to create the object.

2. When a new file object has been created, the metadata about this new file is persisted to a key-value store, which serves as a checkpoint location if there are system failures.

3. Next, the information pertaining to the file object, or file objects, will then be published to an event stream that the `cloudFiles` data source reads from.

4. Upon reading from the event stream, the Auto Loader process in Databricks will fetch the data pertaining only to those new, unprocessed file objects in cloud storage.

5. Lastly, the Auto Loader process will update the key-value store, marking the new files as processed in the system.

This implementation of notification-based file processing avoids the expensive and inefficient directory listing process, ensuring that the process can recover from failures and that files are processed exactly once.

Using Auto Loader with DLT

Databricks Auto Loader can be used to create a streaming table in a DLT pipeline. Now that we know what's going on behind the scenes, building a robust, scalable streaming table that can scale to billions of files can be done with just a few lines of Python code. In fact, for data sources that append new files to cloud storage, it's recommended to always use Auto Loader to ingest data. Let's take a streaming DataFrame definition from the preceding section and combine it with the DLT dataset annotation to define a new data stream in our pipeline:

```python
@dlt.table(
    comment="Raw cloud files stream of completed taxi trips"
)
def yellow_taxi_events_raw():
    return (spark.readStream
                .format("cloudFiles")
                .option("cloudFiles.format", "json")
                .option("cloudFiles.path", schema_path)
                .load(raw_landing_zone_path))
```

One thing to note is that in the preceding code snippet, we've provided two cloud storage paths. The first storage path, `schema_path`, refers to the cloud storage path where schema information and the key-value store will be written. The second storage location, `raw_landing_zone_path`, points to the location where new, unprocessed files will be written by the external data source.

> **Important note**
>
> It's recommended to use an external location governed by Unity Catalog so that you can enforce fine-grained data access across different users and groups within your Databricks workspace.

Now that we have a reliable and efficient way of ingesting raw data from cloud storage input sources, we'll want to transform the data and apply the output to downstream datasets in our data pipeline. Let's look at how the DLT framework makes applying downstream changes simple and straightforward.

Applying changes to downstream tables

Traditionally, Delta Lake offered a `MERGE INTO` command, allowing change data capture to be merged into target tables by matching on a particular condition. However, if the new data happened to be out of order, the merged changes would result in incorrect results, leading to an inaccurate and misleading output. To remediate this problem, data engineering teams would need to build complex reconciliation processes to handle out-of-order data, adding yet another layer to a data pipeline to manage and maintain.

APPLY CHANGES command

DLT offers a new API to automatically apply changes to downstream tables, even handling out-of-order data based on a set of one or more sequence columns. **Slowly changing dimensions (SCDs)** are dimensions in traditional data warehousing that allow the current and historical snapshot of data to be tracked over time. DLT allows data engineering teams to update downstream datasets in a data pipeline with changes in the upstream data source. For example, DLT allows users to capture SCD Type 1 (which does not preserve previous row history) and SCD Type 2 (which preserves historical versions of rows).

DLT offers a Python API as well as SQL syntax to apply change data captures:

- `APPLY CHANGES` – for pipelines written using SQL syntax

- `apply_changes()` – for pipelines written using Python

Let's imagine that we have a table that will record room temperatures published from smart thermostats throughout the day, and it's important to preserve a history of temperature updates. The following code snippet will apply SCD Type 2 changes to an output table in our data pipeline, using the `apply_changes()` API:

```python
import dlt
import pyspark.sql.functions as F
dlt.create_streaming_table("iot_device_temperatures")
dlt.apply_changes(
    target = "iot_device_temperatures",
    source = "smart_thermostats",
    keys = ["device_id"],
    sequence_by = F.col("sequence_num"),
    apply_as_deletes = F.expr("operation = 'DELETE'"),
    except_column_list = ["operation", "sequence_num"],
    stored_as_scd_type = "2"
)
```

Furthermore, DLT will capture high-level operational metrics about the data changes that are applied during the completion of an `apply_changes()` command. For instance, the DLT system will track the number of rows that were updated, inserted, or deleted for each execution of the `apply_changes()` command.

The DLT reconciliation process

Behind the scenes, DLT will create two dataset objects to accurately apply table changes to pipeline datasets. The first data object is a hidden, backend Delta table that contains the full history of changes. This dataset is used to perform a reconciliation process that is capable of handling out-of-order row updates that are processed. Furthermore, this backend table will be named using the provided name parameter in the `APPLY CHANGES` or `apply_changes()` function call, concatenated with the `__apply_changes_storage_` string.

For example, if the name of the table was `iot_readings`, it would result in a backend table being created with the name `__apply_changes_storage_iot_readings`.

This particular table will only be visible if the DLT pipeline publishes the dataset to the legacy Hive Metastore. However, Unity Catalog will abstract these low-level details away from end users, and the dataset will not be visible from the Catalog Explorer UI. However, the table can *still* be queried using a notebook or from a query executed on a SQL warehouse.

Secondly, the DLT system will create another dataset – a view using the name provided for the `apply_changes()` function. This view will contain the latest snapshot of a table with all the changes applied. The view will use a column, or combination of columns, specified as table keys to uniquely identify each row within the backend table. Then, DLT uses the column or sequence of columns specified in the `sequence_by` parameter of the `apply_changes()` function to order the table changes for each unique row, picking out the latest row change to calculate the result set for the view.

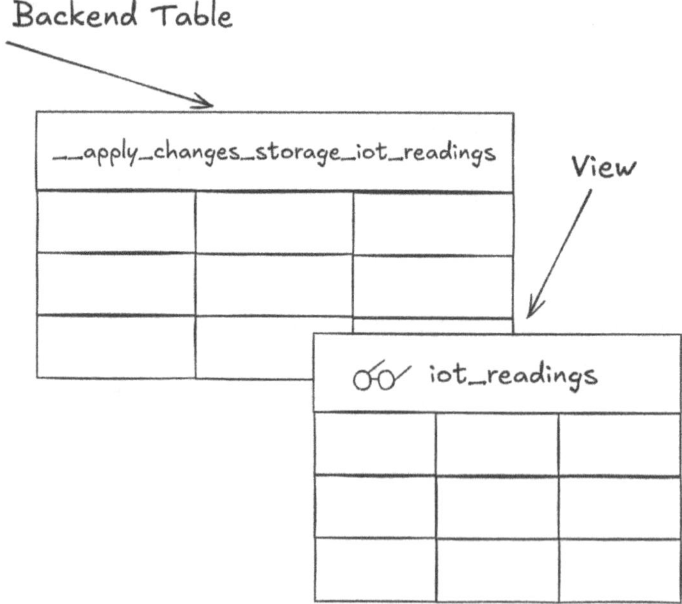

Figure 2.2 – DLT creates a backend table to apply table changes, as well as a view to query the latest data

As you can see, DLT makes it extremely simple to keep downstream data sources in line with the data changes occurring in the source. With just a few parameter changes, you can use the powerful `apply_changes()` API to apply SCD data.

Now that we understand how we can leverage the DLT framework to define data transformations and apply changes to downstream tables, let's turn our attention to how we can add strong data governance on top of our pipeline datasets.

Publishing datasets to Unity Catalog

DLT offers two methods for storing datasets in the Databricks Data Intelligence Platform – the legacy Hive Metastore and Unity Catalog.

As described in *Chapter 1*, Unity Catalog is a centralized governance store that spans all of your Databricks workspaces within a particular global region. As a result, data access policies can be defined once in a centralized location and will be consistently applied across your organization.

However, within the context of a DLT pipeline, these two methods of storing the output datasets are mutually exclusive to one another – that is, a particular DLT pipeline cannot store some datasets in the Unity Catalog and others in the Hive Metastore. You must choose a single metastore location for the entire data pipeline output.

Why store datasets in Unity Catalog?

Unity Catalog is the new best-of-breed method for storing data and querying datasets in the lakehouse. You might choose landing data in a data pipeline into Unity Catalog over the Hive Metastore for several reasons, including the following:

- The data is secured by default.
- There is a consistent definition of access policies across groups and users versus defining data access policies for every individual workspace.
- Open source technology with no risk of vendor lock-in.

Furthermore, Unity Catalog offers a Hive-compatible API, allowing third-party tools to integrate with a Unity Catalog metastore as if it were the Hive Metastore.

Creating a new catalog

One major difference between Unity Catalog and the Hive Metastore is that the former introduces a three-level namespace when defining tables. The parent namespace will refer to the catalog object. A catalog is a logical container that will hold one to many schemas, or databases.

One of the first steps in building a new DLT pipeline is to define a centralized location to store the output datasets. Creating a new catalog in Unity Catalog is simple. It can be done using a variety of methods, such as through the Catalog Explorer UI, using SQL statements executed from within a notebook, or using the Databricks REST API.

We'll use the Databricks Catalog Explorer UI to create a new Catalog:

1. First, navigate to the Catalog Explorer by clicking on the **Catalog Explorer** tab in the navigation sidebar.

2. Next, click the **Create Catalog** button.

3. Give the catalog a meaningful name.

4. Select **Standard** as the catalog type.

5. Finally, click on the **Create** button to create the new catalog.

Assigning catalog permissions

As previously mentioned, one of the benefits of using Unity Catalog is that your data is secured by default. In other words, access to data stored in the Unity Catalog is denied by default unless explicitly permitted. To create new tables in the newly created catalog, we'll need to grant permission to create and manipulate new tables.

> **Important note**
>
> If you are the creator and owner of a target catalog and schema objects, as well as the creator and owner of a DLT pipeline, then you do not need to execute the following GRANT statements. The GRANT statements are meant to demonstrate the types of permissions needed to share data assets across multiple groups and users in a typical Unity Catalog metastore.

First, let's grant access to use the catalog. From a new notebook, execute the following SQL syntax to grant access to use the newly created catalog, where my_user is the name of a Databricks user and chp2_transforming_data is the name of the catalog created in the previous example:

```sql
%sql
GRANT USE CATALOG, CREATE SCHEMA ON CATALOG `chp2_transforming_data`
TO `my_user`;
```

Next, we'll need to create a schema that will hold the output datasets from our DLT pipeline. From the same notebook, execute the following SQL statement to create a new schema:

```sql
%sql
USE CATALOG `chp2_transforming_data`;
CREATE SCHEMA IF NOT EXISTS `ride_hailing`;
USE SCHEMA `ride_hailing`;
```

Execute the following statement to grant permission to create materialized views within the newly created schema:

```
%sql
GRANT USE SCHEMA, CREATE TABLE, CREATE MATERIALIZED VIEW ON SCHEMA
`ride_hailing` TO `my_user`;
```

By now, you should see how simple yet powerful Unity Catalog makes applying consistent data security to your data pipeline datasets, providing data stewards with a variety of options to enforce dataset permissions across their organization. Let's turn our attention to how we can configure some of the advanced features and settings of a DLT pipeline.

Data pipeline settings

Up until now, we've only discussed how to use the DLT framework to declare tables, views, and transformations on the arriving data. However, the computational resources that execute a particular data pipeline also play a major role in landing the latest data in a lakehouse.

In this section, we're going to discuss the different data pipeline settings and how you can control computational resources, such as the cluster, at runtime.

The following pipeline settings can be configured directly from the DLT UI or using the Databricks REST API.

The DLT product edition

The data pipeline product edition tells the DLT framework what set of features your data pipeline will utilize. Higher product editions will contain more features, and as a result, Databricks will assess a higher price (a DBU).

Databricks offers three types of product editions for DLT pipelines, ranked in order of feature set, from the least features to the most:

1. **Core:** Core is the base product edition. This product edition is meant for streaming workloads that only append new data to streaming tables. Data expectations (data quality enforcement is discussed in the next chapter) and utilities to apply change data capture are not available in this product edition.

2. **Pro:** The Pro product edition is the next edition above Core. This production edition is designed for streaming workloads that append new data to streaming tables and apply updates and deletes using APPLY CHANGES command. However, data quality expectations are not available in this product edition.

3. **Advanced**: The Advanced product edition is the most feature-rich product edition. Data quality expectations are available in this production edition, as well as support for appending new data to streaming tables and applying inserts, updates, and deletes that have occurred in the upstream data sources.

There may be times when your requirements change over time. For example, you might require strict data quality enforcement to prevent downstream failures in third-party **business intelligence (BI)** reporting tools. In scenarios like these, you can update the product edition of an existing DLT pipeline at any time, allowing your data pipeline to adapt to changes in your feature requirements and budget.

Pipeline execution mode

DLT offers a way to inform a system that the changes to a data pipeline are experimental. This feature is called data pipeline environment mode. There are two available environment modes – **development** and **production**. The main difference is the behavior of the computational resource.

In development environment mode, a data flow task will not be automatically retried if a failure is encountered. This allows a data engineer to intervene and correct any programmatic errors during ad hoc development cycles.

Furthermore, during a failure in development mode, the cluster executing the data pipeline updates will remain up. This allows a data engineer to view the driver logs and cluster metrics of the cluster, and it also prevents a lengthy cluster re-provisioning and re-initialization of the cluster runtime for each pipeline execution, which, depending upon the cloud provider, could take 10 to 15 minutes to complete. It's expected to have short and iterative development and testing cycles, which assist data engineers in their development life cycle by keeping the cluster up and running.

The data pipeline environment mode can be set from the DLT UI by clicking the environment mode toggle switch at the very top navigation bar of a data pipeline in the DLT UI.

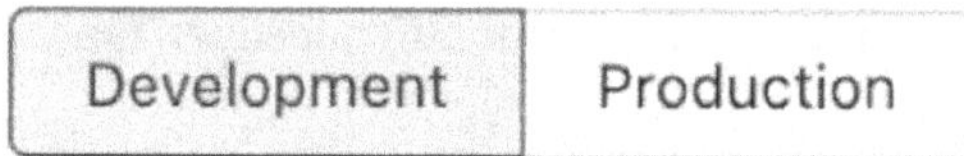

Figure 2.3 – DLT pipeline execution mode can be set using the toggle switch from the UI

Alternatively, the environment mode can also be set using the Databricks REST API. In the following code snippet, we'll use the Python requests library to send a PUT request to the Databricks DLT pipelines REST API that will set the development mode of a DLT pipeline. Note that the endpoint URL will change, depending on your Databricks workspace deployment, and the code snippet is just an example:

```python
import requests

response = requests.put(
```

```
    "https://<your_databricks_workspace>/api/2.0/pipelines/1234",
    headers={"Authorization": f"Bearer {api_token}"},
    json={
        "id": "1234",
        "name": "Clickstream Pipeline",
        "storage": "/Volumes/clickstream/data",
        "clusters": [{
            "label": "default",
            "autoscale": {
                "min_workers": 1,
                "max_workers": 3,
                "mode": "ENHANCED"}
        }],
        "development": True,
        "target": "clickstream_data",
        "continuous": False
    }
)
```

Databricks runtime

DLT is a version-less product feature on the Databricks Data Intelligence Platform. In other words, Databricks manages the underlying **Databricks Runtime (DBR)** that a data pipeline uses for its cluster.

Furthermore, Databricks will automatically upgrade a data pipeline cluster to use the latest stable runtime release. Runtime upgrades are important because they introduce bug fixes, new performance features, and other enhancements. This can mean that your data pipelines will execute faster, translating to less time and money spent to transform the latest data in your lakehouse.

You might even be eager to test out the latest performance features. Each DLT pipeline has a **Channel** setting that allows data engineers to select one of two channel options – **Current** and **Preview**. The Preview channel allows data engineers to configure a data pipeline to execute using the latest, experimental runtime that contains the new performance features and other enhancements. However, since this is an experimental runtime, it's not recommended that data pipelines running in production should use a Preview channel of the Databricks runtime. Instead, it's recommended to use the former option, Current, which selects the latest stable release of the Databricks runtime.

Furthermore, the DLT system will proactively catch runtime exceptions for data pipelines deployed in production mode. For example, if a new runtime release introduces a runtime bug, also referred to as a runtime regression, or a library version conflict, DLT will attempt to downgrade the cluster to a lower runtime that was known to execute data pipelines successfully, and it will retry executing the pipeline update.

The following diagram illustrates the automatic runtime upgrade exception handling.

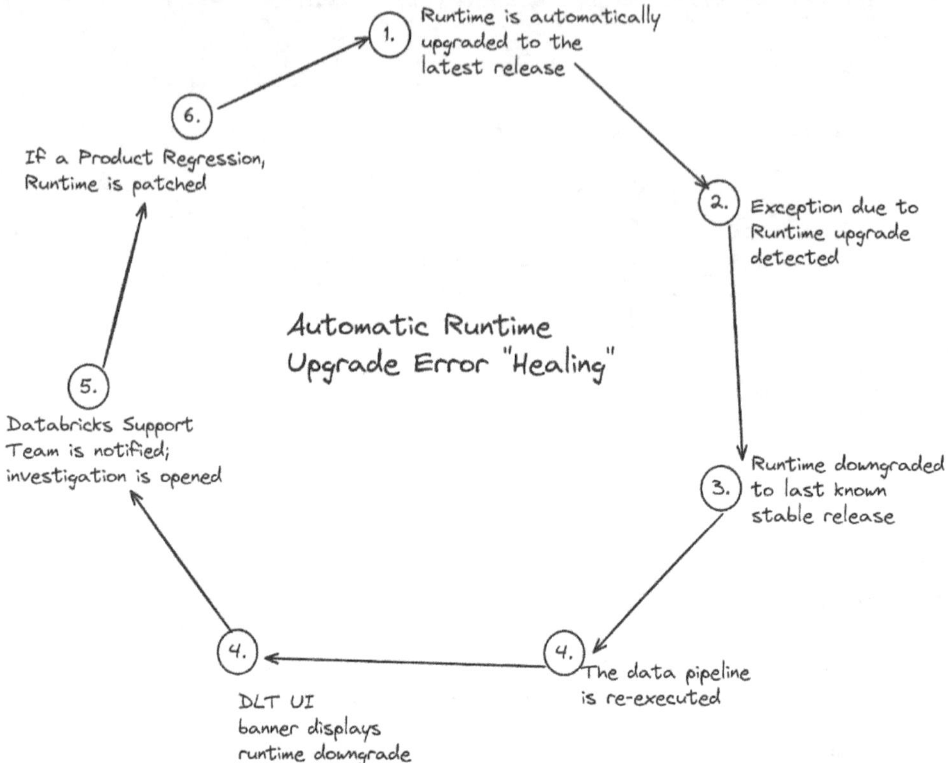

Figure 2.4 – In production mode, DLT will attempt to rerun a failed data pipeline execution using a lower Databricks runtime release

Pipeline cluster types

Each data pipeline will have two associated clusters – one to perform the dataset updates and one to perform the table maintenance tasks.

The settings for these two types of clusters are expressed in the pipeline settings of a pipeline, using a JSON cluster configuration definition. There are three types of cluster configurations that can be expressed in the pipeline settings – the update cluster configuration, the maintenance cluster configuration, and a third option that acts as a default cluster configuration, applying generalized settings to both update and maintenance clusters. The schema for this JSON configuration closely follows that of the Databricks Clusters REST API.

In addition to configuring the physical attributes of a cluster, such as the number of worker nodes and virtual machine instance types, the cluster configuration can also contain advanced Spark configurations. Let's walk through a sample cluster configuration together.

The following example contains two separate cluster configurations – a default cluster configuration that will be applied to both update and maintenance DLT clusters, as well as another cluster configuration that will be applied only to the update DLT cluster.

In the first cluster configuration, we'll specify that the cluster configuration will be the default cluster configuration using the `label` attribute. This means that the cluster configuration will be applied to DLT clusters used to update the datasets and for clusters created to run table maintenance tasks. Then, we'll enable autoscaling for our DLT clusters, specifying that all clusters will begin provisioning a cluster with a single virtual machine but can grow up to five virtual machines in total as processing demands increase. We'll also specify that an enhanced version of the cluster autoscaling algorithm should be used.

In the second set of cluster configurations, we'll specify that the cluster configuration should be applied only to DLT update clusters using the `label` attribute again. Then, we'll specify which instance types to provision for the update cluster driver and worker nodes. For the driver node, which orchestrates tasks, we'll specify that the `i4i.2xlarge` EC2 instance type should be used, while all worker nodes should use the `i4i.xlarge` EC2 instances. Lastly, we'll also enable a Databricks Runtime performance feature, called **Auto-Optimized Shuffle** (**AOS**). AOS will automatically size the number of Spark shuffle partitions at runtime, which can improve performance during wide Spark transformations such as joins, aggregations, and merge operations.

> **Important note**
>
> In the following example, we've chosen to illustrate the cluster configuration settings using virtual machine instances for the AWS cloud. However, if your workspace is in a different cloud provider, we'd suggest using Delta cache accelerated VM instances of similar sizes – eight cores for the driver node and four cores for the worker nodes (`https://docs.databricks.com/en/optimizations/disk-cache.html`):

```
{
    "clusters": [{
        "label": "default",
        "autoscale": {
            "min_workers": 1,
            "max_workers": 5,
            "mode": "ENHANCED"}
    },
    {
        "label": "updates",
        "node_type_id": "i4i.xlarge",
        "driver_node_type_id": "i4i.2xlarge",
        "spark_conf": {"spark.sql.suffle.partitions": "auto"}
    }]
}
```

As you can see, cluster configurations are a powerful tool that provides data engineers with the ability to apply either generalized cluster settings, target specific cluster settings, or do a combination of both. This is a great way to tune clusters for specific workloads and yield additional performance for your DLT pipelines.

A serverless compute versus a traditional compute

Data pipelines can be executed using clusters configured with a traditional compute or a serverless compute.

A traditional compute gives a user the most control over computational resources. However, with a traditional compute, the user will need to manage several aspects of the underlying cluster. For example, data engineering teams will need to configure cluster attributes such as the auto-scaling behavior, whether the pipeline should be executed using the Photon engine or the legacy Catalyst engine in Spark, as well as optional cluster tagging. Furthermore, traditional compute allows the user to have full control over the VM instance types that are selected for the driver and worker nodes of the cluster. As we saw in the previous section, the VM instance types can be specified under the pipeline settings by listing specific instance types within the JSON configuration. For example, the following cluster configuration specifies the i4i.xlarge and i4i.2xlarge EC2 instance types for all update clusters within a DLT pipeline:

```
{
    "clusters": [{
        "label": "updates",
        "node_type_id": "i4i.xlarge",
        "driver_node_type_id": "i4i.2xlarge"
    }]
}
```

However, DLT pipelines configured to use a serverless compute will abstract away all the underlying cluster settings, such as the cluster VM instance types, the number of worker nodes, and the autoscaling settings. As the name *serverless compute* suggests, the computational resources will be provisioned and managed by Databricks in the Databricks cloud provider account. Behind the scenes, Databricks will maintain a pool of pre-provisioned computational resources so that cluster provisioning is fast. As soon as an update for a data pipeline is triggered, the DLT system will create a logical network inside of the Databricks cloud provider account and initialize a cluster to execute the pipeline's data flow graph. Databricks will automatically select the VM instance type, the Photon execution engine, and the autoscaling behavior.

As an added layer of security, there is no communication permitted between logical networks or from the external internet, and the computational resources are never reused across serverless workloads. When the data pipeline processing has been completed and the cluster has been terminated, the computational resources are released back to the cloud provider and destroyed.

You might choose a serverless compute to remove the infrastructure overhead of maintaining and updating multiple cluster policies, as well as to also take advantage of fast cluster provisioning when reacting to spikes in processing demands is critical. Plus, serverless execution enables other platform features, such as updating materialized views in continuous processing mode (processing modes are covered in the next section).

Loading external dependencies

Data pipelines may need to load external dependencies, such as helper utilities or third-party libraries. As such, DLT offers three ways to install runtime dependencies for a data pipeline:

- From a notebook cell, using the `%pip` magic command (`https://docs.databricks.com/en/notebooks/notebooks-code.html#mix-languages`)

- Loading a module from a workspace file or Databricks repo

- Using a cluster initialization script

The popular Python package manager `pip` can be used to install Python modules from any notebook in a data pipeline's source code, via the `%pip` Databricks magic command. `%pip` is the simplest method for installing library dependencies in a data pipeline. At runtime, the DLT system will detect all notebook cells containing `%pip` magic commands and execute these cells first, before performing any pipeline updates. Furthermore, all notebooks for a declared data pipeline's source code will share a single virtual environment, so the library dependencies will be installed together in an isolated environment and be globally available to all notebooks in a data pipeline's source code. Conversely, the notebooks for a data pipeline cannot install different versions of the same Python library. For example, the following code sample will use the `pip` package manager to install the popular libraries `numpy`, `pandas`, and `scikit-learn`, as well as a custom Python library from a Databricks Volumes location:

```
%pip install numpy pandas scikit-learn /Volumes/tradingutils/tech-
analysis-utils-v1.whl
```

As a best practice, these dependency installation statements should be placed at the very top of a notebook, so that it's easier to reference pipeline dependencies quickly.

Alternatively, library dependencies can also be installed as a Python module. In this scenario, the library can be installed and loaded in a DLT pipeline as either a workspace file or from a Databricks Repo, if the module is version-controlled using a Git provider, such as GitHub or Bitbucket.

Lastly, cluster initialization scripts can also be used to install external dependencies. These scripts are run after a cluster has provisioned the VMs and installed the Databricks runtime, but before the data pipeline begins execution. For example, this type of dependency installation might be applicable in a scenario where firmwide libraries need to be consistently installed across all data engineering platforms.

> **Important note**
>
> You may have noticed that the preceding options only covered installing Python dependencies. DLT does not support installing JVM libraries, since it only offers the Python and SQL programming interfaces.

Data pipeline processing modes

The data pipeline processing mode determines how frequently the tables and materialized views within a pipeline are updated. DLT offers two types of pipeline processing modes – **triggered** processing mode and **continuous** processing mode.

Triggered processing mode will update the datasets contained within a pipeline once and then immediately terminate the cluster that was provisioned to run the pipeline, releasing the computational resources back to the cloud provider and thereby terminating additional cloud costs from being assessed. As the name suggests, triggered processing mode can be run in an ad hoc manner and will execute immediately from a triggering event, such as the event of a button clicked on the DLT UI by a user or an invocation to the Databricks REST API.

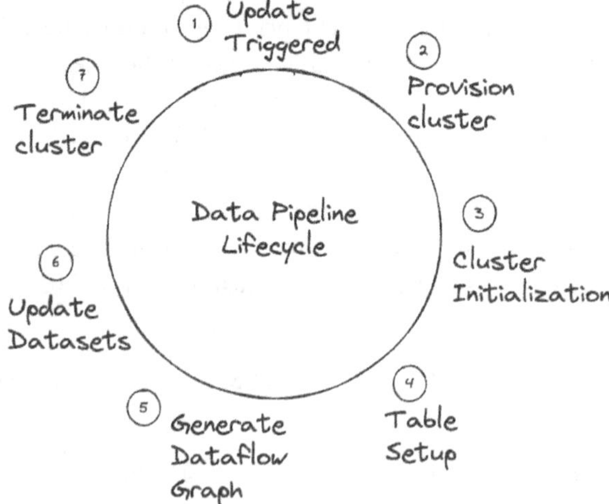

Figure 2.5 – A triggered data pipeline will refresh each dataset and then immediately terminate the cluster

Triggered processing mode can also be triggered to run using a `cron` schedule, which can be configured from the UI or via the REST API. As shown in *Figure 2.6*, a recurring schedule can be created by clicking on the **Schedule** drop-down button in the DLT UI, clicking the **Add schedule** button, and finally, selecting the desired time to trigger a pipeline update. Each day, the datasets within the pipeline will be refreshed at the scheduled time.

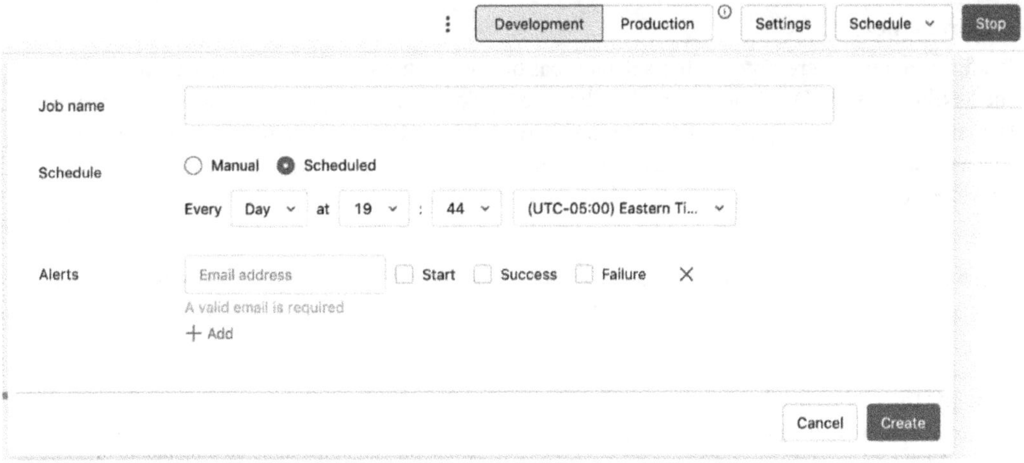

Figure 2.6 – DLT pipelines can be scheduled to refresh datasets based on a repeating schedule

Conversely, continuous processing mode will provision computational resources to refresh datasets within a pipeline but will continue to execute indefinitely, processing data and refreshing the tables and materialized views as data arrives from the source. A continuous processing pipeline will keep the computational resources running and will continue to incur cloud costs, with the trade-off of minimal data staleness. This type of pipeline mode should be selected when data latency is prioritized over cloud compute costs for a particular data pipeline.

Fortunately, the pipeline processing mode and other pipeline settings can be updated throughout the lifecycle of a data pipeline, allowing the pipeline to be flexible around processing latency and compute costs. For example, an economic downturn may force an organization to prioritize cost savings over latency but may again emphasize latency later down the road.

Let's use everything that we've learned together in this chapter and build a DLT pipeline that will apply SCD Type 2 changes to downstream datasets in our data pipeline.

Hands-on exercise – applying SCD Type 2 changes

In this hands-on exercise, we'll use Databricks Auto Loader to incrementally load JSON files that are written to a raw landing zone in a cloud storage account. Next, we'll transform downstream columns and join data ingested from an external Postgres database.

> **Important note**
>
> Reading data from a remote Postgres database is optional. This step is intended to demonstrate the flexibility of the Databricks Data Intelligence Platform, showing you how easy it is to read structured data from a remote RDBMS and combine it with semi-structured data. If you do not have a Postgres database, a static DataFrame containing the taxi driver information is provided for you.

If you haven't done so, you will need to clone the accompanying notebooks from this chapter's GitHub repo, located at `https://github.com/PacktPublishing/Building-Modern-Data-Applications-Using-Databricks-Lakehouse/tree/main/chapter02`.

Let's start by importing the data generator notebook, titled `Generate Mock Taxi Trip Data`. This notebook will create a mock dataset containing fictitious information about taxi trips. Once the mock dataset has been generated, this notebook will store the taxi trip dataset as multiple JSON files in our cloud storage account, which will be later ingested by our DLT pipeline. Attach the taxi trip data generator notebook to an all-purpose cluster and execute all the cells to generate mock data.

Next, let's create our DLT pipeline definition. Create a new notebook by clicking the workspace table on the left sidebar, clicking on the **Add** dropdown, and selecting **Notebook**. Rename the notebook with a meaningful name, such as `Taxi Trips DLT Pipeline`. We'll declare the datasets and transformations for our DLT pipeline in this notebook.

Next, import the DLT Python module to access the DLT function decorators to define datasets and dependencies, as well as the PySpark functions module:

```python
import dlt
import pyspark.sql.functions as F
```

We'll need to create a streaming table that will ingest taxi trip JSON data that has been written to a landing zone on cloud storage. Let's start by defining a new streaming table that uses the `cloudFiles` data source to listen for new file events in the raw landing zone:

```python
# This location keeps track of schema changes
SCHEMA_LOCATION = "/tmp/chp_02/taxi_data_chkpnt"
# This location contains the raw, unprocessed trip data
RAW_DATA_LOCATION = "/tmp/chp_02/taxi_data/"


@dlt.table(
    name="raw_taxi_trip_data",
    comment="Raw taxi trip data generated by the data generator
notebook"
)
def raw_taxi_trip_data():
    return (
        spark.readStream.format("cloudFiles")
```

```
                .option("cloudFiles.format", "json")
                .option("cloudFiles.schemaLocation", SCHEMA_LOCATION)
                .load(RAW_DATA_LOCATION) )
```

As new taxi trip data arrives, our DLT pipeline will efficiently load the data using Auto Loader, fetching only the information pertaining to the unprocessed files.

Now that we've ingested the raw taxi trip data, we can begin applying the recorded changes to downstream tables. Let's first define a target streaming table to apply SCD Type 2 changes that have been reported by the mock taxi trip data source:

```
# Define a new streaming table to apply SCD Type 2 changes
dlt.create_streaming_table("taxi_trip_data_merged")
```

Next, we'll leverage the `apply_changes()` function covered earlier to instruct the DLT system on how changes should be applied, which columns to omit in the downstream table, and which SCD type to use. Add the following function call to the notebook:

```
dlt.apply_changes(
    target="taxi_trip_data_merged",
    source="raw_taxi_trip_data",
    keys = ["trip_id"],
    sequence_by = F.col("sequence_num"),
    apply_as_deletes = F.expr("op_type = 'D'"),
    except_column_list = ["op_type", "op_date", "sequence_num"],
    stored_as_scd_type = 2
)
```

For our last step, we'll transform a few of the columns in our upstream tables, such as rounding columns with a `float` data type to two decimal places, as well as splitting the `trip_distance` column into a column with miles as the unit of measurement and another column with kilometers as the unit of measurement. Next, we'll connect to a remote Postgres database and read the latest taxi driver information. If you have access to a Postgres database, you can import the notebook, titled `Generate Postgres Table`, and execute the cells to generate a table to test with. Our final streaming table, which enriches our data and joins the latest taxi driver reference data, will look like the following:

```
@dlt.table(
    name="raw_driver_data",
    comment="Dataset containing info about the taxi drivers"
)
def raw_driver_data():
    postgresdb_url = f"jdbc:postgresql://{POSTGRES_
HOSTNAME}:{POSTGRES_PORT}/{POSTGRES_DB}"
    conn_props = {
        "user": POSTGRES_USERNAME,
```

```
        "password": POSTGRES_PW,
        "driver": "org.postgresql.Driver",
        "fetchsize": "1000"
    }
    return (
        spark.read
            .jdbc(postgresdb_url,
                  table=POSTGRES_TABLENAME,
                  properties=conn_props))

@dlt.table(
    name="taxi_trip_silver",
    comment="Taxi trip data with transformed columns"
)
def taxi_trip_silver():
    return (
        dlt.read("taxi_trip_data_merged")
            .withColumn("fare_amount_usd",
                        F.round(F.col("trip_amount"), 2))
            .withColumn("taxes_amount_usd",
                        F.round(F.col("trip_amount") * 0.05, 2))
            .withColumn("trip_distance_miles",
                        F.round(F.col("trip_distance"), 2))
            .withColumn("trip_distance_km",
                        F.round(F.col("trip_distance")
                        * 1.60934, 2)) # 1 mile = 1.60934 km
    ).join(
        dlt.read("raw_driver_data"),
        on="taxi_number",
        how="left"
    )
```

In this last function definition, we make use of the `dlt.read()` function to retrieve earlier dataset declarations. Behind the scenes, the DLT framework will add the datasets to the dataflow graph, creating the dependencies between the `taxi_trip_data_merged` and `taxi_trip_silver` datasets.

Now, it's time to create our DLT pipeline. Attach the notebook in the previous step to an all-purpose cluster and execute the notebook cells. When prompted, click on the blue **Create Pipeline** button to open the **Pipeline** UI page. Give the pipeline a meaningful name, such as `Taxi Trip Data Pipeline`. Since we are leveraging the `apply_changes()` function, we will need to select the **Advanced** product edition. Ensure that the **Triggered** processing mode radio button is selected. To view the backend table that is created by the `apply_changes()` function, select the Hive Metastore for the storage location, and provide a target schema to store the pipeline datasets. Accept the remainder default values, and then click the **Create** button to create the pipeline.

Finally, run the newly created pipeline by clicking the **Start** button in the DLT UI. Soon, you will see a data flow graph that ingests changes from the raw JSON data, enriches downstream columns, and joins the remote structured data from the Postgres database.

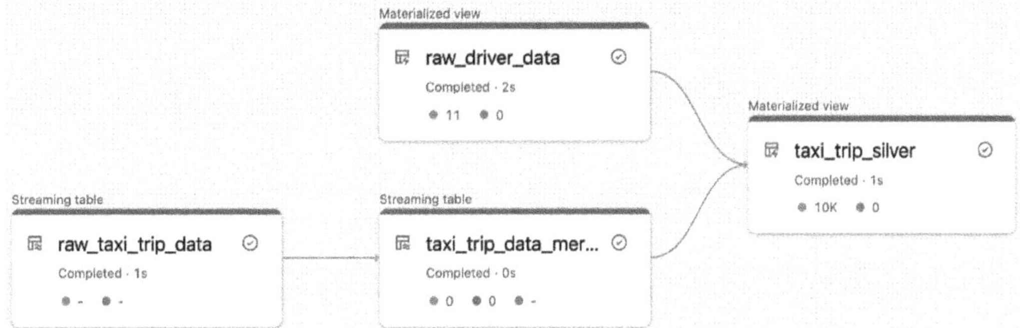

Figure 2.7 – A data flow graph generated by the DLT system

As data is changed in the mock taxi trip data source, the full history of DML changes is picked and applied to a target `taxi_trip_data_merged` table. The output of our data pipeline will be a curated streaming table that contains information about the taxi cab ride, as well as information about the taxi driver and taxi vehicle. Best of all, with just a few lines of code, we deployed a fully scalable, cost-efficient data pipeline that can easily process billions of files.

Summary

In this chapter, we looked at how DLT can simplify our data pipelines by abstracting away many of the low-level details of processing data in Spark. We saw how Databricks Auto Loader solves the scalability problem of stream processing files from cloud storage. With just a few lines of code, we deployed a scalable backend system to efficiently read new files as soon as they appear in a cloud storage location. When it came to applying data changes to downstream datasets within our pipeline, the DLT framework once again simplified data reconciliation when data events were published late or out of order. We also saw how we could apply slowly changing dimensions with just a few parameter changes in the `apply_changes()` API. Finally, we uncovered the details of data pipeline settings, optimizing the pipeline compute based on the computational requirements and DLT feature set that we needed in the data pipeline. We also saw how DLT can automatically handle pipeline failures for us and proactively take action and attempt to fix certain runtime exceptions.

In the next chapter, we'll look at how we can use *expectations* in DLT to enforce data quality rules on data throughout each hop in our data pipeline, taking action whenever the data quality rules have been violated.

3

Managing Data Quality Using Delta Live Tables

This chapter introduces several techniques for managing the data quality of datasets in a data pipeline. We'll introduce **expectations** in **Delta Live Tables** (**DLT**), which is a way to enforce certain data quality constraints on arriving data before merging the data into downstream tables. Later in the chapter, we'll look at more advanced techniques such as quarantining bad data for human intervention. Next, we'll also see how we can decouple constraints so that they can be managed separately by non-technical personas within your organization. By the end of the chapter, you should have a firm understanding of how you can take measures to ensure the data integrity of datasets in your lakehouse and how to take appropriate action on data not meeting the expected criteria.

In this chapter, we're going to cover the following topics:

- Defining data constraints in Delta Lake

- Using temporary datasets to validate data processing

- An introduction to expectations

- Hands-on exercise: writing your first data quality expectation

- Taking action on failed expectations

- Applying multiple data quality expectations

- Decoupling expectations from a DLT pipeline

- Hands-on exercise – quarantining poor-quality data for correction

Technical requirements

To follow along with this chapter, it's recommended to have Databricks workspace permissions to create an all-purpose cluster and a DLT pipeline using a cluster policy. It's also recommended to have Unity Catalog permissions to create and use catalogs, schemas, and tables. All code samples can be downloaded from this chapter's GitHub repository, located at `https://github.com/PacktPublishing/Building-Modern-Data-Applications-Using-Databricks-Lakehouse/tree/main/chapter03`. We'll be using the NYC yellow taxi dataset, which can be found on the Databricks FileSystem at `/databricks-datasets/nyctaxi/tripdata/yellow`. This chapter will create and run several new notebooks and DLT pipelines using the **Advanced** product edition. As a result, the pipelines are estimated to consume around 10-20 **Databricks Units (DBUs)**.

Defining data constraints in Delta Lake

Data constraints are an effective way of defining criteria that incoming data must satisfy before being inserted into a Delta table. Constraints are defined per column in a Delta table and are stored as additional table metadata.

There are four different types of constraints available within the Databricks Data Intelligence Platform:

- `NOT NULL`: Ensures that the data for a particular column in a table is not null. The `NOT NULL` constraint was first introduced in the `StructField` class definition of Apache Spark.

- `CHECK`: A Boolean expression that must evaluate to `True` for each row before being inserted. Check constraints allow data engineers to enforce complex validation logic that a particular column must satisfy.

- `PRIMARY KEY`: Establishes uniqueness for a particular column across all the rows in a table. The `PRIMARY KEY` constraint is a special kind of constraint as it is purely informative and is not enforced on the incoming data. As we'll see in the following example, a `NOT NULL` constraint must accompany a `PRIMARY KEY` constraint.

- `FOREIGN KEY`: Establishes a relationship between a particular column and another table. Like the `PRIMARY KEY` constraint, a `FOREIGN KEY` constraint is also purely informative.

In addition, only the `NOT NULL` and `CHECK` constraints are enforced on the incoming data.

Constraint	Enforced	Informative
NOT NULL	✔	✘
CHECK	✔	✘
PRIMARY KEY	✘	✔
FOREIGN KEY	✘	✔

Table 3.1 – Data quality constraints can either be enforced or not enforced on the Databricks Data Intelligence Platform

> **Important note**
>
> The PRIMARY KEY constraint and the FOREIGN KEY constraint require the Delta tables to be stored in Unity Catalog, otherwise a runtime error will be thrown.

Let's look at how we can use constraints to define a hierarchical relationship between two Delta tables in our lakehouse. First, create a new SQL-based notebook within your Databricks notebook. Let's start by defining a child table that will contain data about the taxicab drivers, called `drivers`, with a primary key defined on the `driver_id` column. Add the following code snippet to a new notebook cell:

```sql
%sql
CREATE CATALOG IF NOT EXISTS yellow_taxi_catalog;
CREATE SCHEMA IF NOT EXISTS yellow_taxi_catalog.yellow_taxi;
CREATE TABLE yellow_taxi_catalog.yellow_taxi.drivers(
    driver_id INTEGER NOT NULL,
    first_name STRING,
    last_name STRING,
    CONSTRAINT drivers_pk PRIMARY KEY(driver_id));
```

Next, let's define a parent table, `rides`, having a primary key defined for the `ride_id` column and a foreign key that references the `drivers` table. Add the following code snippet below the first notebook cell:

```sql
%sql
CREATE TABLE yellow_taxi_catalog.yellow_taxi.rides(
    ride_id INTEGER NOT NULL,
    driver_id INTEGER,
    passenger_count INTEGER,
    total_amount DOUBLE,
    CONSTRAINT rides_pk PRIMARY KEY (ride_id),
    CONSTRAINT drivers_fk FOREIGN KEY (driver_id)
    REFERENCES yellow_taxi_catalog.yellow_taxi.drivers);
```

Attach the newly created notebook to an all-purpose cluster and execute the notebook cells to create the parent and child tables. Finally, let's navigate to the newly defined tables in Catalog Explorer to generate an **Entity Relationship Diagram** (**ERD**) directly from the Databricks Data Intelligence Platform. From our Databricks workspace, click on **Catalog Explorer** on the left sidebar. Navigate to the `yellow_taxi_catalog` catalog in Unity Catalog, in the preceding example. Click on the defined schema and, finally, click on the parent table. A side pane will expand, displaying metadata about our Delta table. Click on the button titled **View Relationships** to view the ERD.

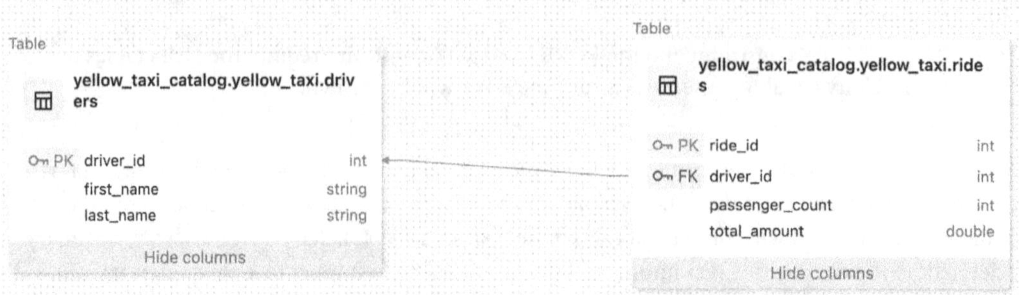

Figure 3.1 – Data constraints can be used to define primary key
and foreign key relationships between Delta tables

As previously mentioned, the primary key and foreign key constraints are purely informative and are not enforced on the incoming data. Instead, it's recommended to implement additional safeguards to ensure the data integrity of a primary key column in a Delta table. Let's look at a few effective strategies we can employ to maintain the integrity of primary key columns defined in our lakehouse tables.

Using temporary datasets to validate data processing

As we'll see in this section, creating a view is an effective method for validating the uniqueness of a primary key column. Additionally, we can also define alerts in the Databricks Data Intelligence Platform to notify the data stewards of potential data quality issues so that they can take appropriate measures to correct the data integrity.

We can leverage a view to validate the uniqueness of the primary key column. Recall the `rides` and `drivers` tables we defined in the previous section. In this example, we're going to define a view on the incoming data to ensure the uniqueness of a primary key column across the `rides` Delta table. Create a new query in Databricks by navigating back to your workspace and right-clicking to open a dialog box. Select **New | Query** to open a new query in the editor. Next, rename the query with a meaningful name, such as `rides_pk_validation_vw`. Finally, add the following query text to the open query and click the **Run** button to validate that the query runs as expected:

```
CREATE VIEW yellow_taxi_catalog.yellow_taxi.rides_pk_validation_vw AS
SELECT *
FROM (
    SELECT count(*) AS num_occurrences
    FROM  yellow_taxi_catalog.yellow_taxi.rides
    GROUP BY ride_id
) WHERE num_occurrences > 1
```

As it turns out, primary key uniqueness is essential in downstream reports for the Yellow Taxi Corporation. Let's create a new alert in the Databricks Data Intelligence Platform to alert our data stewards of possible data corruption so that they can take appropriate action when a duplicate primary key is inserted.

First, let's create a query that will be run by our alert. From the sidebar, click on the **Queries** button and click the **Create query** button, which will take us to the query editor in the Databricks Data Intelligence Platform. Rename the query to something meaningful, such as `Rides Primary Key Uniqueness`. Enter the following SQL text as the query body, click the **Save** button, and select a workspace folder to save the query. Click the **Run** button and ensure that the query runs successfully:

```
SELECT count(*) AS num_invalid_pks
   FROM yellow_taxi_catalog.yellow_taxi.rides_pk_validation_vw;
```

Next, from the sidebar, click on the **Alerts** button to navigate to the **Alerts** UI. Then, click on the **Create alert** button to begin creating a new alert and enter a descriptive name in the **Alert name** textbox, such as `Invalid Primary Key on Rides Table`. In the **Query** dropdown, select the query we just created. Click the **Send notification** checkbox and accept the default settings by clicking the **Create alert** button. In a real-world scenario, this could be an email chain for on-call data engineers or other popular notification destinations such as Slack or Microsoft Teams.

This example is quite practical in real-world data pipelines. However, views require the latest table state to be calculated each time a pipeline is run, as well as the maintenance overhead of having to configure the notification alerts. That's a lot of configuration to maintain, which simply won't scale as we add more tables to our pipelines. What if there's an easier way to declare data quality as a part of our DLT pipeline declaration?

An introduction to expectations

Expectations are data quality rules defined alongside a dataset definition in a DLT pipeline. The data quality rule is a Boolean expression applied to each record passing through a particular dataset definition. The expression must evaluate to `True` for the record to be marked as passing, else it will result in a failed record indicating that the record has not passed data quality validation.

Furthermore, the DLT pipeline will record data quality metrics for each row that gets processed in a data pipeline. For example, DLT will record the number of records that have passed data quality validation, as well as the number of records that have not.

Expectation composition

Each expectation is comprised of three major components: a description, a Boolean expression, and an action to take.

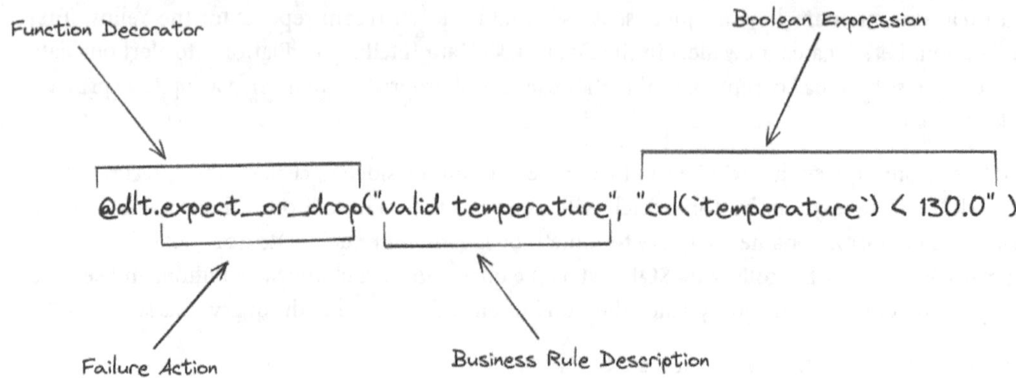

Figure 3.2 – The main components of a DLT expectation

An expectation is declared using a DLT function decorator. The function decorator specifies the type of action that should be taken whenever a particular constraint or set of constraints evaluates to False. Additionally, the function decorator accepts two input parameters, a short description that describes the data quality constraint and a Boolean expression that must evaluate to True for a row to be marked as passing validation.

Hands-on exercise – writing your first data quality expectation

To get a feel for the DLT syntax, let's work through a real-world example of writing a data pipeline for a New York City cab company called the Yellow Taxi Corporation. We'll write a simple data pipeline, enforcing a data quality constraint that can be applied to our incoming NYC Taxi data and warn us when there are records that don't adhere to our data quality specifications. In this scenario, we want to ensure that the incoming trip data does not have any trips with a negative total amount, since it would not be possible for our cab drivers to owe the riders any money.

Generating taxi trip data

Let's begin by logging into our Databricks workspace. For this exercise, you will need to use the accompanying NYC Yellow Taxi trip data generator, which can be downloaded from the chapter's GitHub repo. Either import the data generator notebook into your Databricks workspace or create a new Python notebook with the following code snippet.

First, we'll need to download the dbldatagen Python library, which will help us randomly generate new taxi trip data. Add the following code snippet to your notebook, which uses the %pip magic command to download the library:

```
%pip install dbldatagen==0.4.0
```

Now that the library has been installed, let's define a Python function for generating new taxi trip data according to our schema. We'll specify columns for typical taxi trip details, including the number of passengers, the fare amount, the trip distance, and more:

```python
def generate_taxi_trip_data():
    """Generates random taxi trip data"""
    import dbldatagen as dg
    from pyspark.sql.types import (
        IntegerType, StringType, FloatType, DateType
    )
    ds = (
        dg.DataGenerator(spark, name="random_taxi_trip_dataset",
                         rows=100000, partitions=8)
        .withColumn("trip_id", IntegerType(),
                    minValue=1000000, maxValue=2000000)
        .withColumn("taxi_number", IntegerType(),
                    uniqueValues=10000, random=True)
        .withColumn("passenger_count", IntegerType(),
                    minValue=1, maxValue=4)
        .withColumn("trip_amount", FloatType(), minValue=-100.0,
                    maxValue=1000.0, random=True)
        .withColumn("trip_distance", FloatType(),
                    minValue=0.1, maxValue=1000.0)
        .withColumn("trip_date", DateType(),
                    uniqueValues=300, random=True))

    return ds.build()
```

Now that we've defined a way to randomly generate new trip data, we'll need to define a location to store the new data so that it can be processed by a DLT pipeline. In a new notebook cell, let's create an empty directory on the **Databricks File System (DBFS)** for storing our trip data:

```python
dbutils.fs.mkdirs("/tmp/chp_03/taxi_data")
```

Lastly, we'll need a way to tie everything together. In a new notebook cell, add the following `for` loop, which will call the `generate_taxi_trip_data` function and write the data to the DBFS location:

```python
import random
max_num_files = 100
for i in range(int(max_num_files)):
    df = generate_taxi_trip_data()
    file_name = f"/tmp/chp_03/taxi_data/taxi_data_{random.randint(1,
1000000)}.json"
    df.write.mode("append").json(file_name)
```

Next, create an all-purpose cluster to execute the trip data generator notebook. Once the all-purpose cluster has been created, navigate to the new notebook and click the cluster dropdown in the top navigation bar of the Databricks Data Intelligence Platform. Select the name of the cluster you created and select **Attach** to attach the trip data generator notebook to the cluster and execute all the cells. The taxi trip data generator will append several new JSON files containing the randomly generated trip data to the DBFS location.

Creating a new DLT pipeline definition

Now that we've generated new data, let's create another new notebook for our DLT pipeline definition. Navigate to the workspace tab on the sidebar, drill down to your user's home directory, and create a new notebook by right-clicking and selecting **Add Notebook**.

Give the new notebook a meaningful name such as `Chapter 3 - Enforcing Data Quality`. Begin by importing the DLT Python module as well as the PySpark functions:

```
import dlt
from pyspark.sql.functions import *
```

Next, let's define a bronze table, `yellow_taxi_raw`, that will ingest the taxi trip data that was written to the DBFS location by our taxi trip data generator:

```
@dlt.table(
    comment="The randomly generated taxi trip dataset"
)
def yellow_taxi_raw():
    path = "/tmp/chp_03/taxi_data"
    schema = "trip_id INT, taxi_number INT, passenger_count INT, trip_
amount FLOAT, trip_distance FLOAT, trip_date DATE"
    return (spark.readStream
                .schema(schema)
                .format("json")
                .load(path))
```

For the next layer of our data pipeline, the stakeholders within our organization have asked us to provide a way for their business to report real-time financial analytics of our incoming trip data. As a result, let's add a silver table that will transform the incoming stream of trip data, calculating the expected profits and losses of our cab company, Yellow Taxi Corporation. In this example, we're going to take the total amount that was paid by the passengers and begin to calculate how that money is allocated to fund different parts of the business and calculate potential profits.

Let's define our silver table definition, `trip_data_financials`. The table definition begins just like any normal streaming table definition. We begin by defining a Python function that returns a streaming table. Next, we use the DLT function annotations to declare this function as a streaming table with an optional name, `trip_data_financials`, as well as a comment with descriptive text about the streaming table. Create a new notebook cell, adding the following DLT dataset definition for the silver table:

```python
@dlt.table(name="trip_data_financials",
          comment="Financial information from incoming taxi trips.")
@dlt.expect("valid_total_amount", "trip_amount > 0.0")
def trip_data_financials():
    return (dlt.readStream("yellow_taxi_raw")
                .withColumn("driver_payment",
                            expr("trip_amount * 0.40"))
                .withColumn("vehicle_maintenance_fee",
                            expr("trip_amount * 0.05"))
                .withColumn("adminstrative_fee",
                            expr("trip_amount * 0.1"))
                .withColumn("potential_profits",
                            expr("trip_amount * 0.45")))
```

One thing that you may have noticed in our silver table declaration is a new function decorator for enforcing a data quality constraint. In this case, we want to ensure that the total amount reported in our trip data is greater than zero.

When our data pipeline is triggered to run and update the bronze and silver datasets, the DLT system will inspect each row that is processed and evaluate whether the Boolean expression for our data quality constraint evaluates to `True` for the row:

```python
@dlt.expect("valid_total_amount", "trip_amount > 0.0")
```

Within the body of the function definition, we are using the built-in PySpark `withColumn()` and `expr()` functions to add four new columns to the output of our bronze table – `driver_payment`, `vehicle_maintenance_fee`, `adminstrative_fee`, and `potential_profits`. These columns are calculated by taking a percentage of the original `trip_amount` column. In business terms, we are splitting the total amount that was collected from the passengers into the driver's payment, fees collected to run the company, and potential profits for the company.

In the following section, we'll look at the different types of actions that the DLT system will take if an expectation Boolean expression is evaluated to `False`. By default, the DLT system will simply record that the row failed the Boolean expression for a particular row in the system logs and record the data quality metrics in the system. In our silver table declaration, let's assume the default behavior of logging a warning message.

Running the data pipeline

Let's create a new data pipeline from our dataset declarations in our notebook. Execute the notebook cells and ensure that there are no syntax errors. Next, the Databricks Data Intelligence Platform will prompt you to create a new data pipeline. Click the **Create pipeline** button to create a new DLT data pipeline. Next, under the **Destination** settings, select a catalog and schema in Unity Catalog where you would like to store the pipeline datasets. Under the **Compute** settings, set **Min workers** to **1** and **Max workers** to **2**. Accept the defaults by clicking the **Create** button. Finally, click the **Start** button to execute the data pipeline. You will be taken to a visual representation of the dataflow graph.

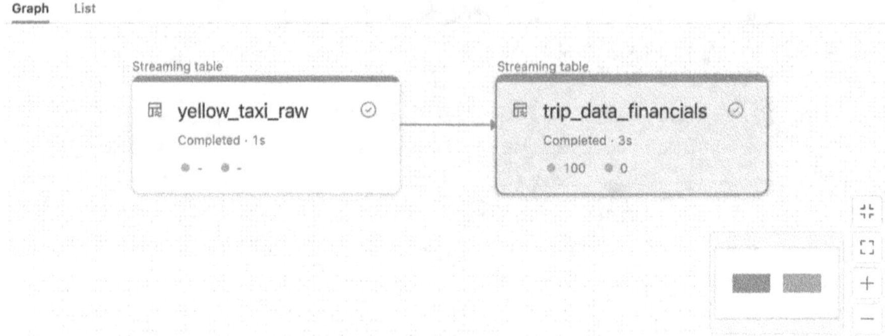

Figure 3.3 – The dataflow graph for our NYC Yellow Taxi Corp. pipeline

Behind the scenes, the DLT system will begin by creating and initializing a new Databricks cluster and begin parsing the dataset definitions in our notebook into a dataflow graph. As you can see, the DLT system will ingest the raw trip data files from our DBFS location into the streaming table, `yellow_taxi_raw`. Next, the system detects the dependency of our silver table, `trip_data_financials`, and will immediately begin calculating our additional four columns in our silver table. Along the way, our data quality constraint is being evaluated on the incoming data in real time.

Let's look at the data quality in real time. Click on the silver table, and the DLT UI will expand a pane on the right-hand side summarizing the silver table. Click on the **Data quality** tab to view the data quality metrics. Notice that the graph is being updated in real time as our data is processed. Of all the data that has been processed by the data pipeline, you'll notice that around 10% has failed the `valid_total_amount` expectation – which is expected. The data generator notebook will purposely publish records with a negative total amount to our cloud storage location. We can easily see how much of our data is validating against our defined data quality criteria and how much is not.

Figure 3.4 – The DLT UI will summarize the data quality metrics of our data pipeline in real time

Congratulations! You've written your first data quality constraint in Delta Live Tables. By now, you should see just how easy yet powerful the DLT framework is. In just a few lines of code, we're able to enforce data quality constraints on our incoming data, as well as to monitor the data quality in real time. This gives data engineering teams more control over their data pipelines.

In the next section, we'll see how data engineering teams can leverage DLT expectations to react to potential data quality issues before leading to potential data corruption.

Acting on failed expectations

There are three types of actions that DLT can take when a particular record violates the data constraints defined on a DLT dataset:

- **Warn**: When DLT encounters an expression violation, the record will be recorded as a metric and will continue to be written to the downstream target dataset.

- **Drop**: When DLT encounters an expression violation, the record will be recorded as a metric and will be prevented from entering the downstream target dataset.

- **Fail**: When DLT encounters an expression violation, the pipeline update will fail entirely until a data engineering team member can investigate and correct the data violation or possible data corruption.

You should always choose one of the actions based on the individual use case and on how you want to handle data that does not meet data quality rules. For example, there may be times when data does not meet the defined data quality constraints but logging the violating rows in the DLT system and monitoring the data quality meets the requirements for a particular use case. On the other hand, there may be scenarios where specific data quality constraints must be met, otherwise the incoming data will break downstream processes. In that scenario, more aggressive action such as failing the data pipeline run and rolling back transactions is the appropriate behavior. In either scenario, the Delta Live Tables framework gives data engineering teams full control to decide the fate of violating rows and the power to define how the system should react.

Hands-on example – failing a pipeline run due to poor data quality

There may be scenarios when you want to immediately halt the execution of a data pipeline update to intervene and correct the data, for example. In this case, DLT expectations offer the ability to immediately fail a data pipeline run using the `@dlt.expect_or_fail()` function decorator.

If the operation is a table update, the transaction is immediately rolled back to prevent contamination of bad data. Furthermore, DLT will track additional metadata about processed records so that data engineering teams can pinpoint which record in the dataset caused the failure.

Let's look at how we can update the earlier example of our Yellow Taxi Corporation data pipeline. In this scenario, having a negative total amount would break downstream financial reports. In this case, rather than simply record the rows that violate the expectation, we'd like to fail the pipeline run, so that our data engineering team can investigate potential issues in the data and take appropriate action such as the manual correction of the data.

In the Delta Live Tables framework, adjusting the behavior of our data pipeline is as simple as updating the function decorator of our silver table definition. Let's update the expectation with the `expect_or_fail` action:

```
@dlt.expect_or_fail("valid_total_amount", "trip_amount > 0.0")
```

The full dataset definition for the silver table, `trip_data_financials`, should look like the following code snippet:

```python
@dlt.table(
    name="trip_data_financials",
    comment="Financial information from completed taxi trips."
)
@dlt.expect_or_fail("valid_total_amount", "trip_amount > 0.0")
def trip_data_financials():
    return (
        dlt.readStream("yellow_taxi_raw")
            .withColumn("driver_payment",
                        expr("trip_amount*0.40"))
            .withColumn("vehicle_maintenance_fee",
                        expr("trip_amount*0.05"))
            .withColumn("adminstrative_fee",
                        expr("trip_amount*0.1"))
            .withColumn("potential_profits",
                        expr("trip_amount*0.45")))
```

Next, let's rerun the trip data generator to append additional files to the raw landing zone in the Databricks file system. Once the trip data generator has finished, navigate back to the Yellow Taxi Corporation data pipeline created earlier and click the **Start** button to trigger another execution of the data pipeline. For this chapter's examples, the trip data generator will randomly generate trip data with negative total amounts.

You should observe for this run of the data pipeline that the data pipeline update failed with an error status.

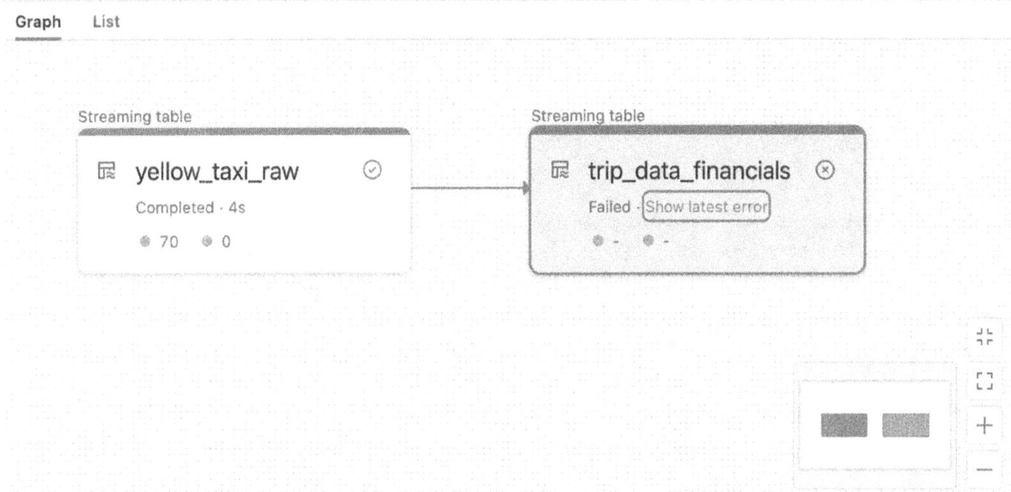

Figure 3.5 – The dataflow graph will update to display an error when the data quality constraint is violated

Expanding the failure message, you can see that the cause of the pipeline failure was a violation of the expectation constraint.

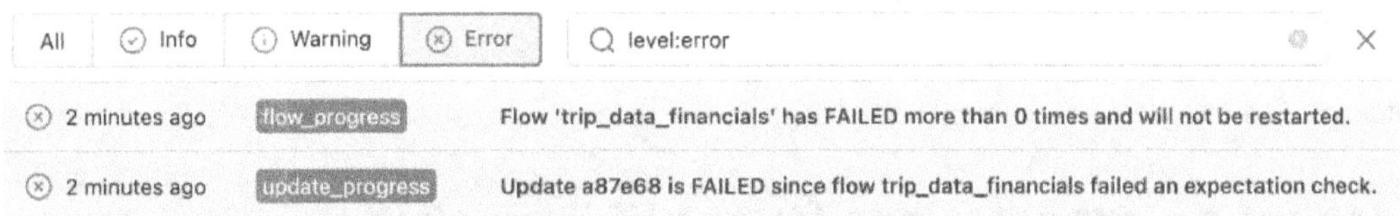

Figure 3.6 – The data pipeline logs will display the failed update due to a violated expectation check

Applying multiple data quality expectations

There may be times when a dataset author may want to apply more than one business rule or data quality constraint on each row of a dataset. In that event, DLT provides a special set of function decorators for specifying multiple data quality constraint definitions.

The `@dlt.expect_all()` function decorator can be used to combine more than one data quality constraint for a particular dataset. Similarly, `expect_all_or_drop()` can be specified when incoming data should be dropped from entering a target table unless all the criteria in the set of data quality constraints are satisfied. Lastly, `expect_all_or_fail()` will fail a run of a data pipeline if any of the criteria in a set of data quality constraints are not met by the incoming data.

Let's look at how we might drop invalid taxicab trip data entries from entering downstream datasets in our pipeline when the values don't pass the validation criteria:

```python
assertions = {
    "total_amount_constraint": "trip_amount > 0.0",
    "passenger_count": "passenger_count >= 1"
}


@dlt.table(
    name="yellow_taxi_validated",
    comment="A dataset containing trip data that has been validated.")
@dlt.expect_all_or_drop(assertions)
def yellow_taxi_validated():
    return (
        dlt.readStream("yellow_taxi_raw")
            .withColumn("nyc_congestion_tax",
                        expr("trip_amount * 0.05")))
```

In the preceding example, we've defined a set of data constraints using the expectations function decorators and we are applying them collectively to the incoming data. Let's imagine that losing a few records of the taxicab trip data will not pose a threat to downstream processes. As a result, we've decided to drop records that don't pass the validation step in our expectation declaration. With just a few extra lines of configuration, our data pipeline can enforce data quality constraints on the incoming data and automatically react to data that doesn't pass the defined criteria.

While we've only looked at data within the context of our DLT data pipeline, let's see how the DLT framework can validate data across multiple systems of data.

Decoupling expectations from a DLT pipeline

Up until now, we've only worked with defining data quality constraints within the table definition. However, there may be scenarios when you'd like to decouple the data quality constraints from data pipeline definitions, allowing the data engineering teams to work separately from the data analyst teams. This is especially useful when a group of non-technical individuals determine the data quality criteria. Furthermore, this design also provides even more flexibility to maintain and change business rules as the business changes. For example, a real-world example would be validating seasonal discount codes that change over time.

Let's imagine that we have a group of non-technical business analysts who would like to interact with the data quality constraints using a UI such as a web portal in a browser window. In that case, we can load and save our data quality constraints into a separate Delta table and then dynamically load the data quality constraints at runtime.

Let's begin by defining a data quality rules table. We'll introduce three columns: a column for the rule name, a column defining the data quality rule expression, and a column identifying the dataset name – everything needed to create an expectation using DLT:

```
%sql
CREATE TABLE IF NOT EXISTS<catalog_name>.<schema_name>.data_quality_
rules
(rule_name STRING, rule_expression STRING, dataset_name STRING)
USING DELTA
```

Let's revisit the previous example for specifying multiple expectations using a Python dictionary. In that example, we defined a `dict` data structure called `assertions`. In this example, let's convert it into a tabular format, inserting the entries into our Delta table. Add the following SQL statement to a new notebook cell:

```
%sql
INSERT INTO
    data_quality_rules
VALUES
    (
        'valid_total_amount',
        'trip_amount > 0.0',
        'yellow_taxi_raw'
    ),(
        'valid_passenger_count',
        'passenger_count > 0',
        'yellow_taxi_raw'
    );
```

Next, within the data pipeline notebook, we can create a helper function that will read directly from our data quality rules table and translate each row to a format that the DLT Expectation can interpret:

```
def compile_data_quality_rules(rules_table_name, dataset_name):
    """A helper function that reads from the data_quality_rules table
and coverts to a format interpreted by a DLT Expectation."""
    rules = spark.sql(f"""SELECT * FROM {rules_table_name} WHERE
dataset_name='{dataset_name}'""").collect()
    rules_dict = {}
    # Short circuit if there are no rules found
    if len(rules) == 0:
        raise Exception(f"No rules found for dataset '{dataset_
name}'")
    for rule in rules:
        rules_dict[rule.rule_name] = rule.rule_expression
    return rules_dict
```

We now have a Delta table that our non-technical data analysts can update using a UI separate from our data pipeline, and we also have a helper function that can read from the Delta table and translate the entries into a format that a DLT expectation can interpret. Let's see how these pieces tie together to create a new dataset in our pipeline that dynamically loads the data quality requirements:

```python
import dlt
from pyspark.sql.functions import *

RULES_TABLE = "<catalog_name>.<schema_name>.data_quality_rules"
DATASET_NAME = "yellow_taxi_raw"

@dlt.table(
    comment="Randomly generated taxi trip data."
)
def yellow_taxi_raw():
    path = "/tmp/chp_03/taxi_data"
    schema = "trip_id INT, taxi_number INT, passenger_count INT, trip_
amount FLOAT, trip_distance FLOAT, trip_date DATE"
    return (spark.readStream
                .schema(schema)
                .format("json")
                .load(path))

@dlt.table(
    name="yellow_taxi_validated",
    comment="A dataset containing trip data that has been validated.")
@dlt.expect_all(compile_data_quality_rules(RULES_TABLE, DATASET_NAME))
def yellow_taxi_validated():
    return (
        dlt.readStream("yellow_taxi_raw")
            .withColumn("nyc_congestion_tax",
                expr("trip_amount * 0.05"))
    )
```

This design pattern provides the flexibility to maintain the data quality rules separately from the data pipeline definition so that non-technical individuals determine the data quality criteria. But what if we have a technical group of individuals who want to stay involved in the quality of the data passing through our data pipeline? Moreover, what if this group of individuals needs to be notified of poor-quality data so that they can intervene and even manually correct the data for the downstream processes to function? Let's take a look at how we might implement such a recovery process in the next hands-on exercise.

Hands-on exercise – quarantining bad data for correction

In this example, we're going to build a conditional data flow for data that doesn't meet our data quality requirements. This will allow us to isolate the data that violates our data quality rules so that we can take appropriate action later or even report on the data that violates the data quality constraints.

We'll use the same Yellow Taxi Corporation example to illustrate building a data quarantine zone concept. Let's start off with a bronze table that ingests the raw JSON data written to the DBFS location by the trip data generator:

```
%py

import dlt
from pyspark.sql.functions import *

@dlt.table(
    name="yellow_taxi_raw",
    comment="The randomly generated taxi trip dataset"
)
def yellow_taxi_raw():
    path = "/tmp/chp_03/taxi_data"
    schema = "trip_id INT, taxi_number INT, passenger_count INT, trip_
amount FLOAT, trip_distance FLOAT, trip_date DATE"
    return (spark.readStream
                    .schema(schema)
                    .format("json")
                    .load(path))
```

Next, let's begin by defining a few data quality rules on incoming data. Let's make sure that the trip data published to our DBFS location is sensible. We'll ensure that the total fare amount is greater than $0 and that the ride has at least 1 passenger, otherwise, we'll quarantine the trip data for further review:

```
data_quality_rules = {
    "total_amount_assertion": "trip_amount > 0.0",
    "passenger_count": "passenger_count >= 1"
}
```

Now, let's apply the two data quality rules to the incoming data by creating another dataset with a calculated column, `is_valid`. This column will contain the results of the data quality rules evaluated for each row:

```
@dlt.table(
    name="yellow_taxi_validated",
    comment="Validation table that applies data quality rules to the
incoming data"
```

```
)
def yellow_taxi_validated():
    return (
        dlt.readStream("yellow_taxi_raw")
            .withColumn("is_valid",
                when(expr(" AND ".join(data_quality_rules.values())),
                lit(True)).otherwise(lit(False)))
    )
```

Finally, we can use the `is_valid` calculated column to split the streaming table into two data flows – a data flow for all incoming data that has passed the data quality assertions and a separate data flow for the incoming data that has not.

Let's define a quarantine table in our data pipeline that will route the data according to the evaluated data quality rules:

```
@dlt.table(
    name="yellow_taxi_quarantine",
    comment="A quarantine table for incoming data that has not met the
validation criteria"
)
def yellow_taxi_quarantine():
    return (
        dlt.readStream("yellow_taxi_validated")
            .where(expr("is_valid == False"))
    )


@dlt.table(
    name="yellow_taxi_passing"
)
def yellow_taxi_passing():
    return (
        dlt.readStream("yellow_taxi_validated")
            .where(expr("is_valid == True"))
    )
```

Finally, create a new DLT pipeline using the new notebook as the source. Provide a meaningful name for the pipeline, such as `Chapter 3 Quarantining Invalid Data`. Select **Core** as the product edition and **Triggered** as the execution mode. Next, select a target catalog and schema in Unity Catalog to store the pipeline datasets. Accept the remaining default values and click the **Create** button to create the new DLT pipeline. Finally, click on the **Start** button to trigger a new pipeline execution run. Notice how the data is split into two downstream tables – one table containing the rows that passed the data quality rules, and a quarantine table containing the rows that have failed the data quality rules.

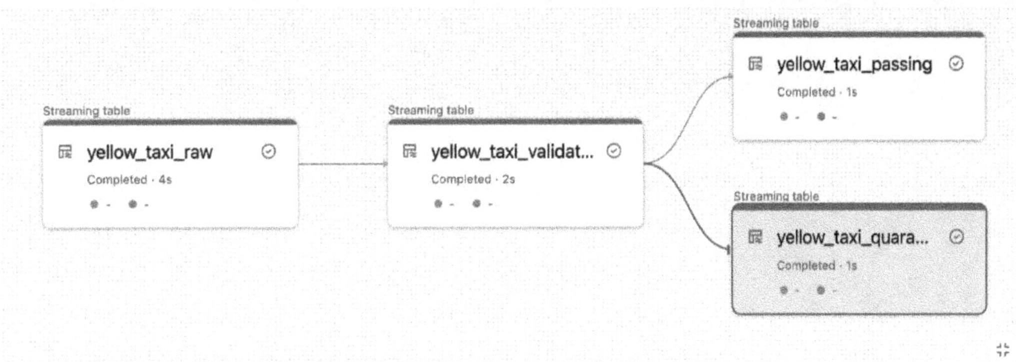

Figure 3.7 – Data that fails data quality rules is split into a quarantine table

By implementing a quarantine table, we can report on the real-time metrics so that stakeholders within our organization can be kept up to date on the quality of our incoming data. Furthermore, the data stewards of our lakehouse can review the data that has not passed the validation logic and even take appropriate action, such as manually correcting the invalid data.

Summary

In this chapter, we covered a lot of topics surrounding the data quality of the data in our lakehouse. We learned how the integrity of a table can be enforced using NOT NULL and CHECK constraints in Delta Lake. We also defined relationships between the tables in our lakehouse using PRIMARY KEY and FOREIGN KEY constraints. Next, we saw how we could enforce primary key uniqueness across our Delta tables using views to validate the data in our tables. We also saw just how easy it was to update the behavior of our data pipeline when incoming rows violated data quality constraints, allowing data engineering teams to react to downstream processes that have the potential to break from poor-quality data. Finally, we saw a practical example of how we can use expectations to create a conditional data flow in our pipeline, allowing our data stewards to quarantine and correct data that doesn't meet the expected data quality.

In the next chapter, we're going to get into more advanced topics of maintaining data pipelines in production. We'll see how we can tune many different aspects of data pipelines to scale to large volumes of data and meet real-time stream processing demands such as high throughput and low latency.

4

Scaling DLT Pipelines

In this chapter, we're going to look at several methods for scaling your **Delta Live Tables** (DLT) pipelines to handle the processing demands of a typical production environment. We'll cover several aspects of tuning your DLT pipelines, from optimizing the DLT cluster settings so that your pipelines can quickly scale to handle the spikes of heavy processing demand to looking at ways we can optimize the data layout of the underlying tables in cloud storage. By the end of this chapter, you should have mastered how DLT clusters can automatically scale out to handle demand. You should also have a good understanding of the impact that table maintenance tasks, which are automatically run in the background by the DLT system, have on the performance of your data pipelines. Lastly, you should understand how to leverage Delta Lake optimization techniques to further improve the execution performance of your DLT pipelines.

We're going to cover the following main topics in this chapter:

- Scaling compute to handle demand
- Hands-on example – setting autoscaling properties using the Databricks REST API
- Automated table maintenance tasks
- Optimizing table layouts for faster table updates
- Serverless DLT pipelines
- Introducing Enzyme, a performance optimization layer

Technical requirements

To follow along with this chapter, you will need Databricks workspace permissions to create and start an all-purpose cluster, as well as access to create a new DLT pipeline using at least a cluster policy. All code samples can be downloaded from this chapter's GitHub repository located at `https://github.com/PacktPublishing/Building-Modern-Data-Applications-Using-Databricks-Lakehouse/tree/main/chapter04`. This chapter will create and run several new notebooks, as well as a new DLT pipeline using the **Core** product edition. As a result, the code samples in this chapter are estimated to consume around 10-15 **Databricks Units** (DBUs).

Scaling compute to handle demand

Different portions of a data pipeline may involve heavy computation as calculations are performed, while other sections of the pipeline don't require as much processing power. To yield the best performance while simultaneously optimizing costs, it's important for any data pipeline to be able to add additional processing power when needed, as well as release computational resources when processing demands shrink over time. Fortunately, Databricks features a built-in autoscaling feature for DLT pipelines, so that **virtual machines** (**VMs**) can be added to and removed from a pipeline cluster to match the processing demands of a data pipeline during its execution period.

In fact, Databricks offers two types of cluster autoscaling modes for DLT pipelines: legacy and enhanced. Both autoscaling modes will automatically add or remove VMs as processing demands increase or decrease throughout a pipeline run. However, *when* the VMs are added and removed differs between the two.

With legacy autoscaling mode, a pipeline cluster will add additional VMs when there has been an increase in processing demand over a sustained period of time. Furthermore, in legacy autoscaling mode, a pipeline cluster will scale down only when VMs are left idle for a period of time and they have no currently executing Spark tasks.

On the other hand, with enhanced autoscaling mode, the DLT system will only add additional VMs if the system *predicts* that adding additional compute resources would speed up the execution of the pipeline update – for example, if the Spark jobs are limited by the number of available CPU cores and would benefit from having additional CPUs to execute a large amount of Spark tasks in parallel. In addition, the enhanced autoscaling feature will proactively look for opportunities for the pipeline cluster to scale down, evicting running Spark tasks and reducing cloud operational costs. During the eviction process, the enhanced autoscaling mode will ensure that evicted Spark tasks are recovered successfully on the remaining, running VMs before terminating the over-provisioned VMs.

Lastly, enhanced autoscaling is only available for clusters used in pipeline update tasks, while the legacy autoscaling mode is used by the DLT system to execute maintenance tasks.

The following table outlines the differences between the two types of autoscaling modes available for DLT pipeline clusters, as well as which DLT tasks are available for each of the autoscaling modes.

Autoscaling Mode	Predictive Autoscaling	Proactive Down Scaling	Update Tasks	Maintenance Tasks
Legacy	✘	✘	✔	✔
Enhanced	✔	✔	✔	✘

Table 4.1 – The differences between autoscaling modes available on DLT pipeline clusters

You can configure the cluster autoscaling mode from either the DLT UI or the Databricks REST API. In the next section, let's use the Databricks REST API to update the autoscaling mode of an existing data pipeline cluster.

Hands-on example – setting autoscaling properties using the Databricks REST API

In this section, you'll need to download the code samples from this chapter's GitHub repository located at `https://github.com/PacktPublishing/Building-Modern-Data-Applications-Using-Databricks-Lakehouse/tree/main/chapter04`. Within the chapter's GitHub repository is a helper notebook titled `Random Taxi Trip Data Generator.py`, which we'll use to generate random bursts of data to a cloud storage landing zone, simulating the unpredictable behavior you could expect in a production environment.

First, let's begin by importing this chapter's pipeline definition notebook, titled `Taxi Trip Data Pipeline.py`, into your Databricks workspace and opening the notebook.

You will notice that we've defined two datasets within our data pipeline. The first dataset uses the Databricks Auto Loader feature to ingest new JSON files as they arrive in our raw landing zone. Once the data has been ingested, a second dataset – our silver table – will contain the result of the transformed taxi trip data with additional columns containing the financial analytics of the taxi trip data:

```
@dlt.table(
    name="random_trip_data_raw",
    comment="The raw taxi trip data ingested from a landing zone.",
    table_properties={
        "quality": "bronze"
    }
)
def random_trip_data_raw():
    raw_trip_data_schema = StructType([
        StructField('Id', IntegerType(), True),
        StructField('driver_id', IntegerType(), True),
        StructField('Trip_Pickup_DateTime',
                    TimestampType(), True),
        StructField('Trip_Dropoff_DateTime',
                    TimestampType(), True),
        StructField('Passenger_Count', IntegerType(), True),
        StructField('Trip_Distance', DoubleType(), True),
        StructField('Start_Lon', DoubleType(), True),
        StructField('Start_Lat', DoubleType(), True),
```

```python
        StructField('Rate_Code', StringType(), True),
        StructField('store_and_forward', IntegerType(), True),
        StructField('End_Lon', DoubleType(), True),
        StructField('End_Lat', DoubleType(), True),
        StructField('Payment_Type', StringType(), True),
        StructField('Fare_Amt', DoubleType(), True),
        StructField('surcharge', DoubleType(), True),
        StructField('mta_tax', StringType(), True),
        StructField('Tip_Amt', DoubleType(), True),
        StructField('Tolls_Amt', DoubleType(), True),
        StructField('Total_Amt', DoubleType(), True)
    ])
    return (spark.readStream
        .format("cloudFiles")
        .option("cloudFiles.format", "json")
        .schema(raw_trip_data_schema)
        .load(raw_landing_zone))
```

Next, attach the notebook to an all-purpose cluster and execute all the notebook cells. Ensure that all the notebook cells are executed successfully. When prompted, create a new DLT pipeline using the **Core** product edition. Select **Continuous** processing mode as the pipeline execution mode. (If you need a refresher, please consult the *Data pipeline settings* section of *Chapter 2* in this book.) Next, select a target Unity Catalog destination to store the output of the data pipeline datasets and accept all the remaining default values. Finally, note the pipeline ID of the newly created data DLT pipeline.

For the next part of this exercise, we'll use a popular Python library, `requests`, to interact with the Databricks REST API. Create a new notebook within your Databricks workspace and begin by importing the `requests` library in the first cell of our notebook:

```python
import requests
```

Next, let's create a new request to the Databricks REST API for updating the cluster settings of our data pipeline. Within the request payload, we'll specify the autoscaling mode, the minimum number of worker nodes for our pipeline cluster, as well as the maximum number of worker nodes. As per the public Databricks documentation, we'll also need to use the PUT verb for updating the settings of our DLT pipeline. Add the following code snippet to the newly created notebook, updating the variables with your environment-specific values:

```python
databricks_workspace_url = "<your_databricks_workspace>"
pipeline_id = "<your_pipeline_id>"
pat_token = "<your_api_token>"
```

```python
response = requests.put(
    f"{databricks_workspace_url}/api/2.0/pipelines/{pipeline_id}",
    headers={"Authentication": pat_token},
    json={
        ...
        "clusters":[{
            "autoscale": {
                "min_workers": 2,
                "max_workers": 5,
                "mode": "ENHANCED"
            }
        }]
        ...
    }
)
print(response.json())
```

Alternatively, you can update the autoscaling mode to ENHANCED for the pipeline by navigating to the pipeline settings from the DLT UI. Now that we've updated our DLT pipeline to use enhanced autoscaling, let's execute a pipeline update. Navigate to the data pipeline UI of the newly created data pipeline. At the top right, select the **Start** button to trigger a pipeline update.

Meanwhile, let's also simulate spikes in processing demand using a random data generator. Import the data generator notebook, titled Random Taxi Trip Data Generator.py, from the chapter's GitHub repository. As the name suggests, Random Taxi Trip Data Generator.py will randomly generate new taxi trip data with varying degrees of volume and frequency, simulating a typical workload in a production environment. Attach the notebook to an all-purpose cluster and click the **Run all** button to execute all the cells. Ensure that the notebook cells have all completed successfully.

Next, switch back to the DLT UI for the pipeline we created. We'll monitor the event log of our pipeline to ensure that our DLT cluster will automatically increase the number of worker instances.

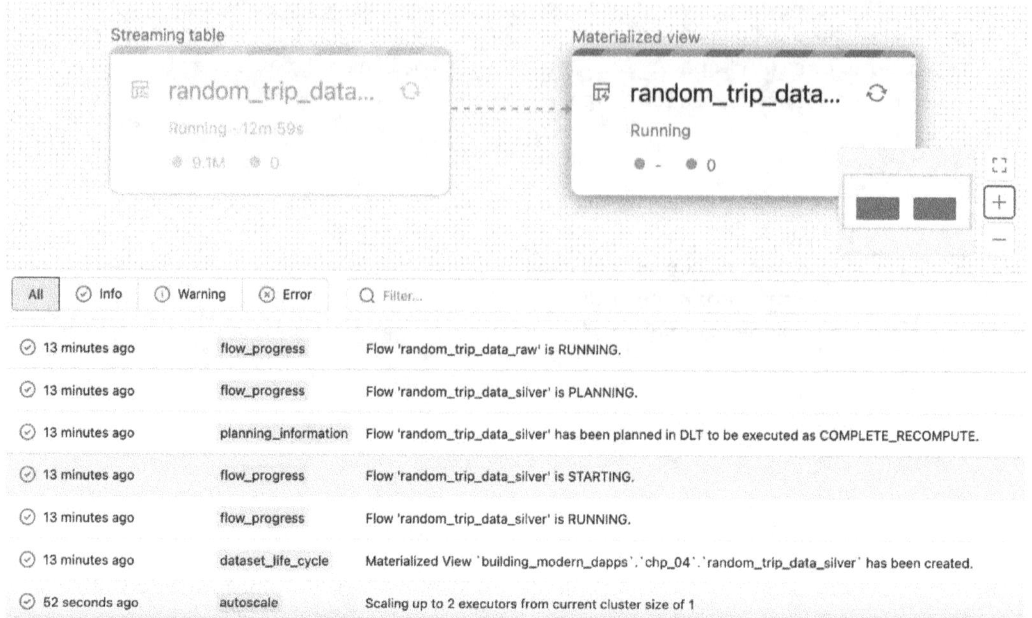

Figure 4.1 – Autoscaling events will be recorded in the event log from the DLT UI

Similarly, monitor the event log to ensure that the DLT update cluster scales back down after the flow of additional data terminates and processing demand dwindles.

By now, you should have a strong foundation in understanding how DLT clusters scale up and down to accommodate the peaks and valleys in processing demands. As you can see, our DLT pipeline will only provision the compute it needs to efficiently keep our datasets up to date and then release additional compute instances to minimize our operational costs. Let's turn our attention to other efficiencies that the DLT system does automatically for us, such as how the DLT system will automatically maintain the optimal state of our underlying Delta tables.

Automated table maintenance tasks

As mentioned in previous chapters, each DLT pipeline will be associated with two clusters – one cluster for performing updates to each of the datasets in a pipeline definition, as well as another cluster for performing maintenance activities to each dataset. These maintenance tasks include executing the Delta `VACUUM` and `OPTIMIZE` operations for each Delta table contained within a data pipeline definition. Previously, data engineers would be responsible for creating and maintaining a separate Databricks workflow that would execute the `VACUUM` and `OPTIMIZE` commands for each Delta table, typically scheduled to run nightly. As you can imagine, as you begin to add more and more tables to a pipeline, this can turn out to be quite a cumbersome task. Fortunately, the DLT framework does this heavy lifting for us right out of the box. Furthermore, each `VACUUM` and `OPTIMIZE` maintenance activity is executed within 24 hours of the last pipeline execution run.

Let's look at each operation individually to understand what overall benefit the maintenance tasks have on the underlying datasets.

Why auto compaction is important

During each new update run for a particular DLT pipeline, the DLT pipeline will initialize a dataflow graph and perform the underlying calculations spelled out in each dataset definition. As a result, new data is either appended or merged into a particular Delta table. Each time the data is written, Apache Spark will distribute the write operation out to the executors, potentially generating many small files as a result. As more updates are executed, more of these small files are created on cloud storage. As downstream processes read these Delta tables, they will need to expend a single Spark task for each unique file that answers a particular table query. More files will result in more Spark tasks – or better put, more work that needs to be done by the Spark engine. This is commonly referred to as the "small files problem," as tables that experience heavy volumes of new data result in many small files, slowing down overall query performance. As a remediation, it would be better to consolidate these small files into larger ones, a process referred to as file compaction.

Fortunately, as data engineers, we don't need to write our own utility for combining smaller files into larger ones. In fact, Delta Lake features a helpful command called OPTIMIZE for doing such maintenance tasks. By default, the Delta Lake OPTIMIZE command will attempt to coalesce smaller files into larger, 1 Gigabyte files.

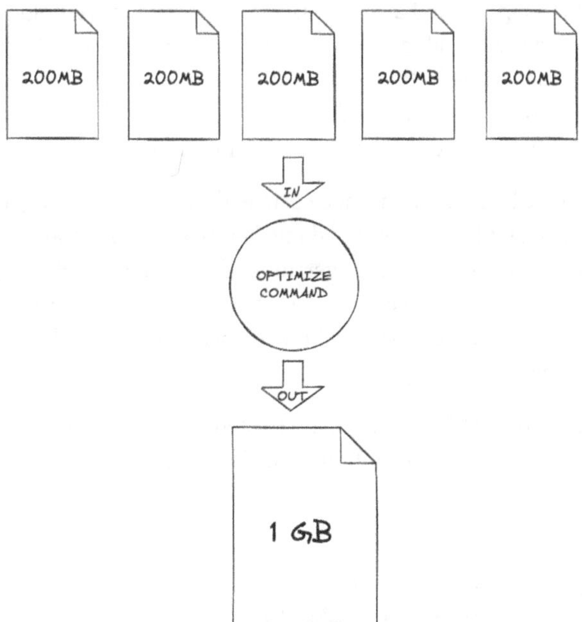

Figure 4.2 – DLT will automatically run the OPTIMIZE command on
Delta tables, coalescing smaller files into larger 1 GB files

Of course, you could choose to disable the auto-optimize feature by disabling the `autoOptimize` table property in the table definition of the DLT pipeline:

```
@dlt.table(
    name="random_trip_data_raw",
    comment="The raw taxi trip data ingested from a landing zone.",
    table_properties={
        "quality": "bronze",
        "pipelines.autoOptimize.managed": "false"
    }
)
```

There might be certain scenarios when you would want to override the default behavior, such as implementing your own table optimization workflow.

As each `OPTIMIZE` maintenance activity is performed, it too will generate additional files for each Delta table. To prevent cloud storage costs from ballooning out of control, we must also take care of removing obsolete table files so that as an organization, we aren't paying for unnecessary cloud storage.

Vacuuming obsolete table files

The `VACUUM` operation is designed to remove table files from previous versions of a Delta table that are no longer in the latest table snapshot and are older than the retention threshold property. By default, the retention threshold for all Delta tables is seven days, meaning that the `VACUUM` operation will remove obsolete table files that are older than seven days from the current snapshot date. At runtime, the `VACUUM` utility will search the Delta table's root directory as well as all of the subdirectories, removing table files older than the retention threshold from cloud storage.

This is a great way to balance both cloud storage costs with the ability to maintain and view older snapshots of a particular Delta table. As mentioned in *Chapter 1*, the time travel feature of Delta Lake relies upon the table history to query previous versions of a Delta table. However, this feature was not designed to support long-term archival use cases, but rather shorter-term table history. So, it's reasonable to expect that we don't need to store all the history of a Delta table and pay the associated storage costs, which could become quite expensive.

Like the auto-optimize feature, a Delta table's history retention threshold is determined by a table property and can be specified in the table definition using the `deletedFileRetentionDuration` table property:

```
@dlt.table(
    name="random_trip_data_silver",
    comment="Taxi trip data transformed with financial data.",
    table_properties={
        "quality": "silver",
        "pipelines.autoOptimize.zOrderCols": "driver_id",
```

```
        "delta.deletedFileRetentionDuration": "INTERVAL 14 days"
    }
)
```

Similarly, the Delta transaction logs – the metadata files that record details about each committed table transaction (covered in *Chapter 1*) – can also lead to unnecessary storage costs. However, these log files are automatically removed during log checkpoint operations (every tenth transaction commit). By default, Delta Lake will retain a maximum of 30 days' worth of table history in the transaction logs.

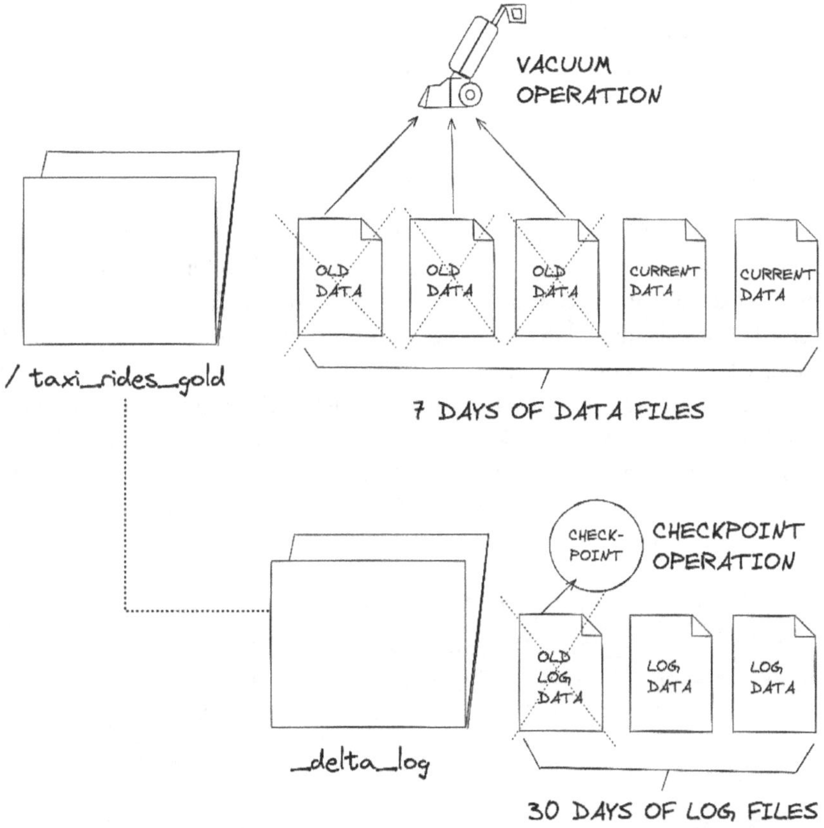

Figure 4.3 – DLT will automatically run a VACUUM operation on all Delta tables

Since the transaction log files contain only metadata information, they are small, containing only a few megabytes of information. However, this history retention can also be configured by setting the `logRetentionDuration` table property:

```
@dlt.table(
    name="random_trip_data_silver",
    comment="Taxi trip data transformed with financial data.",
```

```
table_properties={
    "quality": "silver",
    "pipelines.autoOptimize.zOrderCols": "driver_id",
    "delta.deletedFileRetentionDuration": "INTERVAL 9 days",
    "delta.logRetentionDuration": "INTERVAL 35 days"
}
)
```

Removing obsolete cloud files is a great way to control cloud costs and prevent your organization from paying for unnecessary cloud storage charges. Let's look at how we might be able to optimize other aspects of our DLT pipelines to improve operating efficiency while continuing to drive down operating costs.

Moving compute closer to the data

One of the simplest methods for ensuring that your data pipelines will execute efficiently is to ensure that the DLT pipeline clusters are launched within the same global region as the data that is being processed. This is an age-old tuning concept of moving the hardware closer to the data to minimize network latencies during data processing. For example, you wouldn't want your DLT pipeline cluster to execute in, say, the US West Region of a cloud provider, yet the data is stored in a completely different geographical location, such as the US East Region of the same cloud provider. As a result, this will introduce a considerable amount of network latency to transfer the data across geographical regions, process the data transformations or other calculations, and then store the result back in the original geographical region. Furthermore, most cloud providers will assess data egress and ingress charges associated with the geographical data transfer.

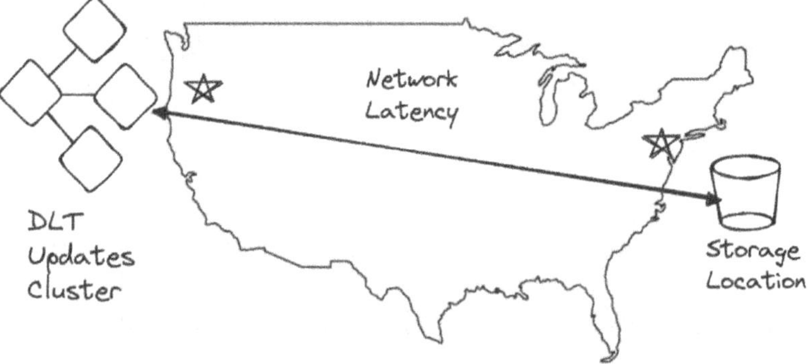

Figure 4.4 – The geographical locations of your DLT cluster and storage container can introduce significant network latencies

The geographical region of a DLT cluster can be set by defining the cloud zone location in the pipeline cluster policy definition. For example, the following code snippet defines a cluster policy that could be used to configure DLT pipeline clusters to launch in the US East Region of the AWS cloud provider:

```
{
    ...
    "aws_attributes.zone_id": "us-east-1",
    "custom_tags.lob": {
        "type": "fixed",
        "value": "ad analytics team"
    }
}
```

By ensuring that your DLT clusters are provisioned in the same geographical region as your organization data, you can make certain that you will be getting the best operating performance out of your pipeline clusters. At the same time, since your pipelines run faster and utilize cloud resources for less time, this translates to dollars saved for your organization. Along with optimizing the computational resources of our data pipelines, we can also organize our table data efficiently to further improve the performance of our data pipeline updates. Let's look at a few other techniques for improving the processing efficiency of our DLT pipelines by optimizing the data layouts of our tables.

Optimizing table layouts for faster table updates

A typical DLT pipeline might include one or more datasets that append new data and update existing data with either new values or even delete rows altogether. Let's take an in-depth look into this latter scenario and analyze what happens "under the hood" so that we can optimize our DLT datasets for faster performance as we add new data to our DLT tables.

Rewriting table files during updates

During a table update, the DLT engine will perform two scans to identify all the rows that match a particular update condition and rewrite the changed table data accordingly. During the first table scan, the DLT engine will identify all table files that contain rows that match a predicate clause in an `apply_changes()` (or `APPLY CHANGES` if using SQL) expression, for example.

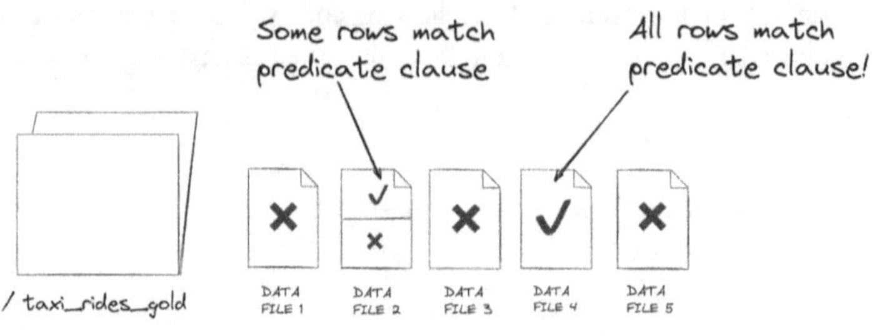

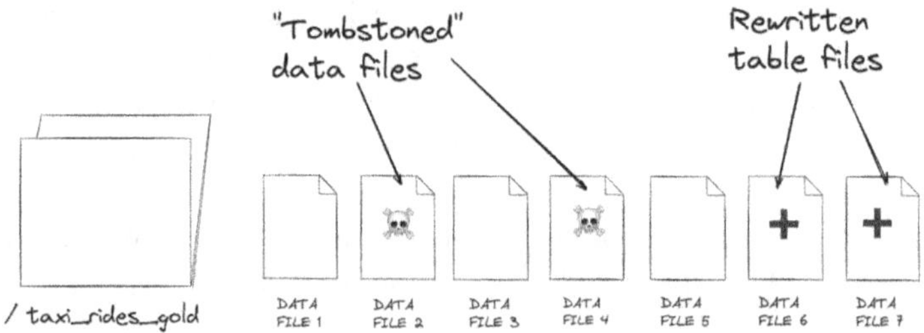

Figure 4.5 – DLT will apply changes to the target DLT table by identifying matching rows using a matching operation

Next, the DLT engine will compile a list of all table files that contain these rows. Using this list of table files, the DLT engine will rewrite each of these files containing the newly updated row(s) in a second table scanning operation. As you can imagine, as you add more data to a DLT table, the process of locating these matching rows and identifying the list of files to rewrite can get quite expensive over time. Fortunately, Delta Lake has a few features up its sleeves that we can use to optimize this search process and speed up the matching process.

Data skipping using table partitioning

One way to speed up this search process is to limit the search space for the DLT engine. One such technique is to use Hive-style table partitioning. Table partitioning organizes related data into physically separate subdirectories within a table's root storage location. The subdirectories correspond to one or more table columns.

During the matching process, the DLT engine can eliminate entire subdirectories that don't match the predicate condition, removing the need to scan unnecessary data.

Partitioning a table with MERGE columns, the columns used to apply data changes to the table, can dramatically boost the performance of the update process. On the other hand, since table partitioning creates physically separate directories, table partitioning can be difficult to get correct and expensive to change, requiring the entire table to be rewritten to adjust the partitioning scheme.

Another challenge is identifying a table partitioning scheme that will result in partition directories that are evenly balanced with the same amount of data. It's quite easy to end up partitioning a table by MERGE columns, but then end up in a scenario where some partition directories contain small amounts of data, while other partition directories contain massive amounts of data. This is commonly referred to as **data skew**. Still, table partitioning is a powerful tool in your data pipeline tuning arsenal. Let's look at how we might be able to combine table partitioning with another table optimization technique to further boost our pipeline performance.

Delta Lake Z-ordering on MERGE columns

One way to optimize the table layout of a Delta table is to organize the data within each of the table files so that it can be read efficiently during file-scanning operations. This is commonly referred to as data clustering. Fortunately, Delta Lake features a data clustering algorithm known as Z-order clustering. Z-order clustering will write the table data by clustering relevant data together, forming a "Z"-shaped pattern. Storing the table data according to this pattern will improve the probability that the DLT engine will skip past irrelevant data within a table file and only read data that matches merge conditions during the update matching process.

Traditionally, without Z-order clustering, Delta Lake will store the data in a linear pattern. As a result, during the update matching process, Delta Lake will need to open each file of the table and scan each of the rows in a linear sorting order. Sometimes, only a single row might match the merge condition. In turn, the DLT engine will read all the unnecessary rows that do not match, only to find maybe 1 or 2 rows that do match the update condition.

By clustering the data within a file using the Z-order clustering technique, the DLT engine can pinpoint where in a particular file the relevant data exists, limiting the amount of data that it must scan. For large tables that require a lot of scanning, this can improve the update process of a DLT pipeline dramatically.

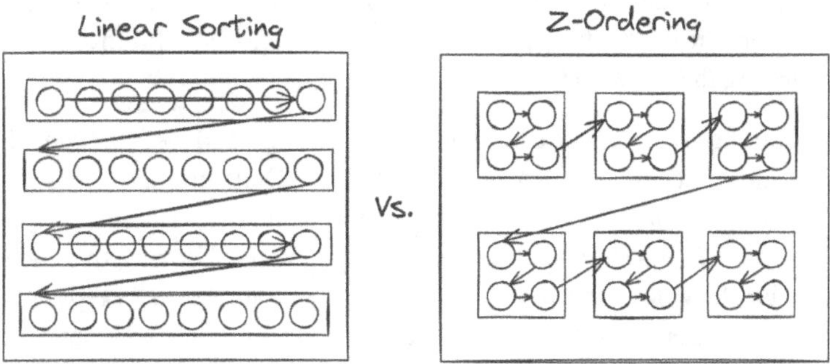

Figure 4.6 – Z-order clustering data within table files can be visualized as data clusters forming "Z" shapes

Z-order clustering can be enabled on DLT datasets by setting the appropriate table property within the dataset definition. Let's look at how we might configure the Z-order clustering for our silver table, `yellow_taxi_transformed`, which receives many updates throughout the day.

We first begin by defining the dataset like any dataset within our DLT pipelines. You'll notice that we've included a name for the dataset, `yellow_taxi_transormed`, as well as a comment, which adds some descriptive text about the table. However, within the DLT function annotation, we've added a couple more parameters where we can set the table properties for this dataset. In the table properties parameter, we've added a couple of attributes that will describe our dataset to the DLT engine. First, we've added a table property describing the quality of this dataset, which is a silver table in our medallion architecture. Next, we've also added another table property that specifies which table columns we would like to apply a Z-order clustering:

```
import dlt


@dlt.table(
    name="yellow_taxi_transformed",
    comment="Taxi cab trip data containing additional columns about
the financial data.",
    table_properties={
        "quality": "silver",
        "pipelines.autoOptimize.zOrderCols": "zip_code, driver_id"
    }
)
```

During the execution of our daily maintenance tasks, the maintenance task will dynamically parse these Z-order columns and will run the following Z-order command on the underlying Delta table behind this DLT dataset:

```
OPTIMIZE yellow_taxi_transformed
    ZORDER BY (zip_code, driver_id)
```

So, which table columns should you Z-order your DLT tables by and how many columns should you specify? A good range is anywhere from 1 to 3 columns, but no more than 5 columns. As you add more columns, it will complicate the data clustering within the table files, diminishing the returns on any possible data skipping that could occur.

Furthermore, you should strive to choose columns that are numerical in data type. The reason for this is that whenever new data is written to a Delta table, the Delta engine will capture statistical information about the first 32 columns – column information such as the minimum value, maximum value, and number of nulls. This statistical information will be used during the update searching process to effectively locate which rows match the update predicate. For data types such as strings, this statistical information does not provide very useful information, since there cannot be an average string, for example. However, there can be an average for a column with a float data type, for instance.

In addition, columns that are used in APPLY CHANGES predicates, join columns, and columns where aggregations are performed all serve as ideal Z-order candidates. Lastly, these columns should have a higher cardinality than the columns used to create a table partitioning scheme.

> **Important note**
>
> There may be times when you may want to experiment with different columns or a different set of columns to Z-order your table by. Changing this Z-order scheme is trivial – it's as simple as updating the `table_properties` parameter in the DLT pipeline definition. However, it's important to note that the new Z-order clustering will take effect only on new data that is written to the table. To apply the new Z-order clustering to existing data, the entire table would need to be fully refreshed so that the table files can be reorganized according to the clustering pattern. As a result, you may want to balance the time and cost it will take to rewrite the table data with the performance benefits that you may get from the table Z-order optimization.

As you can see by now, Z-order optimization is a great way to optimize the layout of your DLT tables to boost the performance of your data pipelines. Having an effective data layout can improve the data skipping of the DLT engine and limit the amount of data that the DLT engine needs to scan to apply updates to target tables within your pipelines. Combined with Hive-style table partitioning, this is a great way to ensure you are squeezing the best performance out of your data pipelines, leading to shorter execution times and less time and money spent keeping update clusters up and running.

However, what if you are only updating a small amount of data within a particular table file? That translates to rewriting an entire file for the sake of updating maybe 1 or 2 rows, for example. Let's look at how we might be able to optimize the performance of our DLT pipelines further to avoid this costly operation.

Improving write performance using deletion vectors

During a table update, the DLT engine applies the update by rewriting the matched file with the newly changed rows in the new, target file. In this type of table update strategy, known as **Copy-on-Write (COW)**, the rows not receiving any updates need to be copied over to the new file, as the name suggests. For table updates that require only a few rows to change across many files, this can be largely inefficient.

A better optimization technique would be to keep track of all the rows that have changed in a separate data structure and write the newly updated rows into separate file(s). Then, during a table query, the table client can use this data structure to filter out any of the updated rows. This technique is called **Merge-on-Read (MOR)** and is implemented in Delta Lake using a feature called deletion vectors.

Deletion vectors are a special data structure that keeps track of all the row IDs that are updated during an UPDATE or MERGE operation on a Delta table. Deletion vectors can be enabled by setting a table property of the underlying Delta table. Like the statistical information regarding the Delta table columns, deletion vectors are stored alongside the table data on cloud storage.

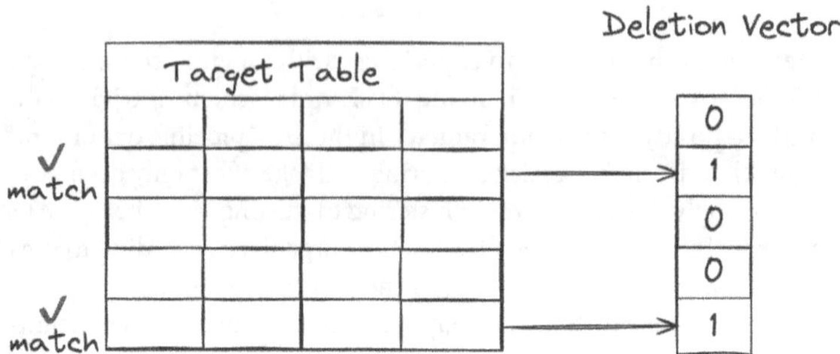

Figure 4.7 – Delta Lake tables will keep track of the row IDs of each row in a separate data structure

Furthermore, deletion vectors can be automatically enabled by default for all new tables created within a Databricks workspace. A workspace administrator can enable or disable this behavior from the **Advanced** tab of the workspace admin settings UI.

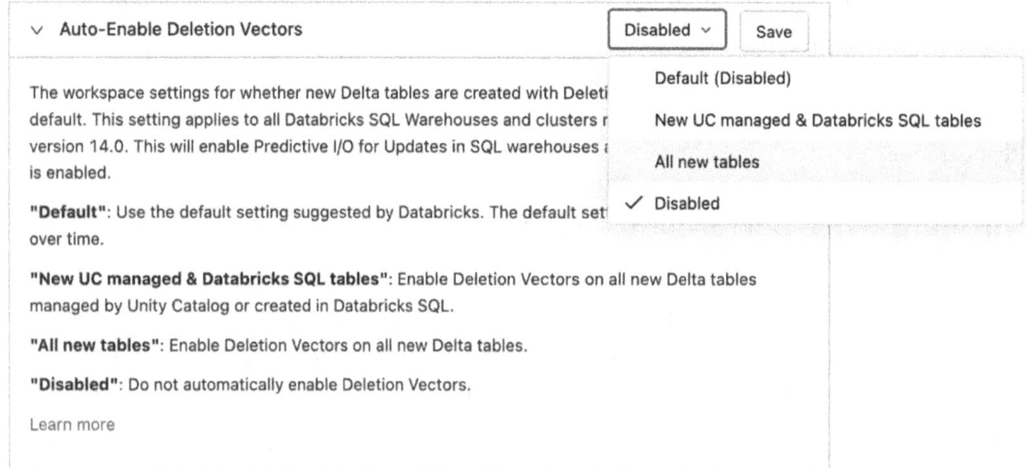

Figure 4.8 – Deletion vectors can be automatically enabled in the Databricks Data Intelligence Platform

Deletion vectors can be explicitly set on a dataset by setting the enableDeletionVectors table property in the DLT table definition:

```
@dlt.table(
    name="random_trip_data_silver",
    comment="Taxi trip data transformed with financial data.",
```

```
    table_properties={
        "quality": "silver",
        "pipelines.autoOptimize.zOrderCols": "driver_id",
        "delta.enableDeletionVectors": "true"
    }
)
```

In addition, deletion vectors unlock a new class of update performance features on the Databricks Data Intelligence Platform, collectively referred to as **Predictive I/O**. Predictive I/O uses deep learning and file statistics to accurately predict the location of rows within files that match an update condition. As a result, the time it takes to scan matching files and rewrite data during updates, merges, and deletes is drastically reduced.

Hive-style table partitioning, Z-order data clustering, and deletion vectors are all great optimization techniques for efficiently storing our table data and improving the speed of our pipeline updates. Let's turn our attention back to the computational resources of our data pipelines and analyze yet another technique for improving the performance of our DLT pipelines in production, particularly in times when the processing demands may spike and become unpredictable.

Serverless DLT pipelines

In *Chapter 2*, we briefly described what serverless DLT clusters were and how they can quickly and efficiently scale computational resources up to handle spikes in demand, as well as scale down to save cloud costs. While we won't cover the architecture of serverless clusters again, we will cover how serverless DLT clusters can help organizations scale their data pipelines as more and more data pipelines are added.

With serverless DLT clusters, the cluster infrastructure and settings are automatically handled by the Databricks cloud provider account. This translates to removing the burden of having to select VM instance types to balance performance with costs. The costs for serverless compute are at a fixed, flat rate, making the costs predictable. In addition, since the computational resources are managed by the Databricks cloud provider account, Databricks can reserve a large amount of VM instances at a discounted price by each cloud provider. These discounted rates can then be passed along to the DLT serverless consumers.

Furthermore, serverless DLT clusters *simplify data pipeline maintenance* by reducing the amount of configuration that's needed per data pipeline. With less configuration, data engineer teams can focus less on the maintenance of their data pipelines and more on what matters to the business, such as changing business logic, data validation, and adding more data pipelines to name a few. In addition, as your data pipelines grow over time and dataset volumes increase over time, you may need to provision more VM instances. Eventually, you may hit the cloud provider limits for certain instance types, which requires an additional process to have these limits increased by the cloud provider. With serverless DLT compute, these limits have already been negotiated with the cloud provider, meaning that the DLT serverless consumers need not be concerned with this burden.

Serverless data pipelines can also help *reduce costs* for data pipelines. For example, with traditional, customer-managed compute, a cluster can only add additional VM instances as quickly as the cloud provider can provision additional instances and routinely run the diagnostic checks. Plus, the Databricks runtime container and user libraries need to be installed on the additional instances, which takes even more time. This can translate to many minutes – sometimes 15 minutes or more depending on the cloud provider – before a DLT cluster can scale out to handle the unpredictable spikes in computational demand. As a result, DLT pipelines running on traditional compute will take much longer to execute as compared to the serverless DLT clusters. With serverless DLT clusters, the VM instances are pre-provisioned with the latest Databricks runtime container already installed and started in a pre-allocated instance pool. During spikes in processing demand, the DLT pipeline can respond with additional resources to meet the demand on the order of seconds rather than minutes. These minutes can add up over many data pipeline runs and over the course of a cloud billing cycle. By driving down the time it takes to scale out with additional resources and being able to aggressively scale down with enhanced autoscaling, serverless DLT pipelines can drastically reduce operational costs while simultaneously improving the efficiency of the ETL processing in your lakehouse.

Removing the infrastructure burden of managing compute settings for data pipelines as well as controlling cloud costs are great motivating factors behind choosing serverless DLT pipelines over traditional, customer-managed compute. However, let's look at another motivation for selecting serverless DLT clusters, such as the performance features that come with this type of computational resource.

Introducing Enzyme, a performance optimization layer

There may be certain scenarios where a data pipeline has been deployed into a production environment. However, down the road, there may be significant changes in the business requirements, requiring the datasets to be recomputed from scratch. In these scenarios, recomputing the historical data of these datasets could be cost prohibitive.

Enzyme, a brand-new optimization layer that is only available for serverless DLT pipelines, aims to reduce ETL costs by dynamically calculating a cost model for keeping the materialized results of a dataset up to date. Like the cost model in Spark query planning, Enzyme calculates a cost model between several ETL techniques from a traditional materialized view in DLT to a Delta streaming table to another Delta streaming table, or a manual ETL technique. For example, the Enzyme engine might model the cost to refresh a dataset using a materialization technique, translating to 10 Spark jobs, each with 200 Spark tasks. This cost model might save two Spark jobs and shave five minutes off the overall execution time as predicted by another modeled ETL technique, so the Enzyme engine will choose the first technique instead.

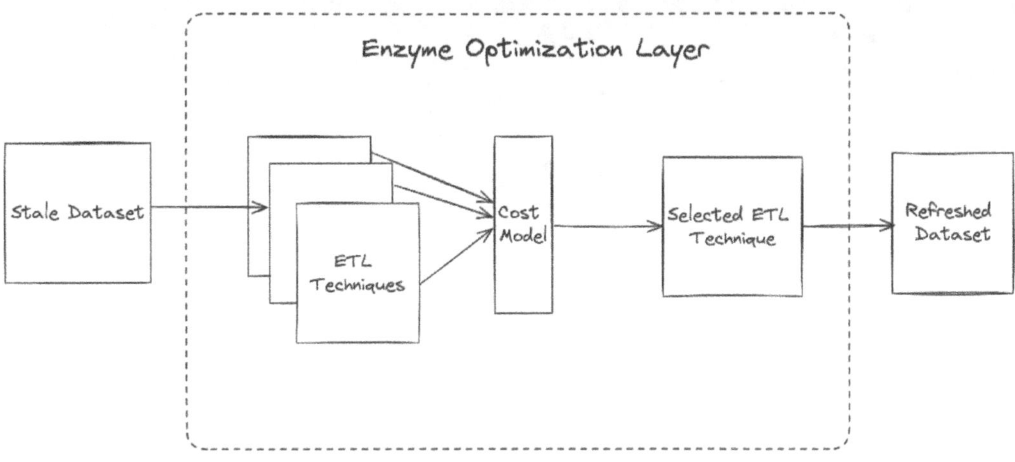

Figure 4.9 – The Enzyme optimization layer will automatically select the most cost-efficient ETL refresh technique using a cost model

The Enzyme layer will dynamically choose the most efficient and cost-effective method for recomputing the results for a given dataset at runtime. Since Enzyme is a serverless DLT feature, it is already enabled by default, removing the need for DLT admins to manage pipeline cluster settings.

By now, you should understand the powerful features that come with serverless DLT pipelines, such as the Enzyme optimization layer, as well as the infrastructure management and cost-saving benefits.

Summary

In this chapter, we looked at various methods for scaling our data pipelines to handle large volumes of data and perform well under periods of high and unpredictable processing demand. We looked at two attributes of scaling our DLT pipelines – compute and data layout. We examined the enhanced autoscaling feature of the Databricks Data Intelligence Platform to automatically scale the computational resources that the data pipelines execute on. We also looked at optimizing how the underlying table data was stored, clustering relevant data within table files and leading to faster table queries and shorter pipeline processing times. Furthermore, we also looked at regular maintenance activities to maintain high-performing table queries, as well as prevent ballooning cloud storage costs from obsolete data files.

Data security is of the utmost importance and is often overlooked until the end of a lakehouse implementation. However, this could mean the difference between a successful lakehouse and making the front page of a newspaper – and not for a good reason. In the next chapter, we'll be taking a look at how we can effectively implement strong data governance across our lakehouse, whether it's within a single geographical region or across a fail-over region on a different part of the globe.

Part 2: Securing the Lakehouse Using the Unity Catalog

In this part, we'll explore how to implement an effective data governance strategy using the Unity Catalog in the Databricks Data Intelligence Platform. We'll look at how you can enforce fine-grained data access policies across various roles and departments in your organization. Lastly, we'll look at how you trace the origins of data assets in Unity Catalog, ensuring that data is coming from trusted sources.

This part contains the following chapters:

- *Chapter 5, Mastering Data Governance in the Lakehouse with Unity Catalog*

- *Chapter 6, Managing Data Locations in Unity Catalog*

- *Chapter 7, Viewing Data Lineage Using Unity Catalog*

5

Mastering Data Governance in the Lakehouse with Unity Catalog

In this chapter, we'll dive into the implementation of effective data governance for the lakehouse using Unity Catalog. We'll cover enabling Unity Catalog on an existing Databricks workspace, implementing data cataloging for data discovery, enforcing fine-grained data access at the table, row and column levels, as well as tracking data lineage. By the end of the chapter, you'll be armed with industry best practices around data governance and will have gained real-world insights for enhancing data security and compliance.

In this chapter, we're going to cover the following main topics:

- Understanding data governance in the lakehouse

- Enabling Unity Catalog on an existing Databricks workspace

- Identity federation in Unity Catalog

- Data discovery and cataloging

- Hands-on lab – data masking healthcare datasets

Technical requirements

To follow along in this chapter, you'll need Databricks workspace permissions to create and start an all-purpose cluster so that you can execute the chapter's accompanying notebooks. It's also recommended that your Databricks user be elevated to an account admin and a metastore admin so that you can deploy a new Unity Catalog metastore and attach it to your existing Databricks workspace. All code samples can be downloaded from this chapter's GitHub repository located at `https://github.com/PacktPublishing/Building-Modern-Data-Applications-Using-Databricks-Lakehouse/tree/main/chapter05`. This chapter will create and run several new notebooks, estimated to consume around 5–10 **Databricks units (DBUs)**.

Understanding data governance in a lakehouse

It's quite common for a lakehouse implementation to leverage multiple processing engines for different use cases. However, each processing engine comes with its own data security implementation and, often, these different data security solutions don't integrate with one another. Where most lakehouses fall short is that due to these multiple security layers, implementing consistent, global data security policies is nearly impossible. Ensuring that the data in your lakehouse is completely and consistently secured and private and that access is only granted to the correct set of users is of the utmost importance when building a data lakehouse. Therefore, having a simple data governance solution that covers all the data in your organization's lakehouse is critical for your organization's success.

Introducing the Databricks Unity Catalog

Unity Catalog is a centralized data governance solution that simplifies securing the data in your lakehouse by organizing workspace object access policies into a single administrative "pane of glass." In addition to access policies, Unity Catalog was designed with strong auditing in mind, allowing administrators to capture all user access patterns to workspace objects so that administrators can observe access patterns, workspace usage, and billing patterns across all Databricks workspaces. Furthermore, Unity Catalog was designed to allow data professionals to discover datasets across your organization, track data lineage, view entity relationship diagrams, share curated datasets, and monitor the health of systems. One of the major strong suites of Unity Catalog is that once your organization's data is in Unity Catalog, it's secured by default – no process, whether it's internal within the Databricks workspace or an external process that interacts with data from outside of the Databricks Data Intelligence Platform, has access to the data unless access has been explicitly granted by a data administrator. Unity Catalog was designed to span across the perimeter of your lakehouse from workspace to workspace and beyond the Databricks workspace, sitting on top of your organization's data so that a single governance model can be simply and consistently applied to all parties accessing your organization's data in the lakehouse.

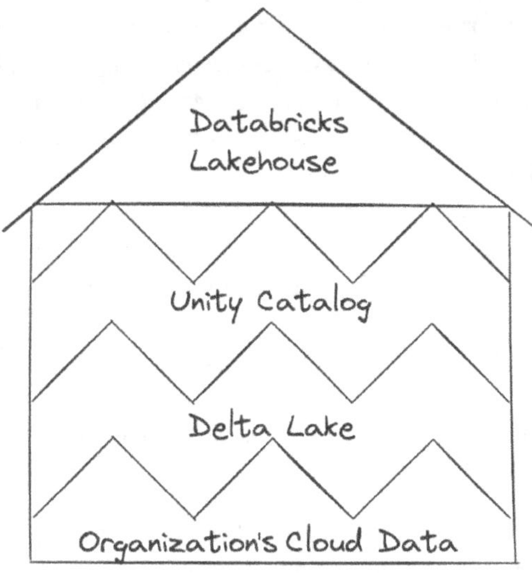

Figure 5.1 – Unity Catalog provides a single, unified governance
layer on top of your organization's cloud data

However, having a global data and workspace object security layer wasn't always as seamless as it is in Unity Catalog today. Let's travel back in time to the lessons learned from the previous security model in Databricks and how Unity Catalog came to fruition today.

A problem worth solving

Previously, data access control policies were defined per workspace using a mechanism known as table **access control lists** (**ACLs**). When these were enforced properly, table ACLs provided a powerful data governance solution. Administrators could define data access policies for different users and groups within a workspace and those access policies could be enforced by the Databricks cluster when executing Spark code that accessed the underlying datasets registered in the **Hive Metastore** (**HMS**).

However, four major problems quickly arose from the table ACL security model. The first problem was that data access policies defined using the table ACL security model needed to be repeated for each unique Databricks workspace. Most organizations prefer to have separate workspaces for each logical work environment – for example, a single workspace for development, another workspace for acceptance testing, and finally, a workspace dedicated to running production workloads. Aside from the repetition of the same shared data access policies, if a data access policy happened to change in one workspace, it often meant that the data access policies across *all* workspaces needed to be changed as well. This led to unnecessary maintenance overhead, as there was not a single location where these data access patterns could be easily defined within the Databricks Data Intelligence Platform.

Secondly, table ACLs were only enforced on the underlying data when interactive notebooks or automated jobs were executed on a table ACL-enabled cluster. A cluster without the table ACL security model enabled could directly access the underlying dataset, bypassing the security model entirely! While cluster policies (covered in *Chapter 1*) could be used to mitigate this issue and prevent any potential nefarious access to privileged datasets, cluster policies are complex to write. They require knowledge of the cluster policy schema as well as experience expressing configuration as JSON, making it difficult to scale across an organization. More often than not, it was quite common for a user to complain to their organization's leaders that they needed administrative workspace access to spin up a cluster of their own liking and complete their day-to-day activities. Once the user was granted administrator workspace access, they too could grant administrator access to other users, and, like a snowball effect, there would be an unreasonable number of administrators for a workspace. This type of bad practice can easily lead to a data leak by side-stepping the table ACL security model using a cluster without table ACLs enabled.

Furthermore, due to the isolation issues of running **Java Virtual Machine** (**JVM**) languages on a shared computational resource, table ACL-enabled clusters limited end users to only running workloads using either the SQL or Python programming languages. Users wanting to execute workloads using the Scala, Java, or R programming languages would need to be granted an exception to use a non-table ACL-enabled cluster, opening a huge hole in the organization's data governance solution.

The fourth major problem that arose had to do with the ability of the HMS to scale. The Databricks Data Intelligence Platform leveraged the HMS to register datasets across a workspace, which allowed users to create new datasets from scratch, organize them in schemas, and even share access to users and groups across an organization. However, as a workspace onboarded thousands of users, those users would need to execute ad hoc queries concurrently, while also executing hundreds or even thousands of scheduled jobs. Eventually, the HMS struggled to keep up with the level of concurrency needed for the most demanding workspaces.

It was clear that there needed to be a huge change and so Databricks set out to completely redesign a data governance solution from scratch.

An overview of the Unity Catalog architecture

One of the primary pain points that Unity Catalog aimed to solve was to implement a complete end-to-end data governance solution that spans all of an organization's workspaces, removing the redundancy of having to redefine data access policies for each Databricks workspace. Instead, with Unity Catalog, data administrators can define data access controls *once* in a centralized location and have the peace of mind that they will be consistently applied across an organization no matter what computational resource or processing engine is used to interact with datasets in Unity Catalog.

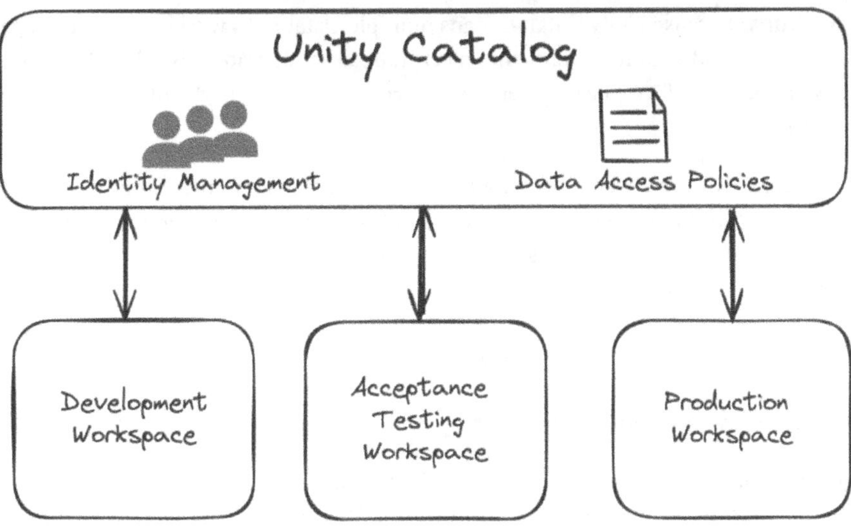

Figure 5.2 – Unity Catalog centralizes data access policies that are then consistently applied across multiple Databricks workspaces

In addition to centralized data governance, Unity Catalog has several other key motivating factors that make it an ideal data governance solution for the modern-day lakehouse:

- **Secure by default**: Users will not have access to read data from any form of compute without using a Unity Catalog-enabled cluster (Unity Catalog clusters are covered in the following section) and having been granted specific access to use and select data from a particular dataset.

- **Comfortable administrator interfaces**: Data access policies in Unity Catalog are tightly integrated with **American National Standards Institute** (**ANSI**) SQL, allowing administrators to express data access permissions on familiar database objects such as catalogs, databases, tables, functions, and views. Data access permissions can also be set using the administrator UI from the Databricks web app, or automated deployment tools such as Terraform.

- **Data discovery**: Unity Catalog makes it easy for data stewards to tag datasets with descriptive metadata, allowing users across your organization to search and discover datasets available to them.

- **Strong auditing**: Unity Catalog automatically captures user-level access patterns and data operations, allowing administrators to view and audit user behavior as they interact with the data in your lakehouse.

- **Data lineage tracking**: Tracing how tables and columns are generated from upstream sources is important in ensuring that downstream datasets are formed using trusted sources. Unity Catalog makes tracking data and workspace assets simple through its strong data lineage APIs and system tables.

- **Observability**: Because Unity Catalog spans multiple Databricks workspaces, it can aggregate system metrics and auditing events into a centralized set of read-only tables for monitoring and system observability called system tables (covered in greater detail in the *Observability with system tables* section).

To implement a security model where the data is secured by default and there is no ability to access the data externally without going through Unity Catalog, Databricks needed to design different clusters based on the user's persona. Let's look at the different cluster types available to users in a Unity Catalog-enabled workspace.

Unity Catalog-enabled cluster types

There are three major types of clusters for a workspace with Unity Catalog enabled:

- **Single-user cluster**: Only a single user or service principal will have permission to execute notebook cells or workflows on this type of cluster. Workloads containing a mixture of Scala, Java, R, Python, and SQL languages can be executed on this type of cluster *only*. Datasets registered in Unity Catalog can be queried from this type of cluster.

- **Shared cluster**: Multiple users or service principals can have permission to execute notebook cells or workflows on this type of cluster. This type of cluster is restricted to only Python, SQL, and Scala workloads. Datasets registered in Unity Catalog can be queried from this type of cluster.

- **Standalone cluster**: A single user or multiple users can attach a notebook and execute notebook cells to this type of cluster. However, datasets registered within the Unity Catalog *cannot* be queried by this type of cluster and will result in a runtime exception if a user attempts to query a dataset registered in Unity Catalog. This type of cluster can be used for reading datasets registered in the legacy HMS.

Now that we've outlined the different types of computational resources you can use to interact with the data in Unity Catalog, let's now turn our attention to how the data and other assets are organized within the Unity Catalog, mainly understanding the Unity Catalog object model.

Unity Catalog object model

It's important to understand the object model within Unity Catalog as it will help users understand the types of objects that can be secured and governed by Unity Catalog. Furthermore, it will also help metastore administrators architect data access policies.

One of the major changes that Unity Catalog introduced is the concept of a three-level namespace. Traditionally, in the HMS, users interacting with the data could reference datasets using a combination of a schema (or database) and a table name. However, Unity Catalog adds a third logical container, called the catalog, which can hold one or more schemas. To reference a fully qualified dataset in Unity Catalog, data practitioners will need to provide the name of the catalog, schema, and table.

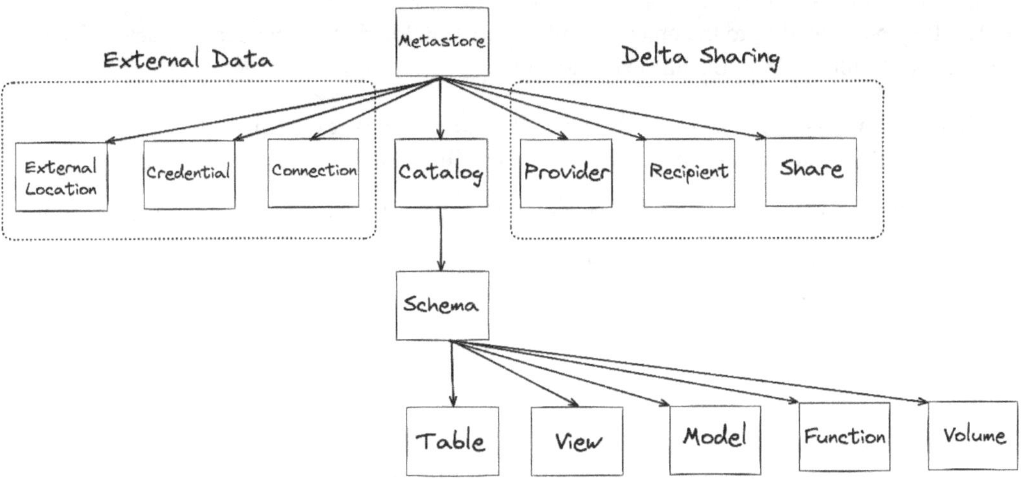

Figure 5.3 – Unity Catalog consists of many different securable objects beyond just a dataset

Let's dive more into the Unity Catalog object model starting with the objects related to organizing physical datasets:

- **Metastore**: The "physical" implementation of Unity Catalog. A particular cloud region can at most contain a single metastore.

- **Catalog**: The top-level container for datasets in Unity Catalog. A catalog can contain a collection of one or more schema objects.

- **Schema**: Serves as the second tier in Unity Catalog. A schema can contain a collection of one or more tables, views, functions, models, and volumes.

- **Table**: The representation of a dataset containing a defined schema and organized into rows and columns.

- **View**: A calculated dataset that can be the result of joining together tables, filtering columns, or applying complex business logic. Furthermore, views are read-only and cannot have data written to them or data updated using **data manipulation language** (DML) statements.

- **Model**: A machine learning model that has been registered to the tracking server using MLflow.

- **Function**: A custom, user-defined function that often contains complex business logic that typically cannot be implemented using the built-in Spark functions alone.

- **Volume**: A data storage location designed for storing structured, semi-structured, or unstructured data (we will cover volumes in greater detail in the following chapter, *Mastering Data Locations in Unity Catalog*).

Next, let's turn our attention to the objects within Unity Catalog that are used to interact with data outside of the Databricks Data Intelligence Platform:

- **Connection**: Represents a read-only connection containing the credentials to access data in a foreign **relational database management system (RDBMS)** or data warehouse.

- **Storage credential**: Represents the authentication credential for accessing a cloud storage location.

- **External location**: Represents a cloud storage location outside of the Databricks-managed root storage location.

Lastly, let's look at the elements of the Unity Catalog object model for sharing and receiving datasets using the Delta Sharing protocol:

- **Provider**: Represents a data provider. This entity creates a collection of one or more curated datasets into a logical grouping, called a *share*. The data provider can revoke access to a shared dataset at any moment.

- **Share**: A logical grouping of one or more shared datasets that can be shared with a data recipient.

- **Recipient**: Represents a data recipient. This entity receives access to a data share and can query the datasets within their workspace.

Now that we've outlined the major building blocks of Unity Catalog, let's look at how we can enable Unity Catalog on an existing Databricks workspace so that administrators can begin taking full advantage of the strong data governance solution.

Enabling Unity Catalog on an existing Databricks workspace

Beginning in early November 2023, all new Databricks workspaces created on **Amazon Web Services (AWS)** or Azure are enabled with Unity Catalog by default, so there is no extra configuration needed if your workspace was created after this date on these two cloud providers. Similarly, at the time of the creation of a new Databricks workspace, a single regional Unity Catalog metastore will be provisioned for your workspace to use. Within the regional metastore is a default catalog having the same name as the workspace and is bound to that workspace only (we'll cover catalog binding in the following section). Furthermore, all users of a newly created workspace will have read and write access to a schema called `default` within this workspace catalog.

> **Important note**
>
> Workspace administrators cannot disable Unity Catalog on a workspace once a Databricks workspace has been enabled for Unity Catalog. However, datasets can always be migrated back to the HMS implementation, but the workspace will always be enabled with a Unity Catalog metastore.

The first step in upgrading an existing Databricks workspace with Unity Catalog is to deploy a new metastore. A metastore is the "physical" implementation of a Unity Catalog. Administrators will need to deploy a single metastore per cloud region for an organization. A metastore can be deployed through a variety of methods, but for simplicity's sake, we'll cover deploying a new metastore using the Databricks UI:

1. First, ensure that you are logged in to the account console located at `https://accounts.cloud.databricks.com`.

2. From the account console, click on the **Catalog** menu item in the sidebar and click the **Create metastore** button to begin deploying a new metastore.

3. Enter a meaningful name for your metastore, choose the appropriate region, and, optionally, select a default storage path where managed datasets should be stored in.

4. Finally, click the **Create** button. After a few minutes, your new metastore will be provisioned in the cloud region of your choosing.

> **Note**
>
> In Databricks, global configurations such as catalog binding, network configurations, or user provisioning are centralized in a single administrative console, sometimes shortened to the "account console."

Now that the metastore has been deployed, the only thing left is to choose which Databricks workspaces you'd like to link the metastore to, enabling Unity Catalog:

1. From the account console, again choose the **Catalog** menu item from the sidebar.

2. Next, click the name of the newly created metastore, followed by the **Assign to workspaces** button.

3. Lastly, click the workspace you would like to enable Unity Catalog on and confirm your selection by clicking the **Assign** button.

Congratulations! You've now enabled Unity Catalog for your existing Databricks workspace, and you can begin to enjoy the peace of mind that your lakehouse data will be governed by a complete data security solution. Equally as important, once you have attached a Unity Catalog metastore to a Databricks workspace, you have now enabled your workspace for identity federation.

Identity federation in Unity Catalog

Whether you've deployed a brand new Databricks workspace or you've manually upgraded an existing workspace to use Unity Catalog, the natural next step is to set up new users so that they log in to the Databricks workspace and take advantage of the benefits of Unity Catalog.

Previously, user management in Databricks was managed within each workspace. Unity Catalog consolidates user management into a single centralized governance pane – the account console. Rather than manage the workspace identities at a workspace level, which can get repetitive if the same users have access to more than one workspace in a Databricks account, identity management is managed at the account level. This allows administrators to define users and their privileges once, and easily manage identity roles and permissions at a global level.

Prior to Unity Catalog, workspace administrators would need to sync organizational identities from the identity provider, such as Okta, Ping, or **Azure Active Directory (AAD)**. With Unity Catalog, the identities are synced across at the account level once using the **System for Cross-domain Identity Management (SCIM)**. Unity Catalog will then take care of syncing across the identities to the appropriate workspace in a process known as **identity federation**. This allows an organization to continue to manage the identities within their organization's identity provider while ensuring that changes are automatically propagated to the individual Databricks workspaces.

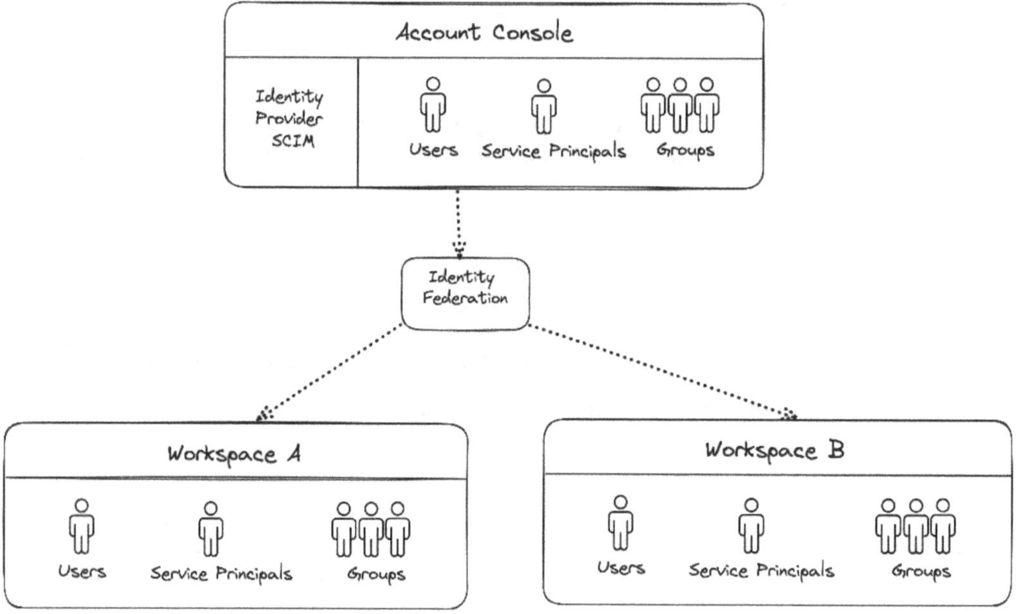

Figure 5.4 – Identities are managed at the account console and will automatically get federated across multiple Databricks workspaces

In fact, the word *administrator* is quite an overloaded term in the context of the Databricks Data Intelligence Platform. Let's take a look at the different administrative roles and the level of entitlement each persona has in a Unity Catalog-enabled workspace:

- **Account owner**: The individual who originally opened the Databricks account. By default, this user will have access to the account console and will be added as both an account admin as well as a workspace admin.

- **Account admin**: A power user who has the privileges to access the account console and make account-level changes, such as deploying a new Unity Catalog metastore, making network configuration changes, or adding users, groups, and service principals to workspaces. This user has the power to grant additional account admins and metastore admins.

- **Metastore admin**: An administrative user who has privileges to make metastore-level changes, such as changing catalog ownership, granting access to users to create or delete new catalogs, or configuring new datasets shared through the Delta Sharing protocol, to name a few. This user does not have access to the account console.

- **Workspace admin**: An administrative user who has privileges to make workspace-level configuration changes, including creating cluster policies and instance pools, creating new clusters and DBSQL warehouses, or configuring workspace appearance settings, to name a few. This user does not have access to the account console.

	Can access account console?	Can make metastore-level changes?	Can make workspace-level changes?
Account Owner	✓	✓	✓
Account Admin	✓	✓	✓
Metastore Admin	✗	✓	✗
Workspace Admin	✗	✗	✓

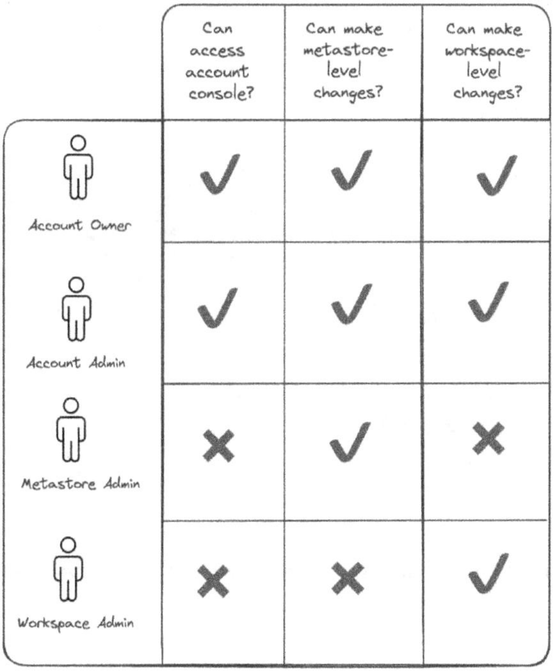

Figure 5.5 – Administrator-level privileges in the Databricks Data Intelligence Platform

To begin provisioning new workspace users, you will need to log in to the account console, located at `https://accounts.cloud.databricks.com/login`. However, only account owners, the individual who originally opened the Databricks organization, or account admins will have access to the admin console.

The first step to begin onboarding new workspace users is to enable **single sign-on** (**SSO**) in the account console. This can be done by navigating to the **Settings** menu of the account console and providing the details of your organization's identity provider. Once you've entered the configuration details, click on the **Test SSO** button to verify connectivity is successful.

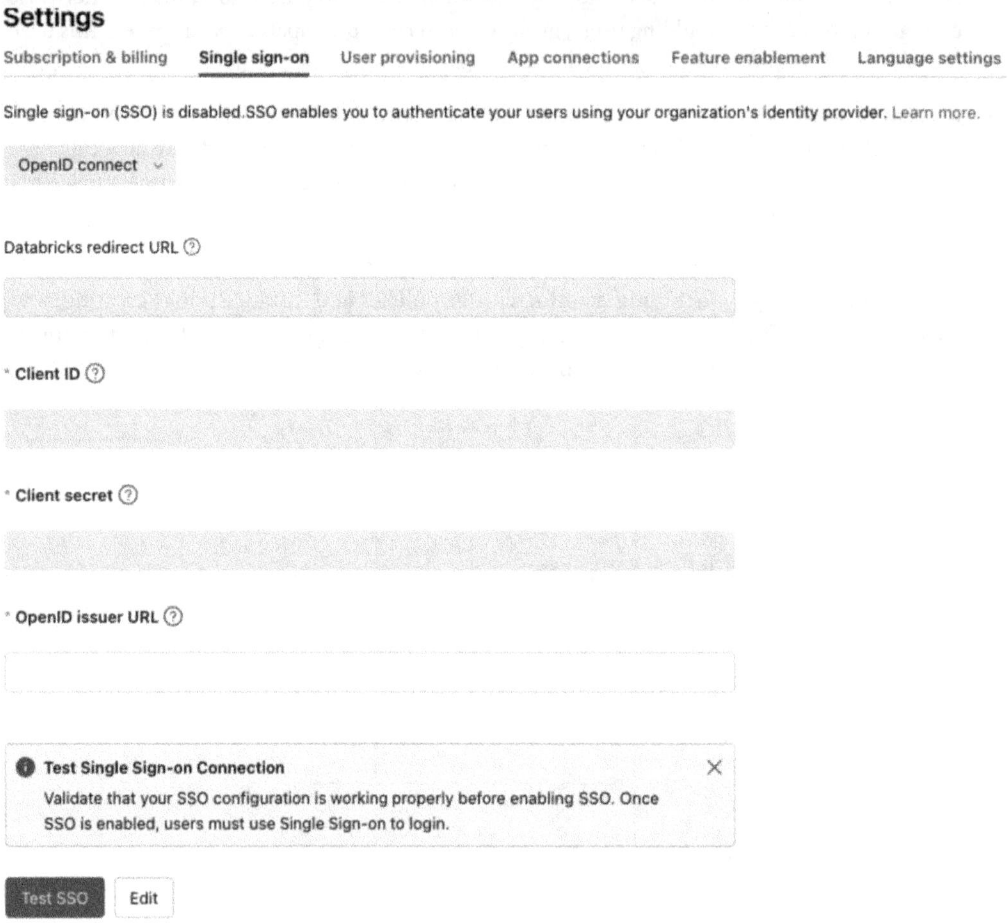

Settings

Subscription & billing   **Single sign-on**   User provisioning   App connections   Feature enablement   Language settings

Single sign-on (SSO) is disabled.SSO enables you to authenticate your users using your organization's identity provider. Learn more.

OpenID connect ⌄

Databricks redirect URL ⑦

* **Client ID** ⑦

* **Client secret** ⑦

* **OpenID issuer URL** ⑦

ⓘ **Test Single Sign-on Connection**   ✕
Validate that your SSO configuration is working properly before enabling SSO. Once SSO is enabled, users must use Single Sign-on to login.

Test SSO   Edit

Figure 5.6 – SSO is required for identity federation to sync with your identity provider

After the identity provider integration has been verified successfully, the next step is to assign users and groups to the appropriate Databricks workspace. If you have a single Databricks workspace, then this is a trivial exercise. However, if there is more than one Databricks workspace, then it will be up to your organization to determine who has access to a particular workspace. You can assign individual users and groups to a Databricks workspace by navigating to the account console, then clicking on the **User Management** tab from the menu item, and assigning users to the appropriate workspace either at the user level or at the group level.

Let's look at how you can promote secure data exploration across your organization.

Data discovery and cataloging

Data tags are useful data cataloging constructs that permit data stewards to link descriptive metadata with datasets and other securable objects, such as catalogs, volumes, or machine learning models, within Unity Catalog. By attaching descriptive tags to datasets and other securable objects, users across your organization can search and discover data assets that may be helpful in their day-to-day activities. This helps to promote collaboration across teams, saving time and resources by not having to recreate similar data assets to reach the completion of a particular activity. Unity Catalog supports tags on the following data objects: catalogs, databases, tables, volumes, views, and machine learning models.

Let's look at an example of how we can apply descriptive tags to our existing taxi trip datasets that will make it easier for users across our organization to search, discover, and use our published datasets in Unity Catalog. Tags can be easily added to a table in Unity Catalog from a variety of methods. The easiest method is directly from the UI using Catalog Explorer in the Databricks Data Intelligence platform. Starting from Catalog Explorer, search for the catalog created in a previous chapter's hands-on exercise that stored data from our DLT pipeline into our `yellow_taxi_raw` dataset. Next, expand the schema and select the `yellow_taxi_raw` dataset to bring up the dataset details. Finally, click on the **Add tags** button to begin adding tag data.

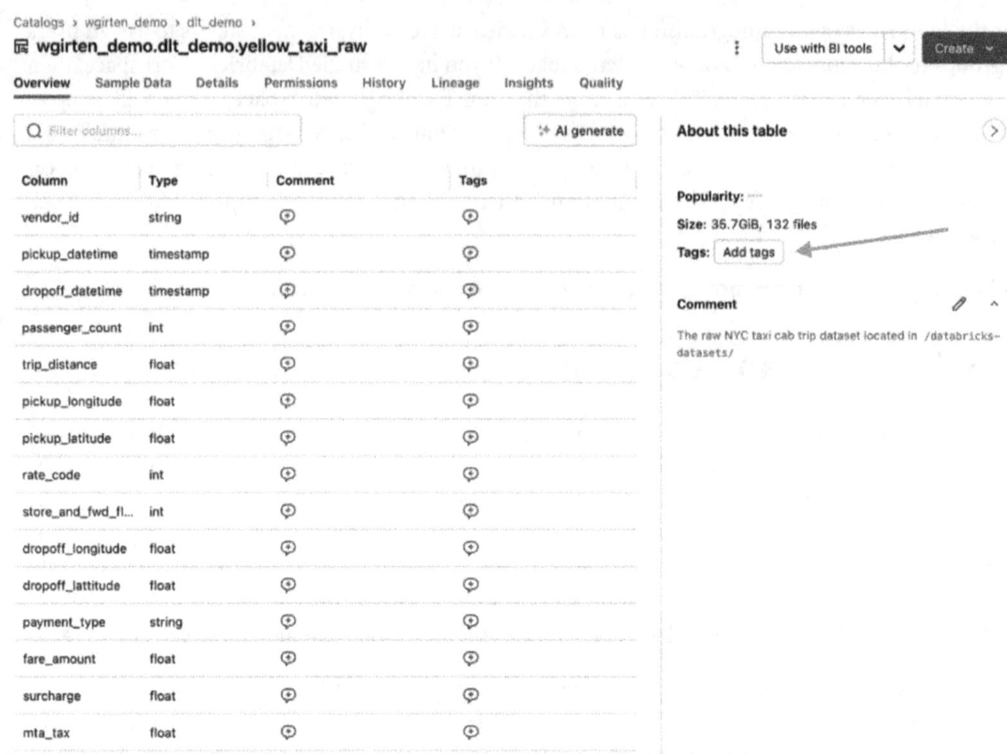

Figure 5.7 – Tags can be added to datasets directly from Catalog Explorer

Tags are added as key-value pairs, with the key serving as a unique identifier, such as a category, and the value containing the contents that you'd like to assign to the securable object. In this case, we'd like to add a few tags to mark the data sensitivity of our dataset as well as a tag for the dataset owner. Add a few tags of your own choosing and click the **Save tags** button to persist your changes to the dataset.

Figure 5.8 – Tags are key-value pairs that help distinguish the dataset from others in Unity Catalog

Similarly, tag data can be added, changed, or removed using SQL syntax as well. In the next example, create a new notebook within your workspace home directory in Databricks, and in the first cell of the notebook, add the following SQL statement. In this example, we'll update the dataset description tag of our dataset:

```
ALTER TABLE yellow_taxi_raw
SET TAGS ('description'='Unprocessed taxi trip data')
```

Lastly, tags support finer granularity and can be added down to the column level for datasets in Unity Catalog. This is useful in scenarios when you might want to distinguish the data sensitivity of a column so that you can dynamically apply a data mask for a view in Unity Catalog.

Add/Edit tags for _c0 column

Key

| data:pii |

Value (optional)

| True |

Figure 5.9 – Tags can be added at the column level for datasets in Unity Catalog

Conversely, users can search for views, tables, or columns that have tags applied by using the following syntax in the **Search** text field of Catalog Explorer: `tag:<case_sensitive_name_of_tag>`.

As you can see, tags are extremely useful in helping promote the discoverability of datasets across your organization and help users distinguish datasets in Unity Catalog from one another.

In addition to discovering datasets across your organization, it's also imperative to know how a dataset is formed and whether upstream sources are trusted. Data lineage is one such method for users to know exactly how the datasets they discover in Unity Catalog are formed and where the different columns originate from.

Tracking dataset relationships using lineage

As data is transformed in your lakehouse by data pipelines, the contents of your organization's datasets can go through a series of evolutions by a variety of processes. This can include processes such as data cleansing, data type casting, column transformation, or data enrichment, to name a few. As you can imagine, the data can deviate quite far from when it was originally ingested from its originating source. It's important for downstream consumers of the data in your lakehouse to be able to verify the validity of your datasets. Data lineage is one mechanism for such validation by allowing users to trace the origin of tables and columns so that you can ensure that you are using data from trusted sources.

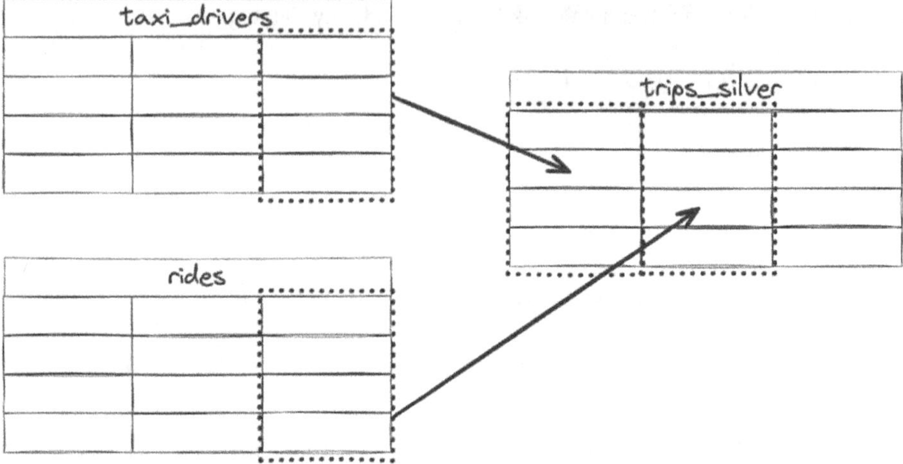

Figure 5.10 – A lakehouse table may be the result of a combination of multiple upstream tables

Data lineage can be viewed from a variety of mechanisms in the Databricks Data Intelligence Platform:

- Directly from Catalog Explorer by viewing the lineage graph

- Retrieved using the Lineage Tracking REST API

- Querying the Lineage Tracking system tables in Unity Catalog

Let's look at how we might be able to trace the origin of a few columns in our downstream table to the upstream sources in Databricks. If you haven't already done so, you can clone this chapter's sample notebooks from the GitHub repository located at `https://github.com/PacktPublishing/Building-Modern-Data-Applications-Using-Databricks-Lakehouse/tree/main/chapter05`. Begin by importing the sample notebook titled `Data Lineage Demo.sql` into your Databricks workspace. Attach the notebook to a running all-purpose cluster and execute all of the notebook cells. The notebook will generate two tables – a parent table and a child table whose columns are constructed from the upstream parent table.

Once the notebook has been executed and the tables have been saved to Unity Catalog, navigate to Catalog Explorer by clicking the **Catalog** menu item from the left-hand navigation menu. From Catalog Explorer, search for the child table by entering the table name in the **Search** text field. Click on the child table to reveal the table details. Finally, click on the blue button titled **See lineage graph** to generate a lineage diagram. You'll notice that the diagram clearly depicts the relationship between the two data assets – the parent table and the child table. Next, click on the column titled `car_description` in the child table. You'll notice that the lineage diagram is updated, clearly illustrating which columns from the parent table are used to construct this column in the downstream child table.

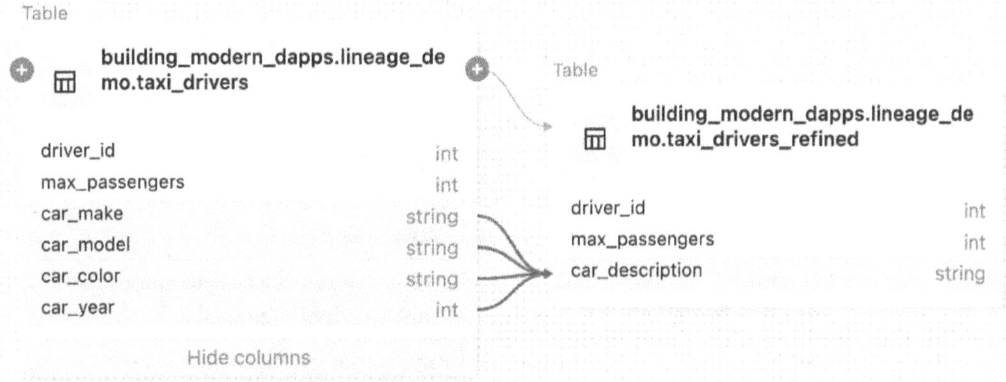

Figure 5.11 – The table lineage graph can be viewed directly from Catalog Explorer

In fact, thanks to the unification nature of Unity Catalog, data lineage can be used to trace data relationships across multiple workspaces. Furthermore, data lineage will capture relationship information in near-real time, so that users can always have an up-to-date view of dataset relationships no matter the Databricks workspace they are using.

Observability with system tables

Strong auditing and system observability is another core strength of Unity Catalog and is implemented in Databricks using system tables. System tables are a set of read-only tables in a Databricks workspace that capture the operational data about activities within your Databricks workspaces. Furthermore, systems tables record data across all workspaces within a Databricks account, serving as a single source of truth to retrieve operational data pertaining to your Databricks workspaces.

System tables record observability information about the following aspects of your Databricks workspaces (the latest list of available system tables can be found at `https://docs.databricks.com/en/admin/system-tables/index.html#which-system-tables-are-available`):

Category	Service	Description
System billing	Billable usage	Captures billing information about utilized computational resources such as warehouses and clusters
	Pricing	Captures historical changes to system service pricing (or **stock-keeping unit (SKU)**)
System access	System audit	Contains event data from workspace services including jobs, workflows, clusters, notebooks, repos, secrets, and more
	Table lineage	Captures data about reads/writes to and from a table in Unity Catalog
	Column lineage information	Captures data about reads/writes to and from a column within a Unity Catalog table
Compute	Clusters	Captures information about clusters – for example, configuration changes over time
	Node type information	Includes hardware information about cluster node types
	SQL warehouse events	Captures changes made to SQL warehousing such as scaling events
System storage	Predictive optimizations	Captures predicative I/O optimizations as they occur during data processing
Marketplace	Marketplace funnel events	Captures marketplace analytical information such as number of impressions and funnel data about dataset listing
	Marketplace listing events	Records marketplace consumer information about dataset listings

Table 5.1 – System tables will record operational information across various parts of the Databricks Data Intelligence Platform

Like all tables in Unity Catalog, there is no access to the system tables by default. Instead, a metastore administrator will need to grant read access (SELECT permissions) to these tables to the appropriate users and groups. For example, to grant permissions for department leaders to track their warehouse scaling events throughout the workday, a metastore admin would need to explicitly grant permissions for the group, dept_leads, to query the SQL warehouse system table:

```
GRANT SELECT ON system.compute.warehouse_events TO dept_leads
```

As you can imagine, very active Databricks workspaces will record many events throughout the day, and over time, these tables can grow to be quite large. To prevent observability information from accumulating to the point of creating a large cloud storage bill, instead, the system information will only be retained for a maximum of one year within your Databricks account.

For use cases where the auditing information is required to be retained in the order of many years, you will need to set up a secondary process to copy the system information into a long-term archival system, for example. Tracking changes to datasets is critical to ensuring strong observability in your lakehouse. Another strong suite of Unity Catalog is that observability extends beyond just datasets and covers all objects that can be secured under Unity Catalog governance.

Tracing the lineage of other assets

As previously mentioned, Unity Catalog implements a single governance solution over your organization's data assets, which extends beyond just tables. With Unity Catalog, you can trace the lineage of other data assets such as workflows, notebooks, and machine learning models, to name a few.

Let's turn our attention to how Unity Catalog can dynamically generate different result sets to queries by evaluating the user and group permissions of a given Databricks user.

Fine-grained data access

Dynamic views are a special type of view within the Databricks Data Intelligence Platform that provides data administrators with the ability to control fine-grained access to data within a dataset. For example, administrators can specify which rows and columns a particular individual may have access to depending upon their group membership. The Databricks Data Intelligence Platform introduces several built-in functions for dynamically evaluating group membership when a particular user queries the contents of a view:

- current_user() returns the email address of the user querying the view

- is_member() returns a Boolean (True or False) of whether the user querying a view is a member of a Databricks workspace-level group

- is_account_group_member() returns a Boolean (True or False) of whether the user querying a view is a member of a Databricks account-level group (as opposed to a workspace-level group)

> **Important note**
>
> For dynamic views created against tables and views in Unity Catalog, it's recommended to use the `is_account_group_member()` function to evaluate a user's membership to a group as it will evaluate group membership at the Databricks account level. On the other hand, the `is_member()` function will evaluate a user's membership to a group that is local to a particular workspace and may provide false or unintended results.

Furthermore, dynamic views also enable data administrators to obfuscate specific column values so that sensitive data is not exfiltrated by accident. Using built-in Spark SQL functions such as `concat()`, `regexp_extract()`, or even `lit()` is a simple yet powerful tool for protecting the contents of the most sensitive datasets on the Databricks platform.

In the next section, we'll look at how we can leverage dynamic views to permit members of a data science team to perform ad hoc data wrangling of a sensitive dataset while simultaneously protecting the contents of columns with **personally identifiable information (PII)** data.

Hands-on example – data masking healthcare datasets

In this example, we'll be creating a dynamic view to restrict data access to certain rows and columns within a dataset. We'll be using the COVID sample dataset located within the Databricks datasets at `/databricks-datasets/COVID/covid-19-data/us-counties.csv`. The dataset contains COVID-19 infection data for US counties during the 2020 global pandemic. Since this dataset can contain sensitive data, we'll apply a simple data mask to prevent the exposure of sensitive data to non-privileged users.

Let's start by defining a few global variables, as well as the catalog and schema that will hold our dynamic views:

```python
CATALOG_NAME = "building_modern_dapps"
SCHEMA_NAME = "dynamic_views_demo"
PERSISTENT_TABLE_NAME = "covid_us_counties"
COVID_DATASET_PATH = "/databricks-datasets/COVID/covid-19-data/us-
counties.csv"

spark.sql(f"CREATE CATALOG IF NOT EXISTS {CATALOG_NAME}")
spark.sql(f"USE CATALOG {CATALOG_NAME}")
spark.sql(f"CREATE SCHEMA IF NOT EXISTS {SCHEMA_NAME}")
spark.sql(f"USE SCHEMA {SCHEMA_NAME}")
```

Next, we'll need to define a persistent table object in Unity Catalog that we will use to create views. Let's start by creating a new table using the sample US Counties COVID dataset:

```
covid_df = (spark.read
              .option("header", True)
              .option("inferSchema", True)
              .csv(COVID_DATASET_PATH))
(covid_df.write
    .mode("overwrite")
    .saveAsTable(f"{CATALOG_NAME}.{SCHEMA_NAME}.{PERSISTENT_TABLE_
NAME}"));
```

Next, let's query the newly created table in Unity Catalog. Note that all columns and rows are returned since we didn't specify any qualifying criteria that would filter the data:

```
spark.table(f"{CATALOG_NAME}.{SCHEMA_NAME}.{PERSISTENT_TABLE_NAME}").
display()
```

Let's create a view that will dynamically evaluate the querying user's group membership in Unity Catalog. In this case, we want to restrict access to certain columns if the user is not a member of the `admins` group. Based upon the group membership, we can give access to a user or we could limit access to the data.

Let's also leverage a built-in Spark SQL function to apply a simple yet powerful data mask to sensitive data columns, allowing only privileged members of the `admins` group access to view the text:

```
RESTRICTED_VIEW_NAME = "covid_us_counties_restricted_vw"
spark.sql(f"""
CREATE OR REPLACE VIEW {RESTRICTED_VIEW_NAME} AS
SELECT
    date,
    county,
    state,
    CASE WHEN is_account_group_member('admins')
        THEN fips
        ELSE concat('***', substring(fips, length(fips)-1,
                                     length(fips)))
    END AS fips_id,
    cases,
    CASE WHEN is_account_group_member('admins')
        THEN deaths
        ELSE 'UNKNOWN'
    END AS mortality_cases
FROM {CATALOG_NAME}.{SCHEMA_NAME}.{PERSISTENT_TABLE_NAME}
""")
```

In the previous view definition, we've limited data access to a particular set of columns within the US Counties COVID dataset. Using dynamic views, we can also limit access to a particular set of rows using a query predicate. In the final view definition, we'll limit which US states a particular user can view based on a user's membership to the `admins` group:

```
COL_AND_ROW_RESTRICTED_VIEW_NAME = "covid_us_counties_final_vw"
spark.sql(f"""
CREATE OR REPLACE VIEW {COL_AND_ROW_RESTRICTED_VIEW_NAME} AS
SELECT
    date,
    county,
    state,
    CASE WHEN is_account_group_member('admins')
        THEN fips
        ELSE concat('***', substring(fips, length(fips)-1,
                                        length(fips)))
    END AS fips_id,
    cases,
    CASE WHEN is_account_group_member('admins')
        THEN deaths
        ELSE 'UNKNOWN'
    END AS mortality_cases
FROM {CATALOG_NAME}.{SCHEMA_NAME}.{PERSISTENT_TABLE_NAME}
WHERE
    CASE WHEN is_account_group_member('admins')
        THEN 1=1
        ELSE state IN ('Alabamba', 'Colorado', 'California',
                        'Delaware', 'New York', 'Texas', 'Florida')
    END
""")
```

Now, members of other groups can perform ad hoc data exploration and other data experimentation. However, we won't inadvertently expose any sensitive healthcare data. For example, let's imagine that there is another group called `data-science`. This group can query the dynamic view, but the results will be different from if a member of the `admins` group queried the view. For example, the following aggregation will return different result sets depending on whether a user is in the `admins` group or the `data-science` group:

```
(spark.table(COL_AND_ROW_RESTRICTED_VIEW_NAME)
    .groupBy("state", "county")
    .agg({"cases": "count"})
    .orderBy("state", "county")
).withColumnRenamed("count(cases)", "total_covid_cases").display()
```

We get the following results:

		state		county		total_covid_cases
	1	California		Alameda		376
	2	California		Alpine		347
	3	California		Amador		357
	4	California		Butte		356
	5	California		Calaveras		353
	6	California		Colusa		350
	7	California		Contra Costa		374
	8	California		Del Norte		344
	9	California		El Dorado		356
	10	California		Fresno		370
	11	California		Glenn		349
	12	California		Humboldt		386
	13	California		Imperial		357
	14	California		Inyo		352
	15	California		Kern		360

Figure 5.12 – Dynamic views can generate customized results based on group membership

By now, you should be able to realize the power of dynamic views within the Databricks Data Intelligence Platform. With just a few built-in functions, we can implement strong data governance across various users and groups interacting with your organization's data in the lakehouse.

Summary

In this chapter, we covered the challenges specific to lakehouse data governance and how Unity Catalog solves these challenges. We also covered how to enable Unity Catalog within an existing Databricks workspace and how metastore admins can establish connections with external data sources. Lastly, we covered techniques for discovering and cataloging data assets within the lakehouse and how annotating data assets with metadata tags can create a searchable and well-organized data catalog.

In the next chapter, we'll explore how to effectively manage input and output data locations using Unity Catalog. You'll learn how to govern data access across various roles and departments within an organization, ensuring security and auditability within the Databricks Data Intelligence Platform.

6

Managing Data Locations in Unity Catalog

In this chapter, we'll explore how to effectively manage data storage locations using securable objects in **Unity Catalog** – objects that allow administrators to grant fine-grained permissions to users, groups, and service principals . We'll cover six types of securable objects for storing data in Unity Catalog: catalogs, schemas, tables, volumes, external locations, and connections. We'll also look at how you can effectively govern storage access across various roles and departments within your organization, ensuring data security and auditability within the Databricks Data Intelligence Platform. Lastly, we'll outline how to organize and structure data across different storage locations within Unity Catalog.

In this chapter, we're going to cover the following main topics:

- Creating and managing data catalogs in Unity Catalog

- Setting default storage locations for data within Unity Catalog

- Creating and managing external storage locations in Unity Catalog

- Hands-on lab – extracting document text for a generative AI pipeline

Technical requirements

To follow along with the examples provided in this chapter, you'll need Databricks workspace permissions to create and start an all-purpose cluster so that you can import and execute the chapter's accompanying notebooks. All code samples can be downloaded from this chapter's GitHub repository located at `https://github.com/PacktPublishing/Building-Modern-Data-Applications-Using-Databricks-Lakehouse/tree/main/chapter06`. It's also recommended that your Databricks user be elevated to a metastore admin (covered in *Chapter 5*) so that you can add and remove external locations, security credentials, foreign connections, and bind catalogs to a Databricks workspace. This chapter will create and run several new notebooks, estimated to consume around 5-10 **Databricks Units (DBUs)**.

Creating and managing data catalogs in Unity Catalog

A **catalog** is the topmost container in the Unity Catalog object model hierarchy for storing data assets. A catalog will contain one or more schemas (or databases), which can contain one or many tables, views, models, functions, or volumes.

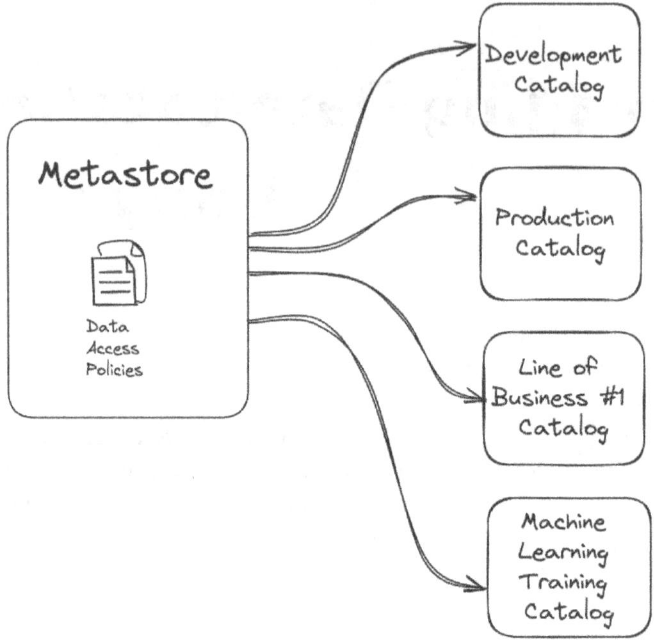

Figure 6.1 – Data is isolated in Unity Catalog using catalogs

A common question is "How many catalogs should my workspace have?" While there is no right or wrong answer to the exact number of catalogs one should create for their workspace, a good rule of thumb would be to break your workspace catalogs up by natural dividing factors such as lines of business, logical work environments, teams, or use cases, for example. Furthermore, you should consider the subset of groups and users who will have permission to use the data assets as a factor in deciding how to create your catalog isolation.

> **Important note**
>
> It is a best practice to not have too few catalogs where you cannot logically divide datasets from one another. Similarly, it's also a best practice to not have too many catalogs within a workspace as it makes it difficult for users to navigate and discover datasets. You should aim to find somewhere in between.

Metastore administrators, or privileged users within Unity Catalog, can grant other users the entitlement to create additional catalogs within a metastore. For example, the following grant statement executed by a metastore administrator will grant the Databricks user, `jane.smith@example.com`, permission to create new catalogs within the metastore attached to their Databricks workspace:

```
GRANT CREATE CATALOG ON METASTORE TO `jane.smith@example.com`;
```

Furthermore, for Databricks workspaces created after November 8th, 2023, a default workspace catalog is created within the Unity Catalog metastore, `<workspace_name>_catalog`. By default, all users in the workspace will have access to this catalog and can create data assets.

Managed data versus external data

When you deploy a Unity Catalog metastore, part of the deployment process includes setting up a new, default cloud storage container at the metastore level. This cloud storage container serves as the *default* location for all data assets created on the Databricks Data Intelligence Platform. For example, when a user creates a new table and they do not specify a `LOCATION` attribute in the **data definition language (DDL)** statement, then the Databricks Data Intelligence Platform will store the table data in the default storage container. As a result, the platform will take care of managing the life cycle of this table, including the data files, metadata, and even characteristics of the table, such as tuning the table layout and file sizes. This type of data asset is referred to as a *managed* table because the Databricks Data Intelligence Platform will manage the life cycle. Furthermore, if the table is dropped, the platform will take care of removing all the table metadata and data files.

However, if the user provides a `LOCATION` attribute in the DDL statement, they will override the default behavior. Instead, the user is explicitly directing the Databricks Data Intelligence Platform to store the data in a location external to the default storage container for Unity Catalog. As a result, this type of data asset is referred to as an *external* table. Databricks will not manage the performance characteristics of the table, such as the size of the files or the layout of the files. Unlike managed tables, if an external table is dropped, only the entry of the table is removed from Unity Catalog and none of the table metadata and data files will be removed from their external location. Instead, the table owner will need to take care of deleting the table files from the cloud location, since they've taken over managing the table life cycle.

Generally speaking, *managed* refers to the Databricks platform managing the life cycle and data will be stored in the default storage container, while on the other hand, *external* means that the object owner is taking control of the object life cycle and the data should be stored in an external storage location.

In fact, there may be good reasons when you wish to create data assets in a different storage location than metastore default location. For example, for privileged datasets containing sensitive data, such as **personally identifiable information (PII)** / **protected health information (PHI)** data, you may wish to store these datasets in a separate storage account. Or perhaps you have a contractual obligation that requires data to be stored separately in an isolated storage account. In any event, it's quite common to have requirements for data isolation. In the next section, let's look at another securable object in Unity Catalog that allows data admins to securely store arbitrary types of data while maintaining strong isolation from traditional tables and views.

Saving data to storage volumes in Unity Catalog

A **volume**, short for a **storage volume**, can be used to store files of various format types. Furthermore, volumes can be stored alongside tables and views in a schema in Unity Catalog. While tables and views are used to store structured data, volumes can be used to store structured, semi-structured, or unstructured data.

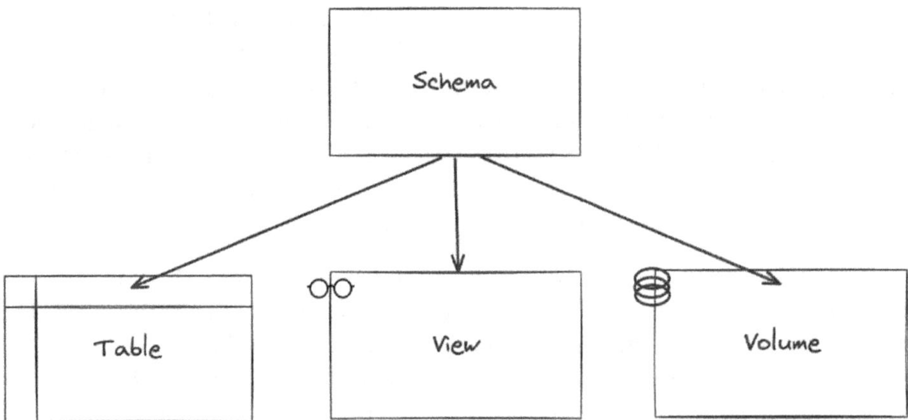

Figure 6.2 – Storage volumes are stored alongside tables and views within a schema in Unity Catalog

Volumes can be managed by the Databricks Data Intelligence Platform, where, once dropped, the storage container, including the entire contents of the storage container, is removed entirely. On the other hand, volumes can be external volumes, meaning the volume owner manages the storage location of the storage volume, and once dropped, the contents of the storage container are not removed.

Storage volumes simplify the storage of files in Unity Catalog by removing the overhead of creating and managing external storage locations and storage credential objects within Unity Catalog. Whereas, external locations would need to be created with an accompanying storage credential, making provisioning and deprovisioning slightly more complex.

Storage volumes provide users of a particular schema the flexibility of storing arbitrary files in a safe and secure storage location that is managed by the Databricks Data Intelligence Platform. By default, storage volumes will persist data in the default storage location of the parent schema. For example, if there was no storage location provided at the time of the schema creation, then the data in a storage volume will be stored in the default storage account for the Unity Catalog metastore. Whereas if the schemas were created with an explicit storage location, then by default the storage volume will store its contents in this cloud location.

A metastore administrator or a privileged user with explicit permission to create a volume within a catalog can create or drop a volume. The following example grants explicit permission for a Databricks user to create volumes on the development catalog:

```
GRANT CREATE VOLUME
    ON CATALOG development_catalog
    TO `jane.smith@example.com`;
```

A fully qualified volume path is constructed using `/Volumes/` followed by the catalog, schema, and volume names. For example, an arbitrary text file can be referenced using the following path:

```
/Volumes/catalog_name/schema_name/volume_name/subdirectory_name/
arbitrary_file.txt
```

In the previous examples, we've let the Databricks Data Intelligence Platform decide how data is stored using schemas, tables, views, and volumes. However, we can set a prescribed cloud location for certain securable objects as well. Let's look at how we can control the storage location using several techniques in Unity Catalog.

Setting default locations for data within Unity Catalog

You can control the storage location of data using several techniques in Unity Catalog:

- **Default location at the catalog level:** When creating a new catalog, data administrators can prescribe a storage location. When creating a data asset, such as a table, and no location is specified, then the data will be stored in the catalog location.

- **Default location at the schema level**: Similarly, you can specify a default location at the schema level. The schema location will override any default location specified at the catalog level. When creating a data asset, such as a table, and no location is specified, then the data will be stored in the schema location.

- **An external location at the table level**: This is the finest-grained control data stewards have over their datasets. The table location will override any default location specified at either the catalog or the schema level.

- **Volume location**: Closely related to external locations (covered in the *Creating and managing external storage locations in Unity Catalog* section), volumes allow control over where the table data gets stored in your cloud storage location.

Isolating catalogs to specific workspaces

By default, when you create a catalog in Unity Catalog, the catalog will be available for metastore admins to grant permissions for users to access across *all* Databricks workspaces using that metastore. However, in certain scenarios, you may want to override this behavior and enforce stronger isolation of datasets residing within a particular catalog. For example, sensitive datasets may only be available for data pipeline processing in a production workspace but should not be available in lower environments such as a development workspace. A feature of Unity Catalog called **catalog binding** helps address this type of scenario. With catalog binding, catalog administrators, such as a metastore administrator or a catalog owner, can control which workspaces have access to a particular catalog. For Databricks workspaces that are not bound to a particular catalog, the catalog will not appear in the search results of the Catalog Explorer UI.

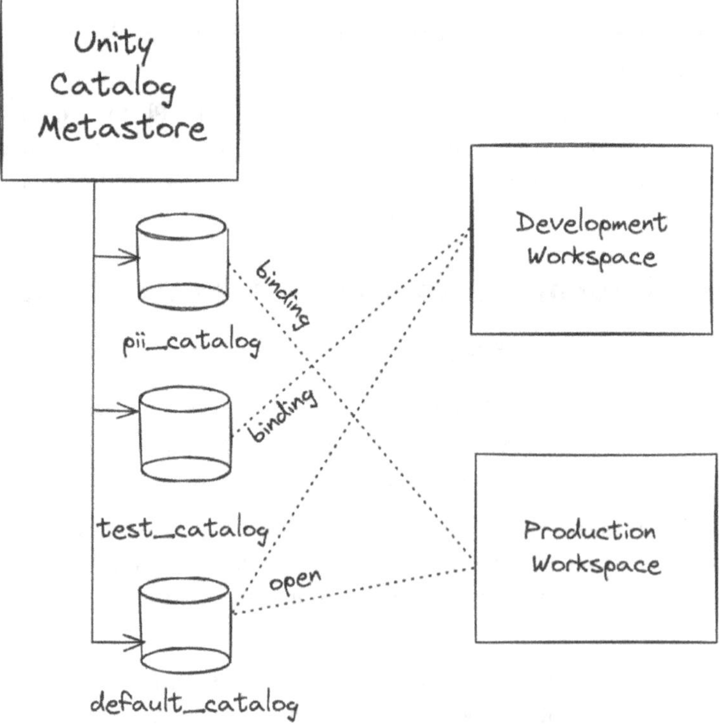

Figure 6.3 – Catalog binding allows data administrators to control
data isolation and isolation levels per workspace

Furthermore, data administrators can prescribe the type of actions that are available to datasets bound to a particular workspace. For example, say that you want to limit the access to read-only for datasets residing within a catalog for a testing environment. Data administrators can change the binding settings of a catalog either from the UI, using the Catalog Explorer in the Databricks Data Intelligence Platform, or using automated tools such as Terraform or the REST API. Let's look at an example of how we could leverage the Databricks REST API to bind our testing catalog, which contains PII data to our production workspace.

First, let's start off by updating the default settings of our catalog so that the catalog is not accessible from all workspaces that use our Unity Catalog metastore. By default, this attribute is set to OPEN, and we would like to isolate our catalog to a prescribed workspace only:

```python
import requests
catalog = "testing_catalog"
response = requests.patch(
    f"https://{workspace_name}/api/2.1/unity-catalog/catalogs/
{catalog}",
    headers = {"Authorization": f"Bearer {api_token}"},
    json = {"isolation_mode": "ISOLATED"}
)
print(response.json())
```

We can also use the Catalog Explorer to verify that the isolation mode of our catalog has been updated with our previous request. From the Databricks workspace, navigate to the Catalog Explorer from the left sidebar menu. Next, type in the name of your catalog in the search box to filter the catalogs and click on the name of your catalog. From the Catalog Explorer UI, verify in the details that the checkbox titled **All workspaces have access** is no longer checked.

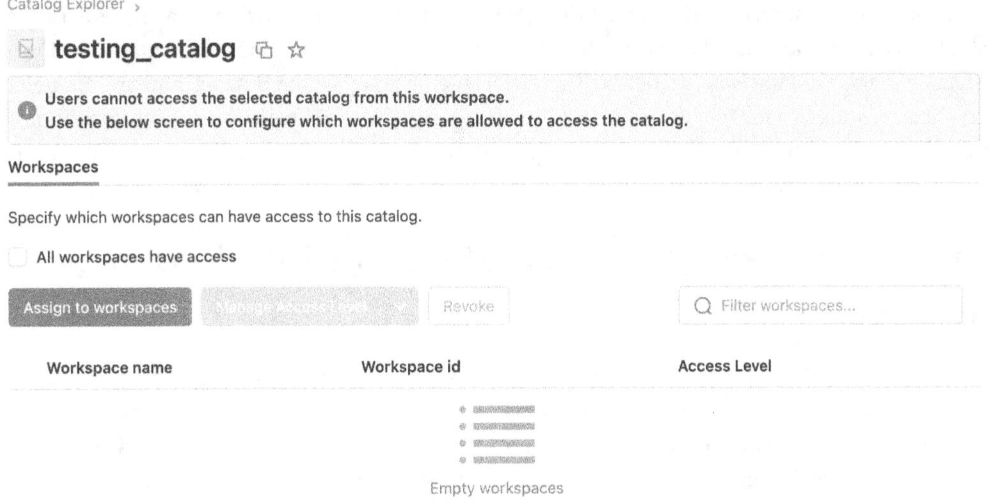

Figure 6.4 – Catalog binding information can be configured from the Databricks UI

Now that our catalog is no longer open for metastore administrators to grant access from all workspaces that use our Unity Catalog metastore, we want to bind the catalog to only the workspaces that we'd like users to have access to.

In the next example, we'll again use the Databricks REST API to allow data administrators in the production workspace to assign read-only access to the datasets in our catalog:

```
response = requests.patch(
    f"https://{workspace_name}/api/2.1/unity-catalog/bindings/catalog/
{catalog}",
    headers = {"Authorization": f"Bearer {api_token}"},
    json = {"add": [{
        "workspace_id": <production_workspace_id>,
        "binding_type": "BINDING_TYPE_READ_ONLY"}]
    }
)
print(response.json())
```

> **Important note**
>
> In the preceding example, we provide the workspace identifier in the payload request for binding a catalog to a workspace in Unity Catalog. If you aren't sure what your workspace identifier is, you can quickly find it by inspecting the URL of your Databricks workspace. The workspace identifier can be found in the first URI segment of the URL to your Databricks workspace and follows the `https://<workspace_name>.cloud.databricks.com/o=<workspace_id>` pattern. The workspace identifier will be the numerical value immediately following the `o=` URL parameter.

By now, you should understand the impact that catalog binding has in allowing data administrators the ability to control how our data is accessible and further isolate datasets in the Databricks Data Intelligence Platform. However, there may be certain scenarios in which data administrators need to control the cloud storage location, such as meeting contractual obligations of no co-location of datasets during pipeline processing. In the next section, let's look at how data administrators can assign specific cloud locations for datasets.

Creating and managing external storage locations in Unity Catalog

One of the strong suits of Databricks is the openness of data, meaning users can connect to data stored in a variety of cloud-native storage systems. For example, users can connect to data stored in Amazon's S3 service and join that data with another dataset stored in an **Azure Data Lake Storage (ADLS) Gen2** storage container. However, one of the downsides is that integration with these cloud-native storage services needs complex configuration settings to be set typically at the beginning of a notebook execution, or perhaps in an initialization script when a cluster starts up.

These configuration settings are complex, and at the very minimum need to be stored in a Databricks secret, and authentication tokens would need to be rotated by cloud admins – a very complex maintenance life cycle for an otherwise simple task – loading remote data using Spark's `DataFrameReader`. One of the key benefits that Unity Catalog brings is a securable object called a **storage credential**, which aims to simplify this maintenance task, while also allowing end users the ability to store and connect to datasets that are external to the Databricks Data Intelligence Platform. Cloud admins or metastore admins can store cloud service authentication details in a single place and save end users, who may not be technical, from having to configure complex details of cloud authentication, such as an IAM role identifier. As an example of how complex these configuration details can be, the following code snippet can be used to configure authentication to an ADLS Gen2 container using the configuration that gets set during the code execution:

```
# Connect to data stored in an ADLS Gen2 container
account_name = "some_storage_account"
spark.conf.set(f"fs.azure.account.auth.type.{account_name}.dfs.core.
windows.net", "SAS")
spark.conf.set(f"fs.azure.sas.token.provider.type.{account_name}.
dfs.core.windows.net", "org.apache.hadoop.fs.azurebfs.sas.
FixedSASTokenProvider")

# Use a Databricks Secret to safely store and retrieve a SAS key for
authenticating with ADLS service
spark.conf.set(
    f"fs.azure.sas.fixed.token.{account_name}.dfs.core.windows.net",
    dbutils.secrets.get(scope="sas_token_scope",
    key="sas_ token_key"))
```

Storing cloud service authentication using storage credentials

A **storage credential** is a securable object within Unity Catalog that abstracts away a cloud-native credential for access to a cloud storage account. For example, a storage credential may represent an **Identity and Access Management (IAM)** role on the **Amazon Web Services (AWS)** cloud. A storage credential may also represent a **managed identity** or service principal in the Azure cloud. Once a storage credential has been created, access to the storage credential can be granted to users and groups in Unity Catalog using an explicit grant statement. Like other securable objects in Unity Catalog, there are various methods for creating a new security credential on the Databricks Data Intelligence Platform. For example, a metastore admin may choose to use **American National Standards Institute Structured Query Language (ANSI SQL)** to create the storage credential, or they might use the Databricks UI.

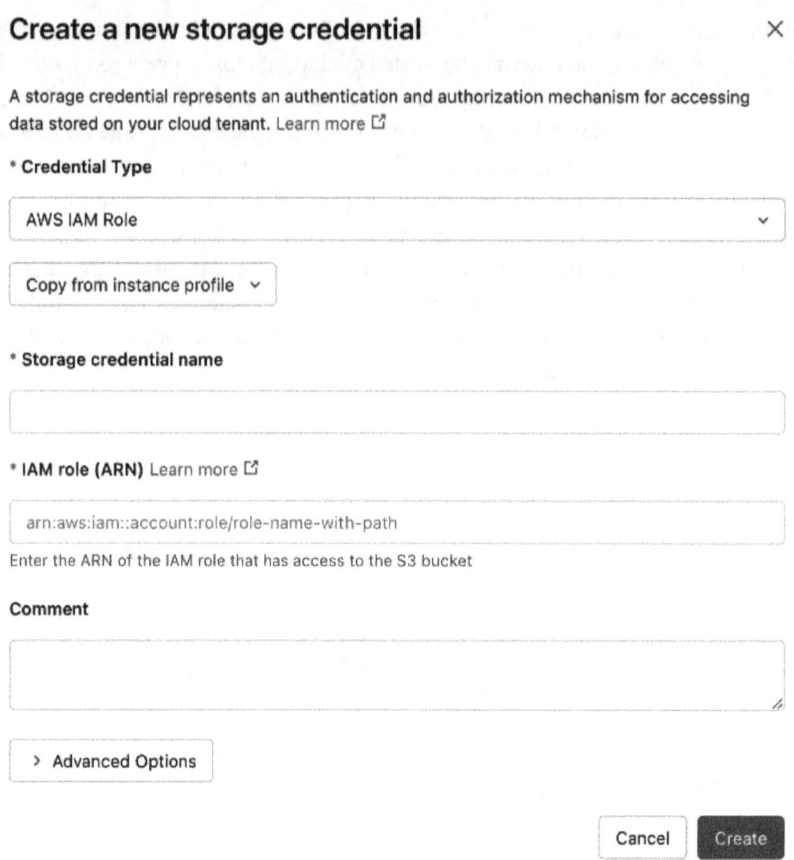

Figure 6.5 – Storage credentials can be created using Databricks UI

Storage credentials are paired with another securable object in Unity Catalog called an **external location**, and the combination is used to store and access data in a specific cloud storage account.

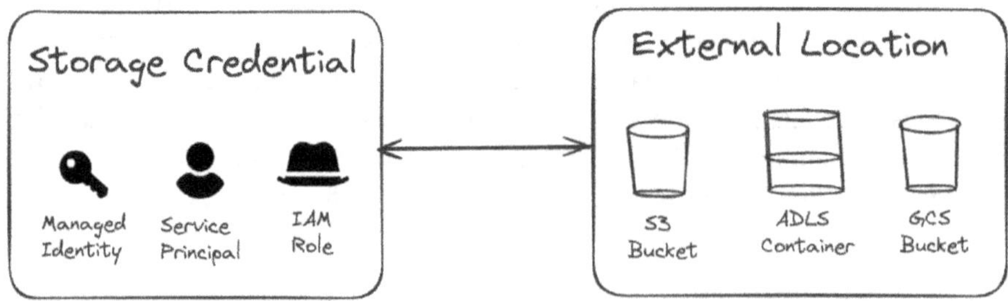

Figure 6.6 – A storage credential encapsulates a cloud identity and is
used by Unity Catalog to access an external storage location

You must be either a Databricks account administrator or a metastore administrator for a Unity Catalog metastore, which will include the `CREATE STORAGE CREDENTIAL` entitlement. The following example uses the Databricks **command-line interface** (**CLI**) tool to create a new storage credential in Unity Catalog using an IAM role in AWS:

```
databricks storage-credentials create \
  --json '{"name": "my_storage_cred", ' \
  '"aws_iam_role": {"role_arn": ' \
  '"arn:aws:iam::<role_identifier>:role/<account_name>"}}'
```

Let's use the SQL API this time to grant permission to the `data-science` group to use the credential for accessing cloud storage:

```
-- Grant access to create an external location using the storage cred
GRANT CREATE EXTERNAL LOCATION
    ON STORAGE CREDENTIAL my_s3_bucket_cred
    TO `data-science`;
```

However, storage containers external to the Databricks Data Intelligence Platform may not be the only source of data that you wish to connect to from your lakehouse. For instance, there may be scenarios in which you may need to connect to an external system, such as an existing data warehouse or a relational database, to cross-reference data. Let's turn our attention to **Lakehouse Federation**, which allows lakehouse users to query datasets outside of the Databricks Data Intelligence Platform.

Querying external systems using Lakehouse Federation

Lakehouse Federation is a feature in the Databricks Data Intelligence Platform that permits users to execute queries on storage systems external to Databricks without needing to migrate the data to the lakehouse. Another securable object in Unity Catalog, called a **connection**, can be used to federate queries to external systems. A connection represents a *read-only* connection to an external system, such as a **relational database management system** (**RDBMS**), such as Postgres or MySQL, or a cloud data warehouse such as Amazon Redshift. This is a great way to query external data to quickly prototype new pipelines in your lakehouse. Perhaps, even, you need to cross-reference an external dataset and don't want to go through the lengthy process of creating another **extract, transform, and load** (**ETL**) pipeline to ingest a new data source just yet.

A list of all connections can be easily viewed in the Databricks Data Intelligence Platform by navigating to the Catalog Explorer, expanding the **Connections** pane, and clicking a **Foreign Connection** to view the details about a previously created connection.

Let's look at an example of how we can use the SQL connection API in Databricks to create a new foreign connection to the MySQL database. Databricks recommends that all credential information be stored in a Databricks secret, which can be easily retrieved from SQL using the `secret()` SQL function and providing the secret scope and secret key:

```
CREATE CONNECTION my_mysql_connection TYPE mysql
OPTIONS (
    host '<fully_qualified_hostname>',
    port '3306',
    user secret('mysql_scope', 'mysql_username'),
    password secret('mysql_scope', 'mysql_password')
)
```

Next, navigate to the **Connections** UI by clicking on the Catalog Explorer in the left-hand side navigation bar, expanding the **External Data** pane, and clicking on the **Connections** menu item. You should now see the newly created connection to the MySQL database and clicking on it will reveal details about the connection.

Connections ›

mysql_connection

Comment:

Owner: john.smith@example.com

URL: jdbc://<fully-qualified-hostname>:3306

Permissions

Create catalog

Grant   Revoke   Type to filter by principal

Principal   Privilege   Object

john.smith@example.com   ALL PRIVILEGES   mysql_connection

Figure 6.7 – Connections to foreign storage systems can be viewed from the Catalog Explorer

Let's connect everything we've learned in the previous sections to build a modern data pipeline capable of powering generative AI use cases.

Hands-on lab – extracting document text for a generative AI pipeline

In this example, we'll look at a typical pipeline used to extract text from documents for the purposes of generative AI. This is a very common architectural pattern, especially for real-world use cases such as training a chatbot over a text corpus. Along the way, we'll see how storage volumes on the Databricks Data Intelligence Platform are a great fit for processing arbitrary files from an external cloud storage location. All code samples can be downloaded from this chapter's GitHub repository located at `https://github.com/PacktPublishing/Building-Modern-Data-Applications-Using-Databricks-Lakehouse/tree/main/chapter06`.

Generating mock documents

The first step in a data pipeline will be a process for generating arbitrary text files to extract text from. Let's begin by creating a new notebook in our Databricks workspace which will be used to train our organization's chatbot. The following code example uses the popular `faker` Python library, to randomly generate the content within our documents, and the `reportlab` Python library, for generating PDF files.

Begin by installing the library dependencies in the first notebook cell using the `%pip` magic command:

```
%pip install faker reportlab
```

Defining helper functions

Let's define a few helper functions that will take a randomly generated paragraph of text and save the text as a document. We'll define three helper functions – one helper function for each document format type – plain text, **Portable Document Format (PDF)**, and **comma-separated values (CSV)**:

1. Let's define the helper function for a plain text file:

    ```python
    from shutil import copyfile

    def save_doc_as_text(file_name, save_path, paragraph):
        """Helper function that saves a paragraph of text as a text
    file"""
        tmp_path = f"/local_disk0/tmp/{file_name}"
        volume_path = f"{save_path}/{file_name}"
        print(f"Saving text file at : {tmp_path}")
        txtfile = open(tmp_path, "a")
        txtfile.write(paragraph)
        txtfile.close()
        copyfile(tmp_path, volume_path)
    ```

2. Next, we define the helper function for a PDF file:

```python
def save_doc_as_pdf(file_name, save_path, paragraph):
    """Helper function that saves a paragraph of text as a PDF
file"""
    from reportlab.pdfgen.canvas import Canvas
    from reportlab.lib.pagesizes import letter
    from reportlab.lib.units import cm
    tmp_path = f"/local_disk0/tmp/{file_name}"
    volume_path = f"{save_path}/{file_name}"
    canvas = Canvas(tmp_path, pagesize=letter)
    lines = paragraph.split(".")
    textobject = canvas.beginText(5*cm, 25*cm)
    for line in lines:
        textobject.textLine(line)
        canvas.drawText(textobject)
    canvas.save()
    print(f"Saving PDF file at : {tmp_path}")
    copyfile(tmp_path, volume_path)
```

3. Lastly, we define the helper function for a CSV file:

```python
def save_doc_as_csv(file_name, save_path, paragraph):
    """Helper function that saves a paragraph of text as a CSV
file"""
    import csv
    tmp_path = f"/local_disk0/tmp/{file_name}"
    volume_path = f"{save_path}/{file_name}"
    print(f"Saving CSV file at : {tmp_path}")
    with open(tmp_path, 'w', newline='') as file:
        writer = csv.writer(file)
        writer.writerow(["Id", "Sentence"])
        i = 1
        for line in paragraph.split("."):
            writer.writerow([i, line])
            i = i + 1
    copyfile(tmp_path, volume_path)
```

This is a great way to simulate a variety of documents you might expect your organization to accumulate over time.

Choosing a file format randomly

Next, we will need to randomly choose the file format to save the generated documents. Let's begin by importing the `faker` library and a few Python utility libraries that we'll use to create unpredictable behavior. We'll also define a few global variables that will be used to determine the characteristics of our randomly generated documents, such as the number of documents to generate, the number of sentences to generate per document, and the types of file formats to store the documents in. Add the following code snippet to the notebook:

```
from faker import Faker
import time
import random


Faker.seed(631)
fake = Faker()


# Randomly generate documents
num_docs = 5
num_sentences_per_doc = 100
doc_types = ["txt", "pdf", "csv"]
volume_path = f"/Volumes/{catalog_name}/{schema_name}/{volume_name}"
```

Next, let's create a simple `for` loop that will serve as the backbone for our random document generator. Within the `for` loop, we'll use the `faker` library to create a paragraph of random text having the number of sentences equal to the number set by our `num_sentences_per_doc` global variable:

```
for _ in range(num_docs):
    paragraph = fake.paragraph(nb_sentences=num_sentences_per_doc)
```

After the paragraph of random text has been generated, it's time to choose what file format to store the text in. We'll leverage the `random` Python library to randomly select a file format type from the list of file formats defined in the `doc_types` global variable. Add the following code snippet to the body of the for-loop:

```
    # Randomly choose a document format type
    doc_type = doc_types[random.randrange(2)]
    print(doc_type)
    if doc_type == "txt":
        doc_name = f"{fake.pystr()}.txt"
        save_doc_as_text(doc_name, volume_path, paragraph)
    elif doc_type == "pdf":
        doc_name = f"{fake.pystr()}.pdf"
        save_doc_as_pdf(doc_name, volume_path, paragraph)
    elif doc_type == "csv":
```

```
doc_name = f"{fake.pystr()}.csv"
save_doc_as_csv(doc_name, volume_path, paragraph)
```

Lastly, we'll add a sleep timer to simulate unpredictable peaks and lulls in the generation of text documents – something that you could expect in a typical production environment. Add the following code snippet to the bottom of the for-loop body:

```
# Sleep for a random interval
sleep_time = random.randint(3, 30)
print(f"Sleeping for {sleep_time} seconds...\n\n")
time.sleep(sleep_time)
```

You'll also notice in the global variables section of the notebook, we've defined a volume path for our process to save the randomly generated documents:

```
volume_path = f"/Volumes/{catalog_name}/{schema_name}/{volume_name}"
```

This is a convenient way to reference a cloud storage location as though it were a local storage path. Plus, we have all the benefits of strong data governance that come with a storage volume in Unity Catalog. For example, all the data is secured by default, and other users or processes cannot read these documents until we have permission to access the data in the storage volume. Finally, let's attach the new notebook to a running all-purpose cluster in the Databricks Data Intelligence Platform and click the **Run all** button at the top of the notebook to begin generating and saving new documents to our storage volume location.

Creating/assembling the DLT pipeline

Now that we've generated some text documents, let's go ahead a create a new DLT pipeline that will stream the randomly generated documents and perform a simple text extraction. Import the notebook titled `Preprocess Text Documents.py` from the chapter's GitHub repository into your Databricks workspace. You'll notice that we define three new streaming tables, all of which are responsible for ingesting the randomly generated text, PDF, and CSV documents. After doing minimal preprocessing, the text field from each of these data sources is extracted and joined in a fourth table, `text_docs_silver`. This fourth table will serve as the input into our chatbot training:

```
@dlt.table(
    name="text_docs_silver",
    comment="Combined textual documents for Generative AI pipeline."
)
def text_docs_silver():
    text_docs_df = dlt.read("text_docs_raw").withColumn(
        "type", F.lit("text"))
    csv_docs_df = dlt.read("csv_docs_raw").withColumn(
        "type", F.lit("csv"))
```

```
pdf_docs_df = dlt.read("pdf_docs_raw").withColumn(
    "type", F.lit("pdf"))
combined_df = text_docs_df.union(csv_docs_df).union(
    pdf_docs_df)
return combined_df
```

After attaching the notebook to a running cluster, you will be prompted to create a new DLT pipeline. Go ahead and create a brand new DLT pipeline (covered in *Chapter 2*), titling the pipeline with a meaningful name, such as doc_ingestion_pipeline. Select **Triggered** for the processing mode and **Core** for the product edition, and accept the remaining defaults. Finally, click **Start** to begin an update execution of the newly created DLT pipeline.

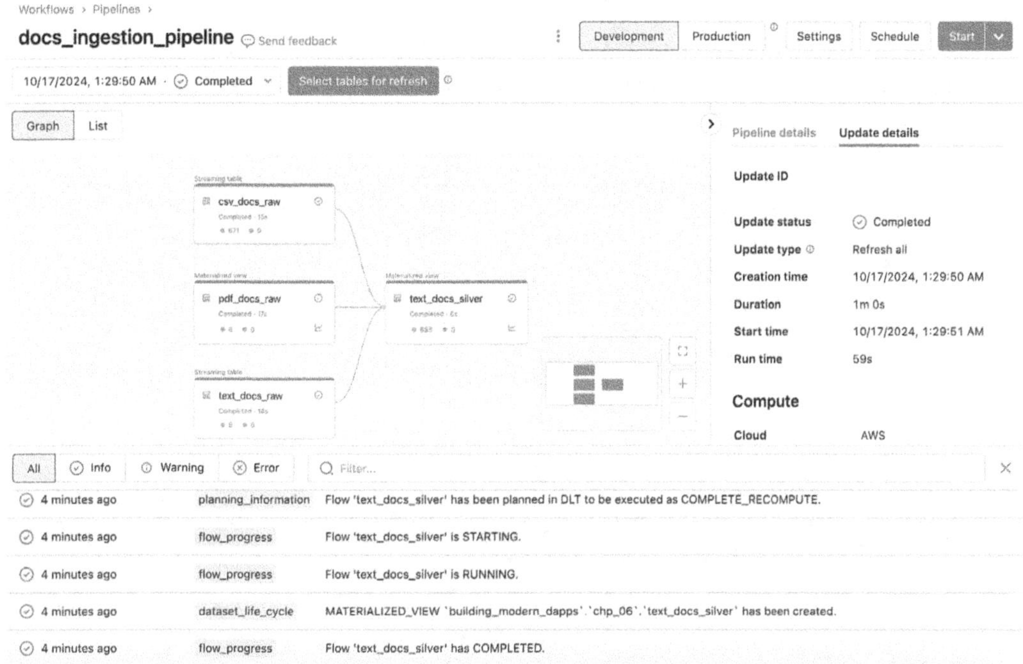

Figure 6.8 – An overview of a DLT pipeline extracting text from arbitrary documents saved to a volume location in Unity Catalog

You should see the DLT pipeline incrementally processing the randomly generated text documents, extracting the text from each of the different file types, and merging them into a consolidated dataset downstream. This is a simple, yet powerful example of how DLT can be combined with a storage volume in Unity Catalog to process arbitrary file formats in a real-world use case.

Summary

In this chapter, we covered a variety of methods for storing data while also maintaining fine-grained access control using different securable objects in Unity Catalog. We covered how data could be stored using catalogs, schemas, tables, views, volumes, and external locations in Unity Catalog. We also saw how organizations could bind catalogs to individual Databricks workspaces to isolate datasets and even set the level of access to read-only. We covered the differences between managed datasets in the Databricks Data Intelligence Platform, as well as how we could set prescribed storage locations for storing data using catalogs, schemas, tables, volumes, and external locations. We covered how external data sources, such as data warehouses, could be queried in place without having to migrate the data using Lakehouse Federation. Lastly, we concluded with a hands-on exercise implementing the start of a generative AI pipeline for extracting text from documents using volumes in Unity Catalog.

Now that we have a solid foundation for storing our data and other assets, in the next chapter, we'll be covering tracking lineage across various objects in the Databricks Data Intelligence Platform.

7

Viewing Data Lineage Using Unity Catalog

In this chapter, we'll dive into the critical role that data lineage plays within the Databricks Data Intelligence Platform. You'll learn how to trace data origins, visualize dataset transformations, identify upstream and downstream dependencies, and document lineage using the lineage graph capabilities of the Catalog Explorer. By the end of the chapter, you'll be equipped with the skills needed to ensure data is coming from trusted sources, and spot breaking changes before they happen.

In this chapter, we're going to cover the following main topics:

- Introducing data lineage in Unity Catalog
- Tracing data origins using the Data Lineage REST API
- Visualizing upstream and downstream data transformations
- Identifying dependencies and impacts
- Hands-on lab – documenting data lineage across an organization

Technical requirements

To follow along with the examples provided in this chapter, you'll need Databricks workspace permissions to create and start an all-purpose cluster so that you can import and execute the chapter's accompanying notebooks. All code samples can be downloaded from this chapter's GitHub repository, located at `https://github.com/PacktPublishing/Building-Modern-Data-Applications-Using-Databricks-Lakehouse/tree/main/chapter07`. This chapter will create and run several new notebooks using an all-purpose cluster and is estimated to consume around 5-10 **Databricks units (DBUs)**.

Introducing data lineage in Unity Catalog

Data lineage refers to the ability to trace relationships across securable objects, such as tables, in **Unity Catalog** (**UC**) so that users can view how data assets are formed from upstream sources and verify downstream dependencies.

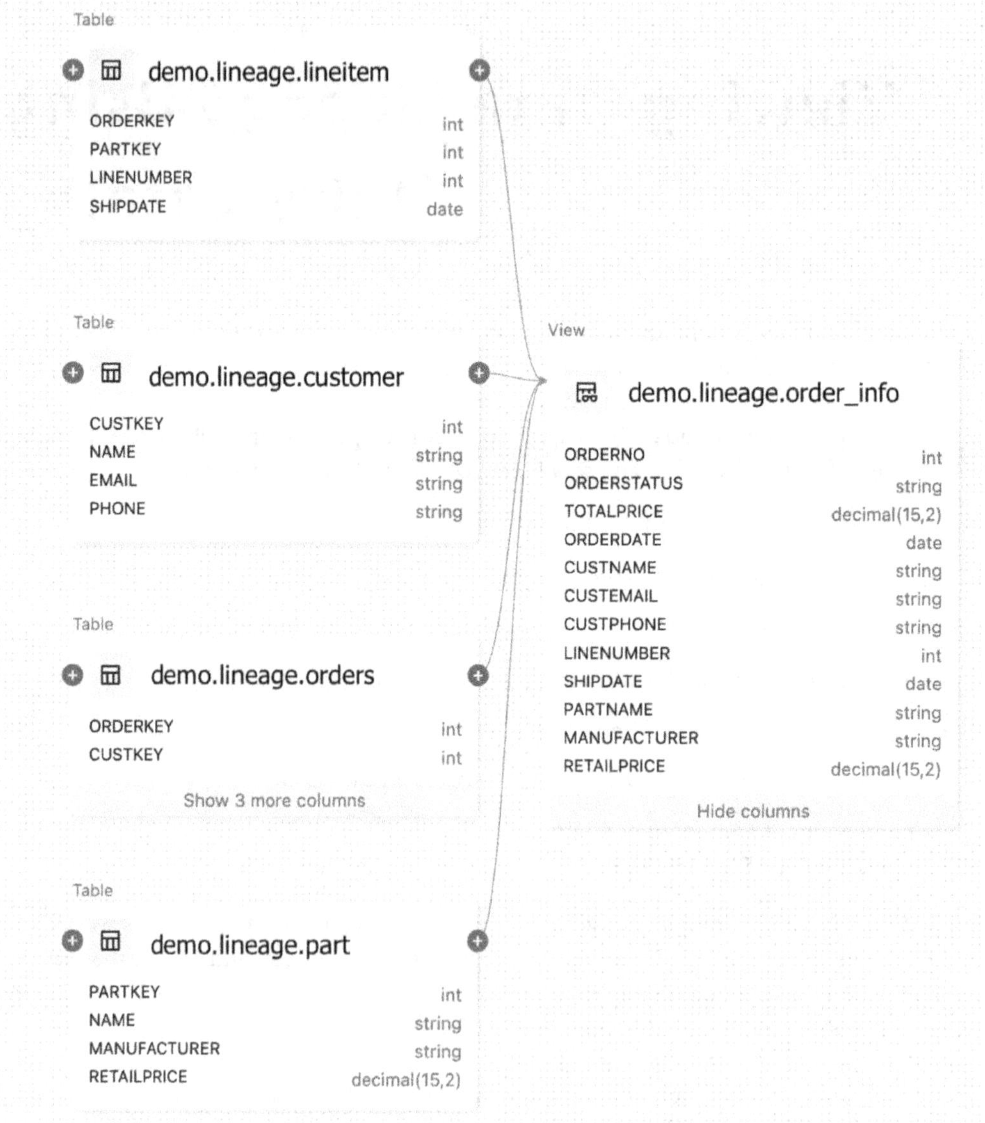

Figure 7.1 – Data lineage traces the flow of data and how it gets transformed over time by internal processes

In Databricks, users can trace the lineage of data assets in near real time so that data stewards can ensure that they are working with the latest assets. Furthermore, data lineage in Unity Catalog spans across multiple workspaces that are attached to the same Unity Catalog metastore, allowing data professionals to get a *complete*, holistic view into how datasets are transformed and are related to one another.

Data lineage can be traced across a variety of securable objects in the Databricks Data Intelligence Platform, including the following objects:

- Queries
- Tables
- Table columns
- Notebooks
- Workflows
- Machine learning models
- **Delta Live Tables** (**DLT**) pipelines
- Dashboards

Like many objects within the Databricks Data Intelligence Platform, you can trace the lineage through a variety of mechanisms, including the Databricks UI, using Catalog Explorer, or by consuming the Data Lineage REST API. In fact, data lineage is automatically captured by the Databricks Data Intelligence Platform and recorded in the system tables (covered in *Chapter 5*). Like other system information that gets preserved in the Databricks system tables, lineage information can accumulate quite a bit. To preserve storage costs, this information is retained for one year by default. For longer lineage storage requirements, it's recommended to set up an alternate process that will append the lineage information to longer-term archival storage. For example, say that an organization needs to retain system auditing information on the order of years, then a long-term archival ETL pipeline would be needed to copy the lineage data into archival storage.

In the coming sections, we'll cover all varieties for viewing lineage across data assets in Databricks.

Tracing data origins using the Data Lineage REST API

Like many securable objects in the Databricks Data Intelligence Platform, there are a variety of ways to retrieve detailed lineage information pertaining to the object. One common pattern for retrieving lineage information about a particular object in Databricks is through the Data Lineage REST API. At the moment, the Data Lineage REST API is limited to retrieving a read-only view of table lineage information as well as column lineage information.

UC Object	HTTP Verb	Endpoint	Description
Table	GET	`/api/2.0/lineage-tracking/table-lineage`	Given a UC table name, retrieves a list of upstream and downstream table connections, as well as information about their related notebook connections
Column	GET	`/api/2.0/lineage-tracking/column-lineage`	Given a UC table name and column name, retrieves a list of upstream and downstream column connections

Table 7.1 – Data Lineage REST API fetches information pertaining to upstream and downstream connections for UC table and column objects

However, it's expected that the Data Lineage REST API will evolve over time, adding additional capabilities for data stewards to retrieve information and even manipulate the end-to-end lineage of data assets within the platform.

Let's look at how we might use the Lineage Tracking API to retrieve information about the upstream and downstream connections for a table created by the dataset generator notebook in this chapter's accompanying GitHub repository, located at `https://github.com/PacktPublishing/Building-Modern-Data-Applications-Using-Databricks-Lakehouse/tree/main/chapter07`.

First, we'll begin by creating a brand-new notebook in our Databricks workspace and importing the `requests` Python library. We'll be exclusively using the Python `requests` library to send data lineage requests to the Databricks REST API and parse the response from the Databricks control plane:

```
import requests
```

Create and start an all-purpose cluster to attach the notebook to and run the notebook cells. You'll need to generate a **personal access token (PAT)** to authenticate with the Databricks REST endpoints and send Data Lineage API requests. It's strongly recommended to store the PAT in a Databricks secret object (`https://docs.databricks.com/en/security/secrets/secrets.html`) to avoid accidentally leaking the authentication details to your Databricks workspace.

> **Important note**
>
> The following code snippets are for illustration purposes only. You'll need to update the workspace name to match the name of your Databricks workspace, as well as the value for the API token.

Let's use the `requests` library to send a request to the Data Lineage API by specifying the fully qualified endpoint:

```
response = requests.get(
    f"https://{WORKSPACE_NAME}.cloud.databricks.com/api/2.0/lineage-
tracking/table-lineage",
    headers={
        "Authorization": f"Bearer {API_TOKEN}"
    },
    json={
        "table_name": FULLY_QUALIFIED_TABLE_NAME,
        "include_entity_lineage": "true"
    }
)
print(response.json())
```

Next, let's include a few helper functions for parsing the response from the Data Lineage API and printing the connection information in a nicely formatted manner that's easy to understand. Add a new cell to your notebook and paste the following helper functions:

```
def print_table_info(conn_type, table_info_json):
    info = table_info_json["tableInfo"]
    print(f"""
        +----------------------------------------------------+
        | {conn_type.upper()} Table Connection Info
        |--------------------------------------------------|
        | Table name: {info['name']}
        |--------------------------------------------------|
        | Catalog name: {info['catalog_name']}
        |--------------------------------------------------|
        | Table type: {info['table_type']}
        |--------------------------------------------------|
        | Lineage timestamp: {info['lineage_timestamp']}
        +----------------------------------------------------+
    """)
    if conn_type.upper() == "UPSTREAMS":
        print(f"""
```

```
    """)

def print_notebook_info(conn_type, notebook_info):
    print(f"""
        +-----------------------------------------------+
        | {conn_type.upper()} Notebook Connection Info:
        |-----------------------------------------------|
        | Workspace id: {str(notebook_info['workspace_id'])}
        |-----------------------------------------------|
        | Notebook id: {str(notebook_info['notebook_id'])}
        |-----------------------------------------------|
        | Timestamp: {notebook_info['lineage_timestamp']}
        +-----------------------------------------------+
    """)
```

Now, let's update the response section of our previous code snippet for fetching table lineage information, but this time, we'll invoke these helper functions:

```
if response.status_code == 200:
    connection_flows = ["upstreams", "downstreams"]
    for flow in connection_flows:
        if flow in response.json():
            connections = response.json()[flow]
            for conn in connections:
                if "tableInfo" in conn:
                    print_table_info(flow, conn)
                elif "notebookInfos" in conn:
                    for notebook_info in conn["notebookInfos"]:
                        print_notebook_info(flow, notebook_info)
```

The output should now be a much more legible response from our Data Lineage API, allowing us to clearly view the upstream and downstream table connections from our table in Unity Catalog.

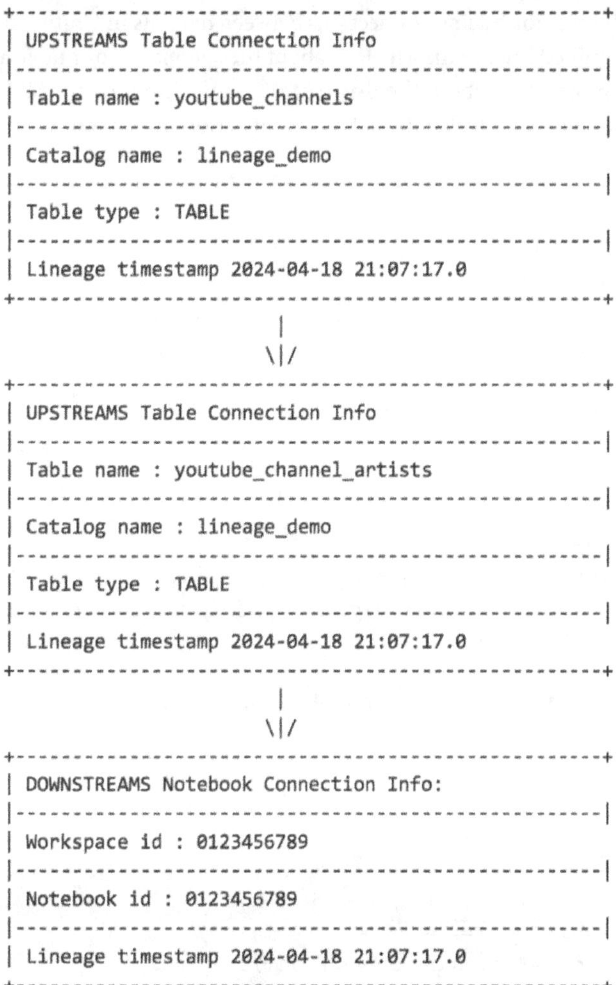

Figure 7.2 – Table lineage response output from the Databricks Data Lineage REST API

The Data Lineage API is great for tracing connections between datasets in Unity Catalog. However, we can also retrieve finer-grained lineage information about the *columns* of our table as well. In the next example, let's retrieve information about the `description` column of our table. Let's also define another helper function to nicely display the column connection information:

```python
def print_column_info(conn_type, column_info):
    print(f"""
        Connection flow: {conn_type.upper()}
        Column name: {column_info['name']}
        Catalog name: {column_info['catalog_name']}
        Schema name: {column_info['schema_name']}
        Table name: {column_info['table_name']}
        Table type: {column_info['table_type']}
        Lineage timestamp: {column_info['lineage_timestamp']}
    """)


column_name = "description"
response = requests.get(
    f"https://{WORKSPACE_NAME}.cloud.databricks.com/api/2.0/lineage-
tracking/column-lineage",
    headers={
        "Authorization": f"Bearer {API_TOKEN}"
    },
    json={
        "table_name": FULLY_QUALIFIED_TABLE_NAME,
        "column_name": column_name
    }
)
if response.status_code == 200:
    if "upstream_cols" in response.json():
        print("| Upstream cols:")
        for column_info in response.json()['upstream_cols']:
            print_column_info("Upstream", column_info)
    if "downstream_cols" in response.json():
        print("| Downstream cols:")
        for column_info in response.json()['downstream_cols']:
            print_column_info("Downstream", column_info)
```

In this scenario, the `description` column in our table is particularly interesting, as it's the result of a concatenation of a text string with two different columns. If you update the previous column lineage requests with a different column name, you'll notice that the number of upstream sources will change to reflect the number of connections specific to that column.

```
+--------------------------------------------------------------------------+
| Column : lineage_demo.api_demo.combined_table.description:
|--------------------------------------------------------------------------|
| Upstream cols:

        Connection flow: UPSTREAM
        Column name : artist_name
        Catalog name : lineage_demo
        Schema name : api_demo
        Table name : youtube_channel_artists
        Table type : TABLE
        Lineage timestamp : 2024-04-18 21:36:09.0

        Connection flow: UPSTREAM
        Column name : category
        Catalog name : lineage_demo
        Schema name : api_demo
        Table name : youtube_channels
        Table type : TABLE
        Lineage timestamp : 2024-04-18 21:36:09.0


+--------------------------------------------------------------------------+
```

Figure 7.3 – Column lineage response output from the Databricks Lineage API

By now, you should feel comfortable working with the Databricks Data Lineage API to trace connections between datasets and even fine-grained data transformations, such as column connections. As you've seen, the requests and responses from the Data Lineage API require experience working with JSON payloads. For some responses, we needed to create helper functions to parse the response into a more readable form.

In the next section, we'll look at using the Databricks UI for tracing dataset relationships, allowing non-technical data stewards the ability to view upstream and downstream sources with just the click of a button.

Visualizing upstream and downstream transformations

In this section, we'll be leveraging the dataset generator notebook to create several datasets in Unity Catalog for working with the Databricks UI to trace dataset lineage. If you haven't done so already, clone this chapter's accompanying GitHub repository, which is located at `https://github.com/PacktPublishing/Building-Modern-Data-Applications-Using-Databricks-Lakehouse/tree/main/chapter07`. Next, either start an existing all-purpose cluster or create a new cluster and begin by attaching the data generator notebook to the cluster. Click the **Run all** button in the top-right corner of the Databricks workspace to execute all the notebook cells, verifying that all cells execute successfully. If you encounter runtime errors, verify that you have the correct metastore permissions to create new catalogs, schemas, and tables in your Unity Catalog metastore.

> **Important note**
>
> You will need to be granted permission to create a new catalog and schema in your Unity Catalog metastore. If this isn't possible, feel free to reuse an existing catalog and schema to generate the sample tables. You will need to update the DDL and DML statements accordingly to match the value within your own Databricks workspace.

The result of the data generator notebook should be three tables in total: `youtube_channels`, `youtube_channel_artists`, and `combined_table`. Data lineage can easily be traced in the Databricks Data Intelligence Platform in a variety of ways. In this example, let's trace the data lineage of a data asset, the `combined_table` table, using the Databricks UI. From your Databricks workspace, click on the **Catalog Explorer** menu tab from the left-hand side navigation menu of the Databricks Data Intelligence Platform. Next, either drill down to the catalog and schema to locate the `combined_table` table, or simply type `combined_table` into the search box at the top of the Catalog Explorer, which will filter the list of data assets matching the text string. Click on the `combined_table` table, which will open the data asset `Overview` details in a separate pane on the right-hand side of the UI.

Figure 7.4 – The data lineage can be traced directly from the Catalog Explorer in Databricks

From the UI pane, click on the **Lineage** tab to expose the details of the data lineage for our table. After navigating to the **Lineage** tab, you should see a summary of all connections related to the `combined_table` dataset, clearly identifying all the upstream sources that are used to construct this table, as well as any downstream dependencies that leverage this table.

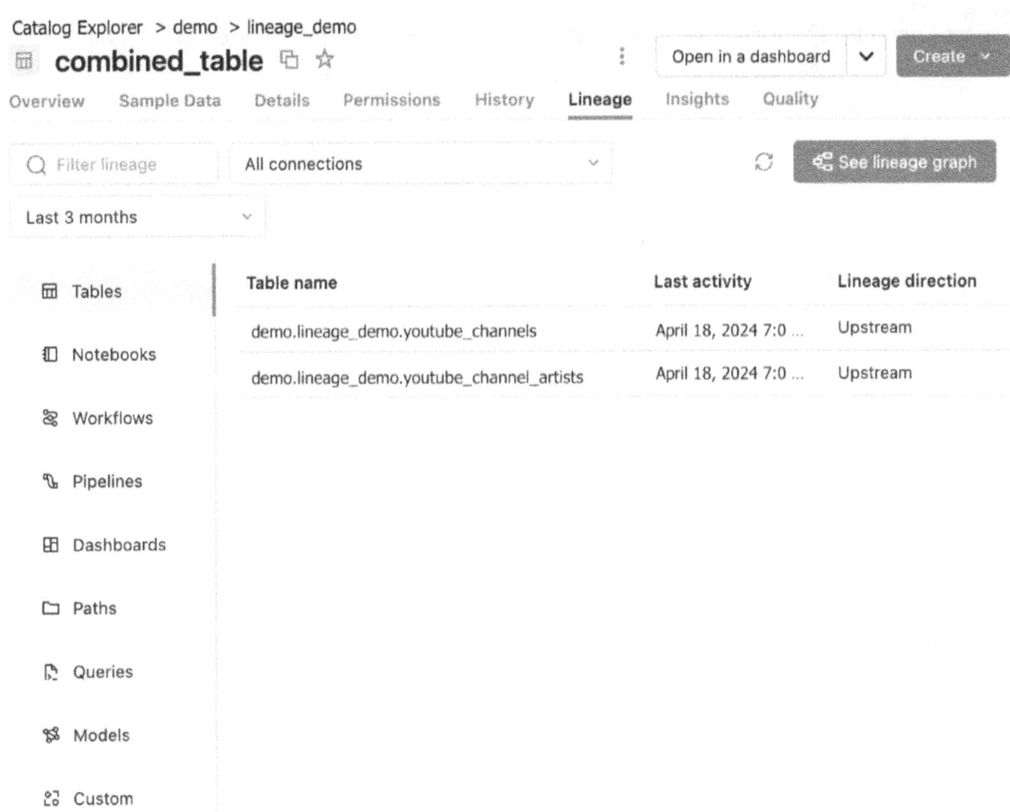

Figure 7.5 – The Lineage tab in the Catalog Explorer contains lineage information about a table

In this case, there should be two rows containing information about the upstream sources – the `youtube_channels` parent table and the `youtube_channel_artists` table. Since we've only recently created this table using our data generator notebook, there shouldn't be any rows with downstream dependencies. As you can imagine, this table will be updated in near real time with a list of all objects that use the dataset in some fashion, clearly identifying any downstream dependents of the data.

Lastly, let's visualize what our table lineage relationships look like. Click on the blue button labeled **See lineage graph** to open the lineage visualization.

You should now clearly see that two upstream tables join to form the `combined_table` table.

Table

demo.lineage_demo.youtube_channels

channel_id	int
num_subscribers	int
language	string
category	string
country_of_origin	string

Hide columns

Table

demo.lineage_demo.combined_table

channel_name	string
artist_name	string
description	string
num_subscribers	int
language	string
category	string
country_of_origin	string

Hide columns

Table

demo.lineage_demo.youtube_channel_artists

artist_id	int
artist_name	string
youtube_channel_id	int
youtube_channel_na...	string

Figure 7.6 – Lineage connection information can be generated by
clicking on connection links on a lineage graph

Next, click on the arrow connecting the upstream table with the downstream table, `combined_table`, to reveal more details about the lineage connection. You will notice that a side pane will open displaying information about the lineage connection, such as the source and target tables, but it will also display how these data assets are used across various other objects in the Databricks Data Intelligence Platform. For instance, the UI pane will list how these datasets are currently being leveraged across notebooks, workflows, DLT pipelines, and DBSQL queries. In this case, we've only generated these tables using our data generator notebook, so it is the only object listed in the lineage connection information.

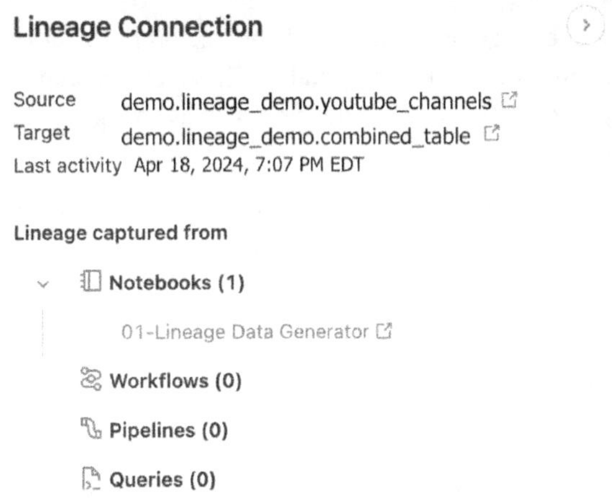

Lineage Connection

Source   demo.lineage_demo.youtube_channels
Target   demo.lineage_demo.combined_table
Last activity Apr 18, 2024, 7:07 PM EDT

Lineage captured from

⌄   ▢ **Notebooks (1)**

          01-Lineage Data Generator

     ⧉ **Workflows (0)**

     ⧉ **Pipelines (0)**

     ⧉ **Queries (0)**

Figure 7.7 – Connection details between datasets can be viewed from the lineage graph

Column lineage can also be traced using the Catalog Explorer. In the same lineage graph, click on various columns in the `combined_table` table to reveal lineage information. For example, by clicking on the `description` table column, the lineage graph will be updated to clearly visualize how the `description` column is calculated. In this case, the column is calculated by concatenating a string of text with the category column from our parent table as well as the artist's name from the child table.

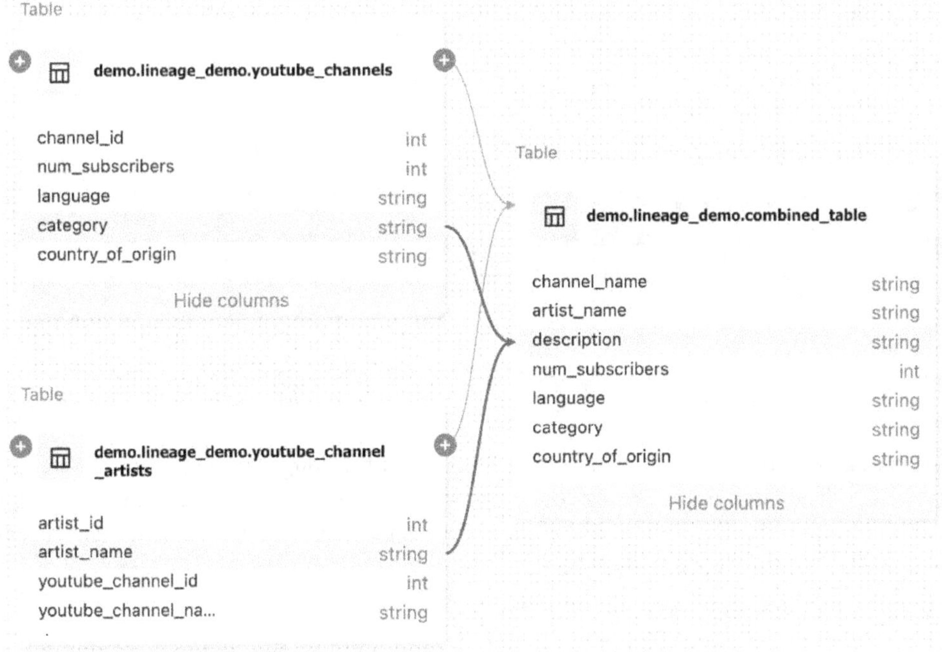

Figure 7.8 – Column lineage can be traced by clicking the column to expose upstream lineage connections

As you can see, generating a lineage graph from the Catalog Explorer provides an accurate snapshot of the latest relationships between datasets in Unity Catalog. These relationships can help us identify the impact data changes have on downstream dependencies, such as changing the data type of a column or dropping a dataset, for example.

In the next section, we'll look at how data lineage can help us identify relationships between our datasets, spot dependent notebooks that leverage these datasets, and avoid introducing breaking changes across our organization.

Identifying dependencies and impacts

In this section, we'll leverage the lineage graph UI from the Catalog Explorer again to better understand how changing the data type and value of a particular column will impact downstream datasets and downstream processes, such as notebooks and workflows, across our Databricks workspaces.

Let's first begin by creating a new notebook in our Databricks workspace that will contain the definition of a new DLT pipeline. The first dataset in our DLT pipeline will ingest raw CSV files containing commercial airline flight information stored in the default **Databricks Filesystem (DBFS)** under the /databricks-datasets directory. Every Databricks workspace will have access to this dataset. Create a new notebook cell and add the following code snippet for the definition of a bronze table in our data pipeline:

```
import dlt
@dlt.table(
    name="commercial_airliner_flights_bronze",
    comment="The commercial airliner flight data dataset located in `/
databricks-datasets/`"
)
def commercial_airliner_flights_bronze():
    path = "/databricks-datasets/airlines/"
    return (spark.readStream
            .format("csv")
            .schema(schema)
            .option("header", True)
            .load(path))
```

We'd like to augment the flight data with information about the commercial airliner jet. Create a new notebook cell and add the following code snippet, which defines a static reference table with information about popular commercial airline jets, including the manufacturer name, airplane model, country of origin, and fuel capacity, to name a few:

```
commercial_airliners = [
    ("Airbus A220", "Canada", 2, 2013, 2016, 287, 287, 5790),
    ("Airbus A330neo", "Multinational", 2, 2017, 2018, 123,
```

```
    123, 36744 ),
    ("Airbus A350 XWB", "Multinational", 2, 2013, 2014, 557,
     556, 44000),
    ("Antonov An-148/An-158", "Ukraine", 2, 2004, 2009, 37,
     8, 98567 ),
    ("Boeing 737", "United States", 2, 1967, 1968, 11513, 7649,
     6875),
    ("Boeing 767", "United States", 2, 1981, 1982, 1283, 764,
     23980),
    ("Boeing 777", "United States", 2, 1994, 1995, 1713, 1483,
     47890),
    ("Boeing 787 Dreamliner", "United States", 2, 2009, 2011,
     1072, 1069, 33340),
    ("Embraer E-Jet family", "Brazil", 2, 2002, 2004, 1671,
     1443, 3071),
    ("Embraer E-Jet E2 family", "Brazil", 2, 2016, 2018, 81,
     23, 3071)
]
commercial_airliners_schema = "jet_model string, Country_of_Origin
string, Engines int, First_Flight int, Airline_Service_Entry int,
Number_Built int, Currently_In_Service int, Fuel_Capacity int"
airliners_df = spark.createDataFrame(
    data=commercial_airpliners,
    schema=commercial_airliners_schema
)
```

Next, we'll save the airline jet reference table to the schema created earlier in Unity Catalog:

```
airliners_table_name = f"{catalog_name}.{schema_name}.{table_name}"
(airliners_df.write
    .format("delta")
    .mode("overwrite")
    .option("mergeSchema", True)
    .saveAsTable(airliners_table_name))
```

Let's add another step to our data pipeline, which will join our static, commercial jet airline reference table with our stream of airline flight data. In a new notebook cell, create the following **user-defined function (UDF)**, which will generate a tail number for each entry in the commercial airline dataset:

```
from pyspark.sql.types import StringType
from pyspark.sql.functions import udf


@udf(returnType=StringType())
def generate_jet_model():
    import random
```

```python
    commercial_jets = [
        "Airbus A220",
        "Airbus A320",
        "Airbus A330",
        "Airbus A330neo",
        "Airbus A350 XWB",
        "Antonov An-148/An-158",
        "Boeing 737",
        "Boeing 767",
        "Boeing 777",
        "Boeing 787 Dreamliner",
        "Comac ARJ21 Xiangfeng",
        "Comac C919",
        "Embraer E-Jet family",
        "Embraer E-Jet E2 family",
        "Ilyushin Il-96",
        "Sukhoi Superjet SSJ100",
        "Tupolev Tu-204/Tu-214"
    ]
    random_index = random.randint(0, 16)
    return commercial_jets[random_index]
```

Lastly, create one more notebook cell and add the following DLT dataset definition for our silver table:

```python
@dlt.table(
    name="commercial_airliner_flights_silver",
    comment="The commercial airliner flight data augmented with
randomly generated jet model and used fuel amount."
)
def commercial_airliner_flights_silver():
    return (dlt.read_stream(
            "commercial_airliner_flights_bronze")
            .withColumn("jet_model", generate_jet_model())
            .join(spark.table(airliners_table_name),
                ["jet_model"], "left"))
```

When prompted, let's create a new DLT pipeline by clicking on the blue button at the bottom of the notebook cell output titled **Create pipeline**. Give the pipeline a meaningful name, such as `Commercial Airliner Flights Pipeline`. Select **Triggered** as the execution mode and **Core** for the product edition. Next, select the target catalog and schema in the previous code sample as a target dataset location for our DLT pipeline. Finally, click the **Start** button to trigger a pipeline update.

Figure 7.9 – The DLT pipeline created for ingesting commercial airline flight data

Let's imagine for a second that there's an external process that aims to calculate the carbon footprint for each commercial flight. In this example, the process is another Databricks notebook that reads the output of our silver table and calculates the carbon dioxide emission for each flight taken across the United States.

Create another notebook within your Databricks workspace and give the notebook a meaningful name, such as Calculating Commercial Airliner Carbon Footprint. Next, let's add a new notebook cell that reads the silver table and calculates the carbon dioxide output using a simple formula:

*Carbon footprint = amount of fuel burned * coefficient / number of passengers*

In this case, we are only interested in calculating the carbon footprint per airliner jet; so, we will avoid dividing by the number of passengers. Add the following code snippet to the newly created notebook, which will assign a calculated carbon footprint per flight entry:

```
# 3.1kg of CO2 is created for every 1kg of fuel used.
# So we multiply the fuel mass above by 3.1 to estimate the CO2
emitted
# Source: https://ecotree.green/en/calculate-flight-co2
# 1 gallon of jet fuel weighs approximately 3.03907 kilograms
def calc_carbon_footprint(fuel_consumed_gallons):
    return (fuel_consumed_gallons * 3.03907) * 3.1
```

Let's imagine again that the fuel capacity amount in the silver table of our DLT pipeline is currently measured in gallons. However, our European business partners want to work with the dataset using liters instead. Let's use the Catalog Explorer to explore the lineage graph of our silver table to better understand what type of impact, converting the unit of measure for the `fuel_capacity` column, would have on the consumers of the dataset. Navigate to the lineage graph by clicking on the Catalog Explorer in the left-hand side navigation bar, filtering the catalogs by entering the name of the catalog in the search text field, and finally clicking on the silver table, `commercial_airliner_flights_silver`.

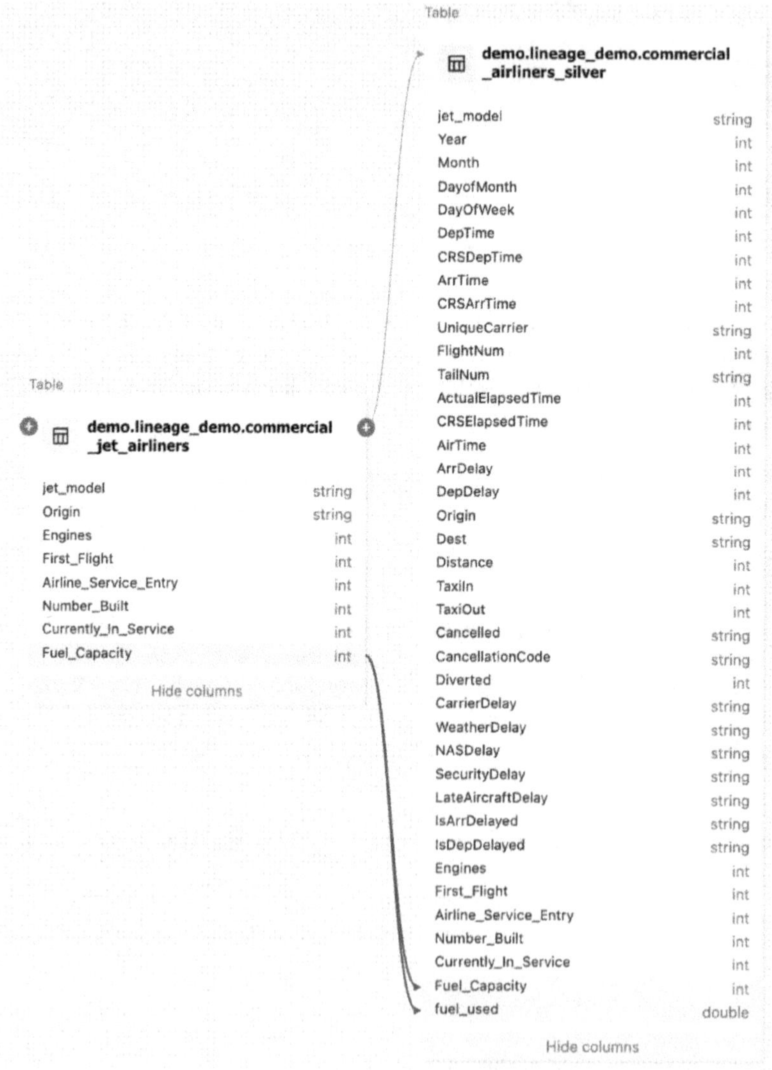

Figure 7.10 – Column lineage can help us understand how changing columns will impact downstream dependencies – an overview

By generating the lineage graph, we were able to see in near real time all the downstream columns that might depend on this column. Furthermore, we can also see a real-time list of all the Unity Catalog objects that depend on this column, such as notebooks, workflows, DLT pipelines, and machine-learning models. So, in effect, we can quickly understand what type of impact changing the unit of measure could have across our organization sharing this dataset.

In the next section, we'll continue with this example to determine an alternative way for updating this dataset to include fuel capacity, distance travel, and arrival times to be European-friendly without impacting any existing consumers of our data.

Hands-on lab – documenting data lineage across an organization

In this section, we'll look at how the system tables in Databricks automatically document how the relationships between our datasets and other data assets change over time. As previously mentioned, Unity Catalog will preserve data lineage across all workspaces that attach to the same Unity Catalog metastore. This is particularly useful in scenarios when organizations need to have strong end-to-end auditing of their data assets.

Let's again begin by creating a new notebook within our Databricks workspace and giving it a meaningful title, such as `Viewing Documented Data Lineage`. Next, let's create a new all-purpose cluster or attach the notebook to an already running cluster to begin executing notebook cells.

Like the Data Lineage API, there are two system tables that provide a read-only view of lineage information in Unity Catalog – the `system.access.table_lineage` table and the `system.access.column_lineage` table. Data lineage system tables automatically document information pertaining to upstream and downstream connections for UC table and column objects.

UC Object	Table Name	Description
Table	`system.access.table_lineage`	Contains a list of upstream and downstream table connections, as well as information about their related notebook connections
Column	`system.access.column_lineage`	Contains a list of upstream and downstream column connections

Table 7.2 – Data lineage system tables capture connections info about tables and columns

Let's query the upstream and downstream lineage information in the previous example. In a new notebook cell, add the following query and execute the cell:

```
SELECT *
  FROM system.access.table_lineage
  WHERE source_table_name LIKE '%commercial_airliners_silver%';
```

We get the following output:

	workspace_id	entity_type	entity_id	entity_run_id	source_table_full_name
1	0123456789	DBSQL_QUERY	635428590	686139344	demo.lineage_demo.commercial_airliners_silver
2	0123456789	NOTEBOOK	1079422676	2060245946	demo.lineage_demo.commercial_airliners_silver
3	0123456789	NOTEBOOK	1079422676	688764655	demo.lineage_demo.commercial_airliners_silver

3 rows | 7.70 seconds runtime   Refreshed now

Figure 7.11 – Lineage information can be queried from the system tables

As you can see from the output, the system table automatically documents connection information about the upstream and downstream sources. In addition, the system tables will automatically capture auditing information, including information about the dataset's creator and the event timestamp of the object creation. This is a great way to document, review, or even report on data lineage across your organization's datasets.

Summary

In this chapter, we covered the various ways that data lineage can be traced across datasets in the Databricks Data Intelligence Platform. We saw how the Data Lineage REST API allowed us to quickly view the upstream and downstream connections of a particular table or column in Unity Catalog. Next, we look at how easy it was to generate a lineage graph using the Catalog Explorer in Unity Catalog. The lineage graph was essential for enabling greater insight into how changes to datasets could impact downstream consumers of the dataset. Lastly, we looked at how the system tables in Unity Catalog provided a way for our organization to document the evolving flow of data asset relationships.

In the next chapter, we'll turn our attention to deploying our data pipelines and all their dependencies in an automated fashion using tools such as Terraform.

Part 3: Continuous Integration, Continuous Deployment, and Continuous Monitoring

In the final part of this book, we'll look at how we can automate the deployment of pipeline changes using popular automation tools such as **Terraform** and **Databricks Asset Bundles** (**DABs**). We conclude the book with a lesson on how you can continuously monitor your DLT pipelines using a variety of tools in the Databricks Data Intelligence Platform.

This part contains the following chapters:

- *Chapter 8, Deploying, Maintaining, and Administrating DLT Pipelines Using Terraform*
- *Chapter 9, Leveraging Databricks Asset Bundles to Streamline Data Pipeline Deployment*
- *Chapter 10, Monitoring Data Pipelines in Production*

8

Deploying, Maintaining, and Administrating DLT Pipelines Using Terraform

In this chapter, we're going to explore how an automation tool such as Terraform can be used to express data pipelines as code, commonly referred to as **Infrastructure as Code (IAC)**, in Databricks. We'll look at how to set up a local Terraform development environment using popular code editors such as VS Code so that we can experiment with deploying different resources to a Databricks workspace. Next, we'll dive into how to represent data pipelines using Terraform and how to configure different aspects of a **Delta Live Tables (DLT)** pipeline. We'll also look at how we can automate the validation and deployment of IaC to different Databricks workspaces, including a production workspace. Lastly, we'll examine industry best practices and future considerations along the way.

In this chapter, we're going to cover the following main topics:

- Introducing the Databricks provider for Terraform

- Setting up a local environment

- Configuring DLT pipelines using Terraform

- Automating DLT pipeline deployment

- Hands-on exercise – deploying a DLT pipeline using VS Code

Technical requirements

To follow along with the examples provided in this chapter, you'll need Databricks workspace permissions to create and start an all-purpose cluster so that you can import and execute the chapter's accompanying notebooks. All code samples can be downloaded from this chapter's GitHub repository located at `https://github.com/PacktPublishing/Building-Modern-Data-Applications-Using-Databricks-Lakehouse/tree/main/chapter08`. This chapter will create and run several new notebooks, as well as run a new DLT pipeline using the product's **Advanced** edition, estimated to consume around 10—15 **Databricks Units (DBUs)**.

Introducing the Databricks provider for Terraform

Terraform is an open source deployment automation tool that can be used to automate the deployment of cloud infrastructure in a repeatable and predictable manner. One reason Terraform is such a popular deployment tool is that it supports deploying infrastructure to the three major cloud providers: **Amazon Web Services (AWS)**, **Azure**, and **Google Cloud Platform (GCP)**. Terraform is centered around the concept of defining IaC where, rather than manually deploying cloud components such as network objects, virtual machines, or storage containers, they are expressed using code files. Furthermore, Terraform files are configuration-driven. Rather than expressing *how* to deploy the infrastructure, cloud administrators focus on expressing *what* changes between environments through configuration. Lastly, Terraform maintains the state of your architecture, meaning that the tool will keep track of the state of cloud resources and will update the state accordingly for each new execution of a Terraform configuration file.

Lastly, Terraform files can be executed directly from your local machine, allowing you to interact with cloud resources remotely.

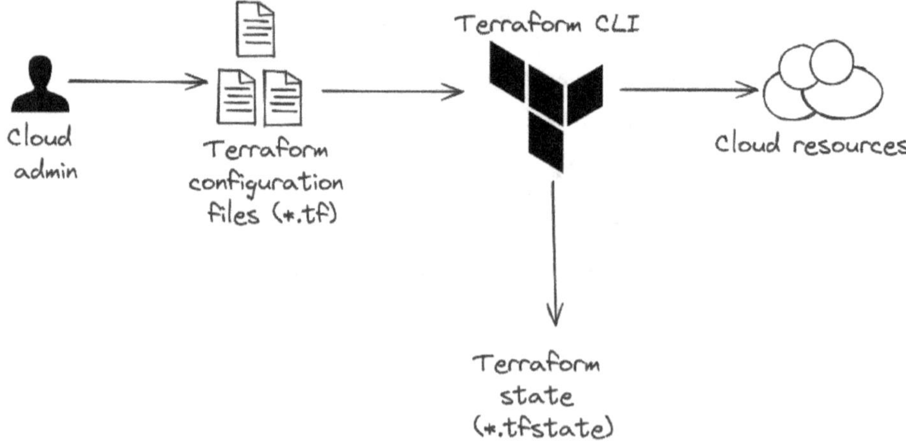

Figure 8.1 – Terraform will reflect environment changes using configuration files

Terraform configuration files define the cloud infrastructure that is applied in the cloud provider, and the infrastructure state is synced back to the local environment. Furthermore, Databricks provides a Terraform provider for deploying Databricks workspaces and workspace objects to the major cloud providers.

A Terraform provider is a plugin for the Terraform tool that enables users to interact with specific APIs. In this case, the Terraform provider interacts with the Databricks REST API, allowing workspace administrators to automate the deployment of even the most complex data processing environments.

There are many advantages to using Terraform to automate the deployment of data pipelines within your organization, including the following:

- It is easy to deploy infrastructure between the major cloud providers, making it trivial to migrate between clouds if need be.
- It is easy to scale to hundreds of data pipelines by focusing on defining configuration rather than manually deploying and maintaining data pipelines.
- Pipeline definition is concise, allowing cloud administrators to focus on expressing what should change, rather than how to deploy infrastructure.

Let's look at how easy it is to get started defining Databricks resources and applying them to targeted workspaces.

Setting up a local Terraform environment

Before we can begin deploying data pipeline objects to our Databricks workspace, we need to install the Terraform **command-line interface** (**CLI**) tool. If you haven't already done so, you will need to download the Terraform CLI, which can be downloaded for free from the HashiCorp website (`https://developer.hashicorp.com/terraform/install`).

Next, we want to organize the Terraform configuration files into a single directory. Let's create a new directory called `chp8_databricks_terraform`.

Within the newly created directory, let's create a brand new Terraform configuration file where we will define our data pipeline and other related workspace objects. Create a new file, naming it `main.tf`.

> **Important note**
> Terraform configuration files use the Terraform language and end with the `.tf` extension.

Importing the Databricks Terraform provider

The first step to using Terraform to deploy Databricks workspace objects is to import the Databricks Terraform provider. If it's your first time using the Terraform provider, Terraform will take care of downloading the Databricks provider from the Terraform Registry. The Terraform Registry is a public hub for downloading third-party providers, modules, and security policies that aid in developing Terraform configuration files to deploy your cloud infrastructure.

Add the following code snippet at the top of the new Terraform configuration file, `main.tf`:

```
terraform {
  required_providers {
    databricks = {
    source = "databricks/databricks"
    }
  }
}
```

This code snippet will instruct the Terraform CLI tool to download and import a Terraform provider called `databricks` that has been published to the Terraform Registry by the Databricks organization.

Now that we've imported the Databricks Terraform provider, we can begin deploying data pipeline objects to our Databricks workspace. But before we can do that, we must first authenticate with our Databricks workspace to make changes, such as creating a new DLT pipeline.

Configuring workspace authentication

If you recall, the Databricks Terraform provider will interact with the Databricks REST API behind the scenes. As a result, the same authentication mechanisms that are used to authenticate with the Databricks REST API and make workspace changes can be applied using Terraform.

In total, there are about nine supported methods for authenticating with a Databricks workspace using the Terraform provider (the latest list can be found here: `https://registry.terraform. io/providers/databricks/databricks/latest/docs#authentication`). A few of the popular authentication methods include the following:

- Using a workspace administrator username and password
- Using a Databricks **Personal Access Token (PAT)**
- Using the Azure CLI or Google Cloud CLI
- If using the Azure cloud provider, using a service principal or managed service identity
- Using the Databricks CLI (user-to-machine authentication)

> **Important note**
>
> Since we are doing local development and testing, in the following example, we'll be generating an OAuth token using the Databricks CLI and logging in to our Databricks workspace manually. However, for production deployments, it's recommended to securely store workspace credentials in a secrets manager such as Azure Key Vault, AWS Secrets Manager, or HashiCorp Vault, to name a few.

There are a couple of options for storing authentication tokens that are used with Terraform – directly within the Terraform configuration file as a part of the Databricks provider import, or on the local machine within a configuration file. We would recommend the latter option to avoid accidental exposure of credentials when checking in code artifacts to your code repository. The easiest method for populating this configuration file is by using the Databricks CLI.

The Databricks CLI supports Windows, Linux, or macOS operating systems, making it a cross-platform-compatible and versatile tool. If your local machine uses macOS or Linux operating systems, you can download the Databricks CLI using the Homebrew package manager using a shell prompt. Or you can easily upgrade the version of an existing Databricks CLI installation. For example, the following commands will install or upgrade an existing Databricks CLI installation using Homebrew on a Mac:

```
$ brew tap databricks/tap
$ brew install databricks
```

On a Windows machine, you can install the Databricks CLI using the popular package manager, `winget` (https://learn.microsoft.com/windows/package-manager/winget/). The following commands will download and install the Databricks CLI using the `winget` utility:

```
$ winget search databricks
$ winget install Databricks.DatabricksCLI
```

Once downloaded, you can configure authentication by executing the `configure` command in the Databricks CLI:

```
$ databricks configure
```

When applying a Terraform configuration file to a target environment, the Terraform CLI will first check to see whether authentication details are provided directly within the configuration file. Otherwise, the Terraform CLI will look for the local Databricks configuration file, which gets stored in a special hidden file called `.databrickscfg` under your user's home folder.

You can also specify a profile name, which is helpful when you have multiple Databricks workspaces and you need to deploy infrastructure components between the different workspaces. Using the profiles, you can store authentication details separately and easily reference them during deployment. You can learn more about creating/testing a profile here: https://docs.databricks.com/dev-tools/cli/profiles.html.

Defining a DLT pipeline source notebook

In the next example, we're going to define a notebook that will contain the start of a simple DLT pipeline and deploy the notebook to your user's workspace directory in a target Databricks workspace.

To construct the workspace location of where to deploy the notebook, we'll need to get your current user in Databricks. Rather than hardcoding this value, we can use the `databricks_current_user` data source, which retrieves the current user's Databricks username at deployment time. Add the following configuration block to the `main.tf` file:

```
data "databricks_current_user" "my_user" {}
```

Next, we'll use the `databricks_notebook` resource to define a new Python notebook, using the previous data source to construct the notebook path. Since the notebook is fairly simple, containing only a single DLT dataset definition, we'll define the notebook contents inline. Add the following configuration block to the `main.tf` file:

```
resource "databricks_notebook" "dlt_pipeline_notebook" {
  path = "${data.databricks_current_user.my_user.home}/chp_8_
terraform/my_simple_dlt_pipeline.py"
  language = "PYTHON"
  content_base64 = base64encode(<<-EOT
    import dlt


    @dlt.table(
        comment="The raw NYC taxi cab trip dataset located in `/
databricks-datasets/`"
    )
    def yellow_taxi_raw():
        path = "/databricks-datasets/nyctaxi/tripdata/yellow"
        schema = "vendor_id string, pickup_datetime timestamp,
dropoff_datetime timestamp, passenger_count integer, trip_distance
float, pickup_longitude float, pickup_latitude float, rate_code
integer, store_and_fwd_flag integer, dropoff_longitude float, dropoff_
lattitude float, payment_type string, fare_amount float, surcharge
float, mta_tax float, tip_amount float, tolls_amount float, total_
amount float"
        return (spark.readStream
                .schema(schema)
                .format("csv")
                .option("header", True)
                .load(path))
    EOT
  )
}
```

Finally, let's add one last block to the `main.tf` configuration that prints the URL to the deployed notebook:

```
output "notebook_url" {
  value = databricks_notebook.dlt_pipeline_notebook.url
}
```

Click **Save** to save the configuration file. In a terminal window, navigate to the directory containing the `main.tf` configuration file.

Applying workspace changes

The first command that should be run is the `terraform init` command, which executes several initialization steps to prepare the current working directory to deploy cloud resources using Terraform. Execute the following command from a terminal window or shell prompt:

```
terraform init
```

Next, the Terraform CLI provides a way for us to validate the effects of a Terraform configuration file before applying the changes. Execute the `validate` command:

```
terraform validate
```

Lastly, we can view the proposed infrastructure changes by listing all of the planned changes in the Terraform plan. Execute the following command to view the proposed Terraform plan:

```
terraform plan
```

You'll notice that there will be a single resource defined in the plan. In this case, it will be the new Databricks notebook containing our DLT dataset definition.

Once we validate that the plan looks good, we can then apply the changes to the target Databricks workspace. Apply the Terraform plan by executing the `apply` command:

```
terraform apply
```

The output will be the full notebook URL to the newly created notebook. Copy the output URL and paste it into a browser window. Verify that there is a new notebook with Python set as the default programming language, containing a single notebook cell with the definition of a single DLT dataset, `yellow_taxi_raw`.

Congratulations! You've written your first Terraform configuration file and you are well on your way to automating the deployment of your Databricks assets across environments. In the next section, we'll expand on the previous example to see how the Databricks Terraform provider can be used to deploy DLT pipelines to workspaces.

Configuring DLT pipelines using Terraform

We will use the `databricks_pipeline` resource in the Databricks Terraform provider to deploy a DLT pipeline to a target Databricks workspace. The `databricks_pipeline` resource is the main building block for our Terraform configuration files. Within this Terraform resource, we can specify many different configuration options that will affect the deployment of our DLT pipeline. For example, we can configure the DLT production edition, a target Unity Catalog location, library dependencies, update cluster sizes, and more. Let's dive into the exact configurations to get a better idea of the type of control you have over the DLT pipeline that gets deployed.

There are several arguments used to define the configuration and behavior of a DLT pipeline using the Databricks provider for Terraform. To get a better picture of the types of arguments, the following sections cover all the available arguments in the Databricks provider for Terraform (the latest version can be found here: `https://registry.terraform.io/providers/databricks/databricks/latest/docs/resources/pipeline`).

Generally speaking, the `databricks_pipeline` arguments can be thought about as falling into one of three possible categories:

- **Runtime configuration**: `name`, `channel`, `development`, `continuous`, `edition`, `photon`, `configuration`, and `library`
- **Pipeline compute configuration**: `cluster`
- **Pipeline dataset storage configuration**: `catalog`, `target`, and `storage`

Let's go through each argument in greater detail to get a better understanding of the effect that our Terraform configuration can have on a target DLT pipeline.

name

The name argument assigns an alphanumeric name to identify a DLT pipeline. The name argument should be a String that can contain mixed-case characters, numbers, spaces, and special characters (including emoji characters). Furthermore, the pipeline name argument doesn't necessarily need to be unique; name uniqueness is not enforced by the Databricks Terraform provider. Upon creation of a DLT pipeline, the Databricks Data Intelligence Platform will assign a unique pipeline identifier to each pipeline, so the name argument is solely used as a convenient way for data engineers to distinguish their DLT pipelines from other pipelines from the DLT UI.

notification

The `notification` argument is used to specify a list of email recipients who will receive an email notification during specific pipeline events. The types of DLT pipeline events that will trigger a notification include `on-update-success`, `on-update-failure`, `on-update-fatal-failure`, and `on-flow-failure`.

channel

The `channel` argument controls the type of Databricks runtime a DLT pipeline update cluster should use. There are only two options to choose from: `CURRENT` and `PREVIEW`. `CURRENT` selects the latest stable Databricks runtime release and is the default option. You may want to choose `PREVIEW` if your DLT pipeline is operating in a development environment, and you'd like to experiment with upcoming performance features and optimizations that haven't made their way into the current Databricks runtime yet.

development

The `development` argument is a Boolean flag that controls whether you want to execute your DLT pipeline in Development mode or not. When set to `true`, Terraform will deploy a DLT pipeline, with the pipeline mode set to **Development**. This will also be reflected on the DLT UI by a toggle button at the top right of the DLT UI.

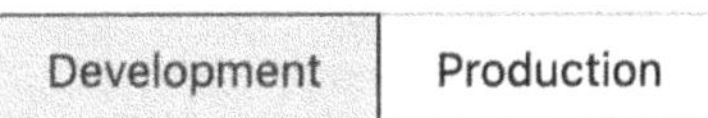

Figure 8.2 – Development mode is visible from the DLT UI as a toggle button

Similarly, when this argument is set to `false`, Terraform will set the pipeline mode to **Production**. If you recall from *Chapter 2*, we mentioned that in Development mode, DLT will not retry pipeline updates in the event of a runtime exception and will also keep the update cluster up and running to help data engineers triage and fix bugs, thereby shortening debugging cycles.

continuous

The `continuous` argument is a Boolean flag that controls the frequency of pipeline update executions. When set to `true`, Terraform will deploy a DLT pipeline that will continuously update datasets within a DLT pipeline. Similarly, when set to `false`, the DLT pipeline will be deployed with a triggered execution mode. In this type of execution mode, a data engineer will need to trigger the start of a pipeline update either by clicking the **Start** button on the DLT UI or by invoking the Pipelines REST API to start a pipeline update.

edition

The `edition` argument selects which product edition you would like to use when deploying a DLT pipeline. There are only three options to choose from: CORE, PRO, and ADVANCED. If you recall from *Chapter 2*, the product edition selects the feature set that you would like to enable when running a DLT pipeline. As a result, the pipeline pricing is reflected in the number of features enabled with an edition. For example, the PRO product edition will enable data engineers to use expectations to enforce data quality but will also incur the highest operational pricing. On the other hand, the CORE product edition may be used to append incoming data to streaming tables and will incur the least amount of operation charges to update.

photon

The `photon` argument is a Boolean flag that controls whether to use a Photon processing engine to update a DLT pipeline. When set to `true`, Terraform will deploy a DLT pipeline with an update cluster having the Photon engine enabled. During the dataset updates, your DLT pipeline can take advantage of this fast, vectorized processing engine that makes joins, aggregations, windows, and sorting much faster than the default cluster. When set to `false`, DLT will create an update cluster using the traditional Catalyst engine in Spark. Due to faster processing and improved performance, enabling Photon execution will incur higher DBU pricing.

configuration

The `configuration` argument allows data engineers to deploy a DLT pipeline with optional runtime configuration. The configuration argument is an optional list of key-value pairs. This argument can be used to populate environment variables, cloud storage locations, or cluster shutdown settings, for example.

library

The `library` argument can be used to install cluster libraries that a DLT pipeline update might depend on in order to apply updates to a pipeline. The `library` argument also adds support for referencing local notebook or arbitrary file dependencies, if data engineers wish to include dependent code artifacts using local files as opposed to build artifacts. For example, the following `library` block could be used to include a custom date utility defined as a Python file in the user's home directory in their workspace:

```
library {
  notebook {
    path = "/Users/<username>/common/utils/date_utils.py"
  }
}
```

cluster

The `cluster` argument controls what cluster is used by the pipeline during an update, maintenance activities, or the default cluster type to use in both update and maintenance tasks. If no `cluster` block is specified, DLT will create a default cluster to use to apply updates to a pipeline's datasets. Furthermore, the `cluster` argument will also contain a `mode` parameter where you can specify what type of autoscaling to use. If you recall, in *Chapter 2*, we described two autoscaling modes in DLT: LEGACY and ENHANCED. For example, the following configuration will create an update cluster that will autoscale from a minimum of three worker nodes to a maximum of eight nodes using the ENHANCED autoscaling algorithm:

```
cluster {
  node_type_id = "i3.xlarge"
  autoscale {
    min_workers = 3
    max_workers = 8
    mode = "ENHANCED"
  }
}
```

catalog

The `catalog` argument determines the catalog to store the output datasets of a DLT pipeline in Unity Catalog. As a DLT pipeline executes the definitions for datasets outlined in a DLT pipeline, these datasets need to have some destination location specified. You can specify a combination of a catalog and a schema (covered in the next section, *target*) or you can specify a cloud storage location – but not both. This argument is mutually exclusive to the following argument, the `storage` argument. Alternatively, data engineers can continue to store a DLT pipeline's datasets in the legacy Hive Metastore specifying the following configuration:

```
catalog {
  name = "hive_metastore"
}
```

> **Important note**
>
> If either the `catalog` or `storage` arguments are changed in a Terraform configuration file and the changes are applied, Terraform will recreate the entire DLT pipeline with the new changes. These values cannot be updated in the original DLT pipeline once deployed.

target

The `target` argument specifies the schema in which to store the output datasets defined in a DLT pipeline. This argument, combined with the previous `catalog` argument, specifies a fully qualified schema in Unity Catalog or the legacy Hive Metastore. Data engineers may choose to use the values set in the `catalog` and `target` arguments as a convenient means for querying the intermediate datasets of a DLT pipeline. This may be for common tasks such as data validation, debugging, or general data wrangling.

storage

The `storage` argument can be used to specify a cloud storage location to store the output datasets and other related metadata for a DLT pipeline. It's important to keep in mind that this argument is mutually exclusive to the preceding argument, the `catalog` argument. The `storage` argument may contain a fully qualified storage location path, a volumes location, or a location in the **Databricks File System (DBFS)**. For example, the following configuration block would create a DLT pipeline whose output datasets would be stored in the DBFS:

```
storage {
  path = "/pipelines/my-dlt-pipeline-output/"
}
```

> **Important note**
>
> The `storage` and `catalog` arguments are mutually exclusive to one another. You may only specify one when authoring a Terraform configuration file.

By now, you should feel confident in using the `databricks_pipeline` resource to declare DLT pipelines using the Databricks provider for Terraform. You should also have a greater understanding of the different types of configuration options available to customize a target DLT pipeline. In the next section, we'll look at how we can automate the deployment of DLT pipelines using existing version control systems so that the latest changes are synchronized across target workspaces as soon as they are made available.

Automating DLT pipeline deployment

Terraform can be combined with automated **Continuous Integration/Continuous Deployment (CI/CD)** tools, such as GitHub Actions or Azure DevOps Pipelines to automatically deploy code changes to your Databricks workspaces. Since Terraform is cross-platform, the target Databricks workspace can be in one of the major cloud providers: GCP, AWS, or Azure. This allows your development team to maintain infrastructure in a single set of code artifacts while also being agile enough to apply the same resources to alternate cloud providers.

Let's walk through a typical CI/CD process that uses the Databricks provider for Terraform to deploy Databricks resources to target workspaces. The CI/CD process will contain two automated build pipelines – one that will be used to validate changes made in feature branches, and a second that will be used to deploy changes that have been approved and merged into the main code branch to Databricks workspaces.

First, a team member creates a new feature branch to track changes to their organization's IaC code base. Once finished, the engineer will open a pull request, requesting one or more peers from their team to review the changes, leave feedback, and approve or reject the changes. Upon opening a pull request, the build pipeline will be triggered to run, which will check out the feature branch, initialize the current working directory using the Terraform `init` command, validate the Terraform plan using the Terraform `validate` command, and generate an output in the form of a Terraform plan. Optionally, this Terraform plan can be automatically included in the pull request as a comment for peers to review.

When the pull request has been approved by their team members, the feature branch can be merged into the main code repository branch – or the `main` branch, for short.

Once the feature branch has been merged into the `main` branch, the build release pipeline is triggered to run. The build release pipeline will check out the latest copy of the `main` branch and apply the changes using the Terraform `apply` command. Upon applying the Terraform plan, new changes to the organization's infrastructure will be reflected in the target Databricks workspace.

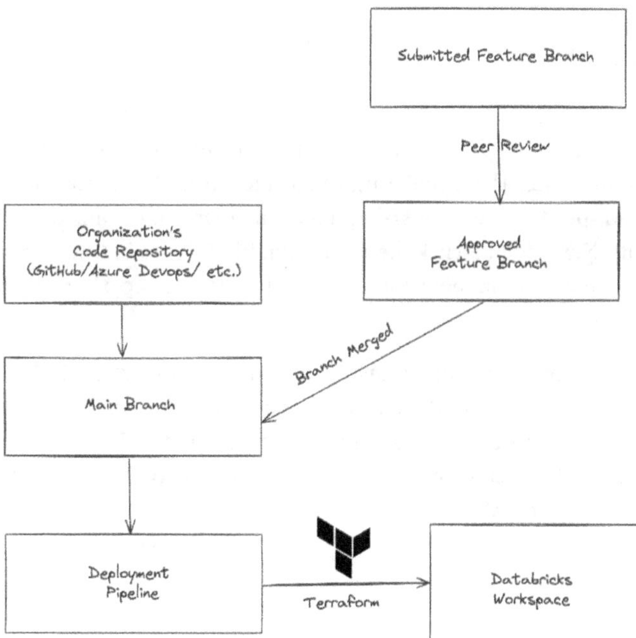

Figure 8.3 – Automatic deployment of Databricks resources using build tools

By now, you should have a complete understanding of how to design an automatic Databricks deployment using tools such as Azure DevOps to synchronize infrastructure changes through Terraform. Let's combine everything that we've learned in the preceding sections to deploy our very own DLT pipeline to a target Databricks workspace using a typical development environment.

Hands-on exercise – deploying a DLT pipeline using VS Code

In this hands-on exercise, we'll be using the popular code editor, **Visual Studio Code** (**VS Code**), to author new Terraform configuration files for deploying a DLT pipeline to a target Databricks workspace. VS Code has gained immense popularity over the years due to its ease of use, light memory footprint, friendly code navigation, syntax highlighting, and code refactoring, as well as a great community of extensions. Plus, VS Code is built around an open source community, meaning it's free to download and use. Furthermore, VS Code is a cross-platform code editor, supporting Windows, macOS, and Linux operating systems. In this hands-on exercise, we'll be using one of the community extensions, the Terraform plugin for VS Code, which is authored by HashiCorp to help assist in the development of Terraform configuration files. For example, the Terraform plugin for VS Code features Terraform syntax highlighting, auto-completion, code formatting, access to Terraform commands from the VS Code command palette, and overall, provides an easy experience navigating Terraform configuration files for deploying Databricks workspace objects.

Setting up VS Code

VS Code can be downloaded from its website located at `https://code.visualstudio.com/download`. If you haven't installed VS Code yet, select the installer download for the operating system that matches your local machine. The installer may take a few minutes to download, depending on your network connection speed. Once the installer has been downloaded, unzip the ZIP file to reveal the downloaded contents. Next, double-click the application file, `Visual Studio Code`, to launch the code editor. Alternatively, you can move the application file to the `Applications` directory of your local operating system.

Next, let's install the Terraform extension by HashiCorp. In a web browser window, navigate to the Terraform extension in the Visual Studio Marketplace website located at `https://marketplace.visualstudio.com/items?itemName=HashiCorp.terraform`. Or you can search for the extension in the Marketplace search box in VS Code. Click the **Install** button to download and install the Terraform extension for VS Code.

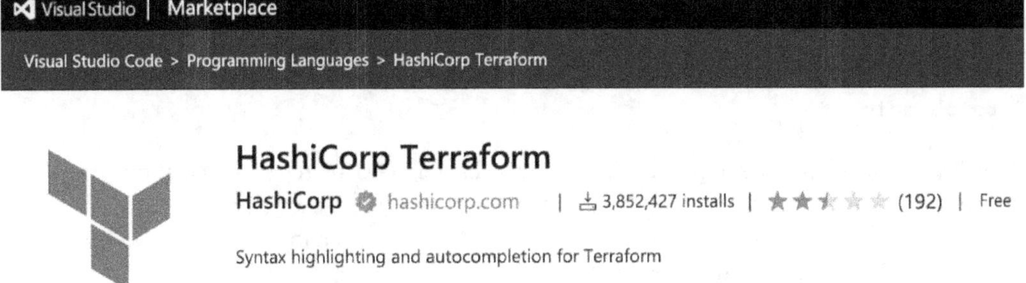

Figure 8.4 – The Terraform extension for VS Code by HashiCorp can
be installed from the Visual Studio Marketplace

You may be prompted to allow your web browser to open the VS Code application on your local machine. If so, click the **Allow** button to open VS Code and install the extension. The extension will be downloaded and installed in just a few minutes. Once the installation has been completed, you should now see menu items for HashiCorp Terraform on the left-hand side navigation bar of VS Code.

Figure 8.5 – The HashiCorp Terraform extension will create new
menu items in the left-hand side navigation bar

Now that the Terraform extension has been successfully installed, the extension will automatically be activated when the code editor detects a Terraform file. You can verify that the extension is activated by a Terraform logo, which will appear in the bottom right-hand corner of the opened Terraform file.

Creating a new Terraform project

Let's create a new directory for our hands-on exercise:

```
$ mkdir chapter_8_hands_on
$ cd chapter_8_hands_on
```

Create an empty Terraform configuration file, titled `main.tf`, either from a shell prompt or using VS Code:

```
$ touch main.tf
```

Optionally, you can clone the sample project from this chapter's GitHub repo, located at `https://github.com/PacktPublishing/Building-Modern-Data-Applications-Using-Databricks-Lakehouse/tree/main/chapter08`. Next, open the directory in VS Code by selecting **File | Open Folder** and navigating to the directory's location.

Defining the Terraform resources

Let's start by expanding the Terraform example introduced in the *Setting up a local Terraform environment* section at the beginning of this chapter. Either copy the existing `main.tf` file or feel free to directly edit the body of the existing `main.tf` configuration file.

First, let's begin by adding a second dataset to the DLT pipeline definition in the `databricks_notebook` resource definition (the code from the *Defining a DLT pipeline source notebook* section has been truncated for brevity in the following code block). We will now have a data pipeline containing two datasets – a bronze layer followed by a silver layer. Update the `databricks_notebook` resource definition in the `main.tf` file with the following definition:

```python
resource "databricks_notebook" "dlt_pipeline_notebook" {
  path = "${data.databricks_current_user.my_user.home}/chp_8_
terraform/taxi_trips_pipeline.py"
...

                  .load(path))


    @dlt.table(
        name="yellow_taxi_silver",
        comment="Financial information from incoming taxi trips."
    )
    @dlt.expect_or_fail("valid_total_amount", "total_amount > 0.0")
    def yellow_taxi_silver():
        return (dlt.readStream("yellow_taxi_bronze")
                    .withColumn("driver_payment",
                            F.expr("total_amount * 0.40"))
                    .withColumn("vehicle_maintenance_fee",
                            F.expr("total_amount * 0.05"))
                    .withColumn("adminstrative_fee",
                            F.expr("total_amount * 0.1"))
                    .withColumn("potential_profits",
                            F.expr("total_amount * 0.45")))
    EOT
```

```
  )
}
```

Next, before we can create a new DLT pipeline, we'll want to define a location in Unity Catalog in which to store the pipeline datasets. Add the following catalog and schema resource definitions to the bottom of the `main.tf` file:

```
resource "databricks_catalog" "dlt_target_catalog" {
  name = "chp8_deploying_pipelines_w_terraform"
  comment = "The target catalog for Taxi Trips DLT pipeline"
}

resource "databricks_schema" "dlt_target_schema" {
  catalog_name = databricks_catalog.dlt_target_catalog.id
  name = "terraform_demo"
  comment = "The target schema for Taxi Trips DLT pipeline"
}
```

Now that we have an updated source notebook containing the definition of our DLT pipeline, as well as a location to store the pipeline datasets, we can define a DLT pipeline. Add the following pipeline definition to the `main.tf` file:

```
resource "databricks_pipeline" "taxi_trips_pipeline" {
  name = "Taxi Trips Pipeline"
  library {
    notebook {
      path = "${data.databricks_current_user.my_user.home}/chp_8_
terraform/taxi_trips_pipeline.py"
    }
  }
  cluster {
    label = "default"
    num_workers = 2
    autoscale {
      min_workers = 2
      max_workers = 4
      mode = "ENHANCED"
    }
    driver_node_type_id = "i3.2xlarge"
    node_type_id = "i3.xlarge"
  }
  continuous = false
  development = true
  photon = false
```

```
  serverless = false
  catalog = databricks_catalog.dlt_target_catalog.name
  target = databricks_schema.dlt_target_schema.name
  edition = "ADVANCED"
  channel = "CURRENT"
}
```

You'll notice that we've defined the location for the notebook containing the DLT pipeline definition, a default cluster to use for pipeline updates and maintenance tasks, as well as other runtime settings such as the Development mode, product edition, channel, and more.

Next, we'll want to orchestrate the updates to our DLT pipeline so that we can trigger runs on a repeated schedule, configure alert notifications, or set timeout thresholds. Add the following workflow definition to the bottom of the `main.tf` file:

```
resource "databricks_job" "taxi_trips_pipeline_job" {
  name = "Taxi Trips Pipeline Update Job"
  description = "Databricks Workflow that executes a pipeline update
of the Taxi Trips DLT pipeline."
  job_cluster {
    job_cluster_key = "taxi_trips_pipeline_update_job_cluster"
    new_cluster {
      num_workers = 2
      spark_version = "15.4.x-scala2.12"
      node_type_id  = "i3.xlarge"
      driver_node_type_id = "i3.2xlarge"
    }
  }
  task {
    task_key = "update_taxi_trips_pipeline"
    pipeline_task {
      pipeline_id = databricks_pipeline.taxi_trips_pipeline.id
    }
  }
  trigger {
    pause_status = "PAUSED"
    periodic {
      interval = "1"
      unit = "HOURS"
    }
  }
}
```

Lastly, we'll want to output the workflow URL of the deployed resource so that we can open the workflow UI easily from a browser. Add the following output definition to the `main.tf` file:

```
output "workflow_url" {
  value = databricks_job.taxi_trips_pipeline_job.url
}
```

Deploying the Terraform project

Before we can begin deploying new resources, the first step is to initialize the Terraform project. Execute the Terraform `init` command in the parent directory either from the VS Code command palette or from a shell prompt:

```
$ terraform init
```

Next, preview the changes in the Terraform file by executing the Terraform `plan` command to view the proposed infrastructure changes:

```
$ terraform plan
```

In total, there should be five new resources created, including the `databricks_notebook` resource, which represents the notebook containing the DLT pipeline definition, the target Unity Catalog's catalog, the target Unity Catalog schema, the `databricks_pipeline` resource, which represents our DLT pipeline, and the `databricks_job` resource, which represents the workflow that will trigger pipeline updates.

After we've validated the plan, we can now deploy our DLT pipeline to a Databricks workspace. Next, execute the Terraform `apply` command to deploy the new infrastructure changes to our workspace:

```
$ terraform apply
```

Once all resource changes have been applied, you should expect Terraform to output the URL to the Databricks workflow.

Copy and paste the workflow URL into a browser window and ensure that the address resolves to the newly created workflow in the target workspace. You'll notice that the new workflow contains a single task for updating the DLT pipeline. The workflow is paused, as outlined in the Terraform configuration. Optionally, you can click the blue **Run now** button to trigger a new, immediate run of the workflow.

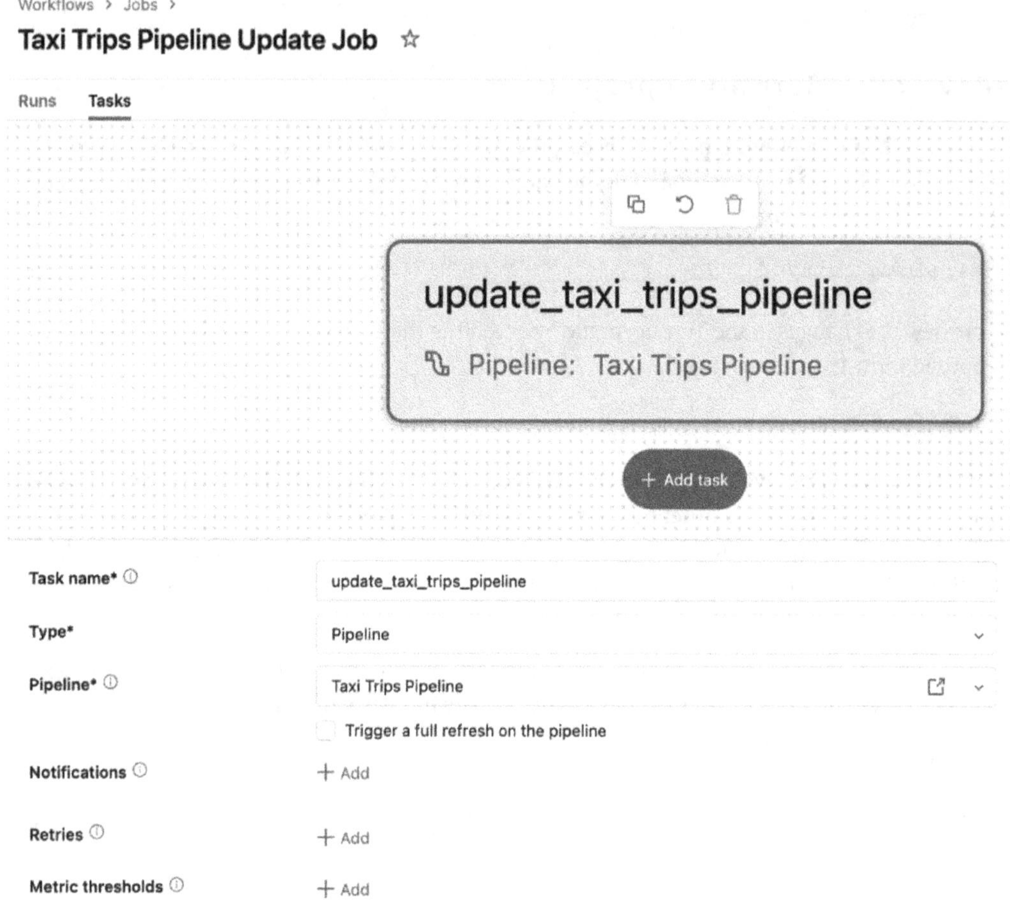

Figure 8.6 – Terraform will output the workflow URL for updating the DLT pipeline

As simple as it was to deploy our changes to the target Databricks workspace, it's just as easy to undeploy the changes. Execute the following command to remove all the resource changes from the target Databricks workspace:

```
$ terraform destroy
```

Confirm the decision by entering the word yes. It may take a few minutes to fully undeploy all of the resources from your Databricks workspace.

As you saw, with just a few keystrokes and a few clicks of the button, it was fast and easy to provision and deprovision resources in a Databricks workspace using the Databricks Terraform provider. Rather than instructing Terraform how to deploy the resources to our target Databricks workspace, we focused on what changes to make through configuration and let the Terraform tool handle the heavy lifting for us.

Summary

In this chapter, we covered how to use the Databricks provider for Terraform to implement a CI/CD process for deploying data pipelines across workspaces. We saw how easy it was to set up a local development environment for working with Terraform configuration files and how easy it was to test our Terraform plans before applying them to a target environment. We also installed the Databricks Terraform provider from the Terraform Registry and imported the provider into Terraform configuration files. Next, we dove into the details of the `databricks_pipeline` resource, which is used by the Databricks Terraform provider to deploy a DLT pipeline to a target workspace. We inspected each argument in the resource specification and saw how we could control the DLT pipeline runtime configuration, the compute settings, and even the location of the output datasets from our pipeline. Lastly, we saw how easy it was to automate our Terraform configuration files by storing them in a version control system such as GitHub and automating the deployment using a build tool such as Azure DevOps Pipelines. We concluded the chapter with a hands-on example of using the Terraform extension with the popular code editor VS Code to deploy a DLT pipeline from your local development environment.

However, Terraform isn't for everyone and it may be the case that it's too complex or too difficult to use for your use case. In the next chapter, we'll dive into **Databricks Asset Bundles** (**DABs**), which is another CI/CD tool that makes it simple to package and deploy Databricks code artifacts for data and machine learning workloads.

9

Leveraging Databricks Asset Bundles to Streamline Data Pipeline Deployment

This chapter explores a relatively new **continuous integration and continuous deployment (CI/CD)** tool called **Databricks Asset Bundles (DABs)**, which can be leveraged to streamline the development and deployment of data analytical projects across various Databricks workspaces. In this chapter, we'll dive into the core concept of **DABs**. We'll demonstrate the practical use of DABs through several hands-on exercises so that you feel comfortable developing your next data analytics projects as a DAB. Lastly, we'll cover how DABs can be used to increase cross-team collaboration through version control systems such as GitHub, and how DABs can be used to simplify even the most complex data analytical deployments.

In this chapter, we're going to cover the following main topics:

- Introduction to Databricks Asset Bundles
- Databricks Asset Bundles in action
- Simplifying cross-team collaboration
- Versioning and maintenance

Technical requirements

To follow the examples in this chapter, it's recommended that you have Databricks workspace administrative privileges so that you can deploy DABs to target workspaces. You'll also need to download and install version 0.218.0 or higher of the Databricks CLI. All the code samples can be downloaded from this chapter's GitHub repository at `https://github.com/PacktPublishing/Building-Modern-Data-Applications-Using-Databricks-Lakehouse/tree/main/chapter09`. In this chapter, we will deploy several new workflows, DLT pipelines, notebooks, and clusters. It's estimated that this will consume around 5-10 **Databricks Units (DBUs)**.

Introduction to Databricks Asset Bundles

DABs provide an easy and convenient way to develop your data and **artificial intelligence (AI)** projects together with YAML metadata for declaring the infrastructure that goes along with it – just like a bundle. DABs provide data engineers with a way to programmatically validate, deploy, and test Databricks resources in target workspaces. This may include deploying workspace assets such as **Delta Live Tables (DLT)** pipelines, workflows, notebooks, and more. DABs also provide a convenient way to develop, package, and deploy machine learning workloads using reusable templates (we'll cover DAB templates later in the *Initializing an asset bundle using templates* section), called MLOps Stacks.

DABs were designed around the principles of expressing **Infrastructure as Code (IaC)** and benefit from using configuration to drive the deployment of architectural components of your data applications. DABs provide a way to check in IaC configuration along with data assets such as Python files, Notebooks, and other dependencies. DABs can also be an alternative if you feel Terraform (covered in *Chapter 8*) is too advanced for your organization's needs within the context of the Databricks Data Intelligence Platform.

DABs share some similarities with Terraform in that both are IaC tools that give users the ability to define cloud resources and deploy those resources in a cloud-agnostic manner. However, there are many differences as well. Let's compare a few of the similarities and differences between DABs and Terraform to get a better feeling of when to choose which tool over the other for your organization's needs:

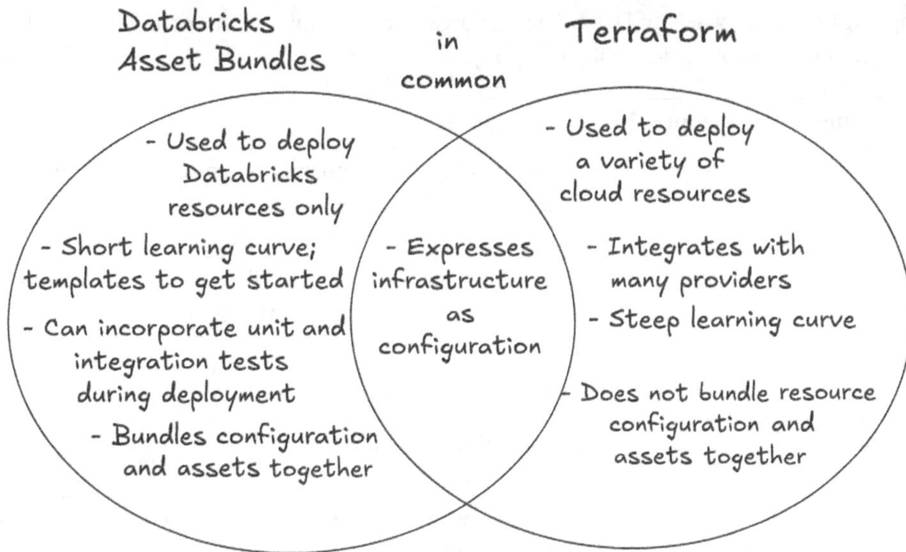

Figure 9.1 – DABs and Terraform are both IaC tools, but they meet very different needs

Before we start writing our very first DAB, let's spend some time getting to know the major building blocks of what makes up a DAB configuration file.

Elements of a DAB configuration file

At the center of a DAB is a YAML configuration file, named `databricks.yml`. This configuration file provides engineers with an entry point for configuring the deployment of their project's resources. The file consists of many composable building blocks that tell the Databricks **command-line interface (CLI)** what to deploy to a target Databricks workspace and how to configure each resource. Each building block accepts different parameters for configuring that component.

Later in this chapter, we'll cover how to decompose the configuration file into many YAML files, but for simplicity's sake, we'll start with a single YAML file. Within this YAML configuration file, we'll declare our Databricks resources, as well as other metadata. These building blocks, or **mappings**, tell the DAB tool what Databricks resource to create, and more importantly, what Databricks REST API to manipulate to create and configure a Databricks resource.

These mappings can be a variety of Databricks resources. For example, a DAB configuration file can contain any combination of the following mappings:

Mapping Name	Required?	Description
`bundle`	Yes	Contains top-level information about the current asset bundle, including the Databricks CLI version, existing cluster identifier, and git settings.
`variables`	No	Contains global variables that will be dynamically populated during the execution of a DAB deployment.
`workspace`	No	Used to specify non-default workspace locations, such as the root storage, artifact storage, and file paths.
`permissions`	No	Contains information about what permissions to grant to the deployed resources.
`resources`	Yes	Specifies what Databricks resources to deploy and how to configure them.
`artifacts`	No	Specifies deployment artifacts, such as Python `.whl` files, that will be generated during the deployment process.
`include`	No	Specifies a list of relative file path globs to additional configuration files. This is a great way to separate a DAB configuration file into several child configuration files.
`sync`	No	Specifies a list of relative file path globs to include or exclude in the deployment process.
`targets`	Yes	Specifies information about the context in addition to the Databricks workspace and details about the workflow, pipeline, and artifacts.

Table 9.1 – Mappings in a databricks.yml file

Let's look at a simple DAB configuration file so that we're familiar with some of the basics. The following example will create a new Databricks workflow called `Hello, World!` that will run a notebook that prints the simple yet popular expression `Hello, World!`:

```
bundle:
  name: hello_dab_world

resources:
  jobs:
    hello_dab_world_job:
      name: hello_dab_world_job
```

```
    tasks:
      - task_key: notebook_task
        existing_cluster_id: <cluster_id>
        notebook_task:
          notebook_path: ./src/hello_dab_world.py

targets:
  dev:
    default: true
    workspace:
      host: https://<workspace_name>.cloud.databricks.com
```

In this simple example, our DAB configuration file consists of three main sections:

- `bundle`: This section contains high-level information about the current DAB – in this case, its name.

- `resources`: This defines a new Databricks workflow with a single notebook task that should be run on an existing cluster.

- `targets`: This specifies information about the target Databricks workspace the workflow and notebook should be deployed to.

Now that we have a strong understanding of the basics of a DAB configuration file, let's look at how we can deploy our Databricks resources under different deployment scenarios.

Specifying a deployment mode

One attribute that's available from within a DAB configuration file is a deployment mode, which allows us to specify an operating mode when we're deploying resources. There are two types of deployment modes available: development and production.

In *development* mode, all resources are marked with a special prefix, `[dev <username>]`, to indicate that the resources are in development. Furthermore, all resources, when available, are deployed with the `dev` metadata tag, to also indicate that the resources are in development. As you may recall from *Chapter 2*, DLT also has a development mode available. When DLT pipelines are deployed using DABs in development mode, all deployed DLT pipelines will be deployed to the target workspace with this development mode enabled.

During the development life cycle, it's also expected that engineers will want to experiment with changes and quickly iterate on design changes. As a result, development mode will also pause all Databricks workflow schedules and enable concurrent runs of the same workflow, allowing engineers to run the workflow in an ad hoc fashion directly from the Databricks CLI. Similarly, development mode gives you the option to specify an existing all-purpose cluster to use for the deployment process, either by specifying the cluster ID as an argument from the Databricks CLI via `--compute-id <cluster_id>` or by adding the cluster ID to the top-level `bundle` mapping of the YAML configuration file.

Let's look at how we might be able to specify a target workspace so that it can be used as a development environment and override all clusters with a default, existing all-purpose cluster:

```
targets:
  dev:
    default: true
    mode: development
    compute_id: <cluster_id>
    workspace:
      host: https://<workspace_name>.cloud.databricks.com
```

Conversely, you can also specify a production mode. In *production* mode, resources won't be prepended with a special naming prefix and no tags will be applied. However, production mode will validate the resources before they're deployed to the target workspace. For example, it will be ensured that all DLT pipelines have been set to production mode and resources that specify cloud storage locations or workspace paths don't point to user-specific locations.

In the next section, we'll roll up our sleeves and dive into using the Databricks CLI to experiment with asset bundles and see them in action.

Databricks Asset Bundles in action

DABs depend entirely on the Databricks CLI tool (see *Chapter 8* for installation instructions) to create new bundles from templates, deploy bundles to target workspaces, and even remove previously deployed resource bundles from workspaces. For this section, you'll need version 0.218.0 or higher of the Databricks CLI. You can quickly check the version of your local Databricks CLI by passing the `--version` argument:

```
databricks --version
```

You should get a similar output as shown in the following *Figure 9.2*:

```
$ databricks --version
Databricks CLI v0.219.0
```

Figure 9.2 - Checking the version of a previously installed Databricks CLI

Once you've successfully installed the recommended version of the Databricks CLI, you can test that the installation was successful by displaying the manual page for the bundle command. Enter the following command to display the available arguments and descriptions from the CLI:

```
$ databricks bundle --help
```

We'll get the following manual page:

```
Databricks Asset Bundles let you express data/AI/analytics projects as code.

Online documentation: https://docs.databricks.com/en/dev-tools/bundles/index.html

Usage:
  databricks bundle [command]

Available Commands:
  deploy        Deploy bundle
  deployment    Deployment related commands
  destroy       Destroy deployed bundle resources
  generate      Generate bundle configuration
  init          Initialize using a bundle template
  run           Run a job or pipeline update
  schema        Generate JSON Schema for bundle configuration
  sync          Synchronize bundle tree to the workspace
  validate      Validate configuration

Flags:
  -h, --help            help for bundle
      --var strings     set values for variables defined in bundle config. Example: --var="foo=bar"

Global Flags:
      --debug           enable debug logging
  -o, --output type     output type: text or json (default text)
  -p, --profile string  ~/.databrickscfg profile
  -t, --target string   bundle target to use (if applicable)
```

Figure 9.3 – The manual page for the bundle command in the Databricks CLI

Before we can begin authoring DABs and deploying resources to Databricks workspaces, we will need to authenticate with the target Databricks workspaces so that we can deploy resources. DABs leverage OAuth tokens to authenticate with Databricks workspaces. Two types of OAuth authentication can be used with DABs – **user-to-machine** (**U2M**) authentication and **machine-to-machine** (**M2M**) authentication.

User-to-machine authentication

U2M authentication involves a human in the loop generating an OAuth token that can be used when you're deploying new resources to a target workspace. This type of authentication involves a user who will log in via a web browser when prompted by the CLI tool. This type of authentication is good for development scenarios where users want to experiment with DABs and deploy resources in non-critical development workspaces.

U2M is the easiest way to authenticate with your Databricks workspace and can be done directly from the Databricks CLI:

```
$ databricks auth login --host <workspace-url>
```

Workspace information such as the workspace's URL, nickname, and authentication details are stored in a hidden file under your user directory on your local machine. For example, on Mac and Linux systems, this information will be written to a local `~/.databrickscfg` file under the user's home directory:

```
; The profile defined in the DEFAULT section is to be used as a fallback when no
  profile is explicitly specified.
[DEFAULT]
host       = https://<dev-workspace>.cloud.databricks.com
cluster_id = 01234567890
auth_type  = databricks-cli

[TEST_ENV]
host       = https://<test-workspace>.cloud.databricks.com
auth_type  = databricks-cli

[PROD_ENV]
host       = https://<prod-workspace>.cloud.databricks.com
cluster_id = 01234567890
auth_type  = databricks-cli
~
~
~
~
~
~
~
~
~
"~/.databrickscfg" 14L, 486B
```

Figure 9.4 – Example of multiple Databricks profiles saved to a local configuration file

You can quickly switch between different Databricks workspaces by passing the `--profile <profile_nickname>` argument using CLI commands. For example, the following command will apply a DAB to a workspace saved under the `TEST_ENV` profile:

```
$ databricks bundle deploy --profile TEST_ENV
```

U2M authentication was designed strictly for development purposes. For production scenarios, this type of authentication is not recommended as it can't be automated and doesn't restrict access to the least set of privileges necessary. In these cases, M2M authentication is recommended.

Let's take a look at this alternative authentication type for when you're automating your DAB deployment in production scenarios.

Machine-to-machine authentication

M2M authentication doesn't involve a human, per se. This type of authentication was designed for fully automated CI/CD workflows. Furthermore, this type of authentication pairs well with version control systems such as GitHub, Bitbucket, and Azure DevOps.

M2M requires the use of service principals to abstract the generation of OAuth tokens. Furthermore, service principals give automated tools and scripts API-only access to Databricks resources, providing greater security than using users or groups. For this reason, service principals are an ideal scenario for production environments.

M2M requires a Databricks account admin to create a service principal and generate an OAuth token from the Databricks account console. Once an OAuth token has been generated under the service principal's identity, the token can be used to populate environment variables such as `DATABRICKS_HOST`, `DATABRICKS_CLIENT_ID`, and `DATABRICKS_CLIENT_SECRET`, which are used in automated build and deployment tools such as GitHub Actions or Azure DevOps.

Initializing an asset bundle using templates

DABs also come with project templates, which allow developers to quickly create a new bundle using predefined settings. DAB templates contain predefined artifacts and settings for commonly deployed Databricks projects. For example, the following command will initialize a local DAB project:

```
$ databricks bundle init
```

From the CLI, the user is prompted to choose a DAB template:

```
demo % databricks bundle init
Search: █
? Template to use:
  default-python (The default Python template for Notebooks / Delta Live Tables / Workflows)
  mlops-stacks
  custom...
```

Figure 9.5 – Initializing a new DAB project using templates from the Databricks CLI

At the time of writing, DABs come with four templates to choose from: `default-python`, `default-sql`, `dbt-sql`, and `mlops-stacks` (`https://docs.databricks.com/en/dev-tools/bundles/templates.html`). However, you also have the option to create organization templates and generate artifacts as a reusable project bundle.

Now that we have a good understanding of the basics of DABs, let's put together everything that we've learned so far and deploy a few resources to a Databricks workspace.

Hands-on exercise – deploying your first DAB

In this hands-on exercise, we're going to create a Python-based asset bundle and deploy a simple Databricks workflow that runs a DLT pipeline in a target workspace.

Let's begin by creating a local directory that we'll be using to create the project scaffolding for our DAB. For example, the following command will create a new directory under the user's home directory:

```
$ mkdir -p ~/chapter9/dabs/
```

Next, navigate to the newly created project directory:

```
$ cd ~/chapter9/dabs
```

Generate a new OAuth token using U2M authentication by entering the following command and completing the **single sign-on (SSO)** login when you're redirected to a browser window:

```
$ databricks auth login
```

Now that our directory has been created and we've authenticated with our target workspace, let's use the Databricks CLI to initialize an empty DAB project. Enter the following command to bring up the prompt for choosing a DAB template:

```
$ databricks bundle init
```

Next, choose default-python from the template chooser prompt. Enter a meaningful name for your project, such as my_first_dab. When prompted to select a notebook stub, select No. Select Yes when you're prompted to include a sample DLT pipeline. Finally, select No when you're prompted to add a sample Python library. The project scaffolding will be created, at which point you can list the directory's contents so that you can have a glance at the generated artifacts:

```
$ cd ./my_first_dab  # a new dir will be created
$ ls -la             # list the project artifacts
```

To navigate to the newly created project files more easily, open the project directory using your favorite code editor, such as VS Code:

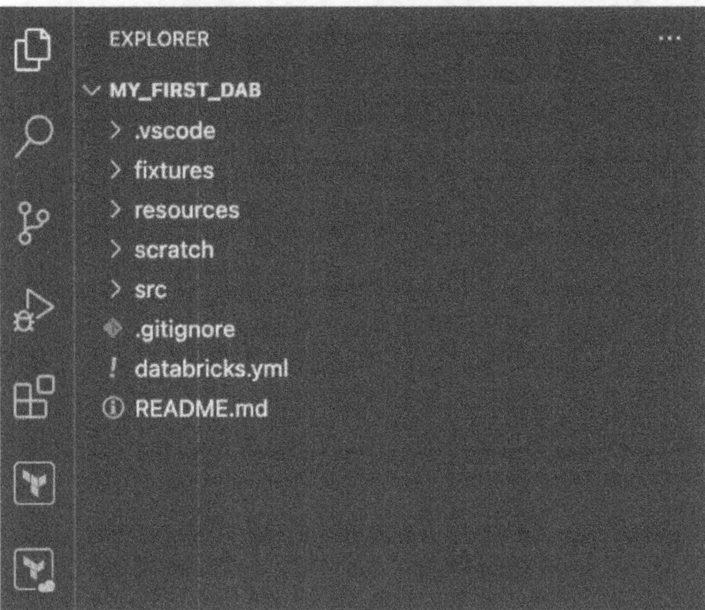

Figure 9.6 – Generated DAB project scaffolding using the default-python template, viewed from VS Code

Go ahead and explore the subdirectories of the generated DAB project for yourself. You should notice a couple of important directories and files:

- `src`: This directory contains the DLT pipeline definition as a notebook file.

- `resources`: DABs can be decomposed into multiple YAML files that pertain to a single resource or a subset of resources. This directory contains the resource definitions for a DLT pipeline and a workflow definition for running the pipeline, including the schedule, notebook task definition, and job cluster attributes.

- `databricks.yml`: This is the main entry point and definition of our DAB. This tells the Databricks CLI what resources to deploy and how to deploy them, and specifies target workspace information.

- `README.md`: This is the project README file and contains helpful information on the different sections of the project, as well as instructions on how to deploy or undeploy the resources.

Open the `dlt_pipeline.ipynb` notebook contained under the `src` directory. Notice that the notebook defines two datasets – a view that reads raw, unprocessed JSON files from the NYC Taxi dataset and a table that filters the view based on rows with a `fare_amount` value of less than 30.

Next, open the `databricks.yml` file. You'll notice that this file has three main sections: `bundle`, `include`, and `targets`.

For simplicity's sake, under the `targets` mapping, remove all sections except for the `dev` section. We'll only be deploying to a development environment for this exercise.

Finally, ensure that the `dev` target is pointing to the correct development workspace. Your `databricks.yml` file should look similar to this:

```
bundle:
  name: my_first_dab
include:
  -resources/*.yml
targets:
  mode: development
  default: true
  workspace:
    host: https://<workspace_name>.cloud.databricks.com
```

Save the changes to the `databricks.yml` file and return to your Terminal window. Let's validate the changes to our DAB project by executing the `validate` command from the Databricks CLI:

```
$ databricks bundle validate
```

Now that our project has been modified to our liking, it's time to deploy the bundle to our development workspace. Execute the following command from your Databricks CLI:

```
$ databricks bundle deploy
```

The Databricks CLI will parse our DAB definition and deploy the resources to our development target. Log in to the development workspace and verify that a new workflow titled `[dev <username>]` `my_first_dab_job` has been created and your Databricks user is listed as the owner.

Congratulations! You've just created your first DAB and deployed it to a development workspace. You're well on your way to automating the deployment of data pipelines and other Databricks resources.

Let's test that the deployment was successful by executing a new run of the deployed workflow. From the same Databricks CLI, enter the following command. This will start an execution run of the newly created workflow and trigger an update of the DLT pipeline:

```
$ databricks bundle run
```

You may be prompted to select which resource to run. For this, select `my_first_dab_job`. If successful, you should see a confirmation message from the CLI that the workflow is currently running. Return to your Databricks workspace and verify that an execution run has indeed been started.

There may be certain scenarios where you need to undeploy resources from a target workspace. To undeploy the workflow and DLT pipeline definitions that were created earlier, we can use the `destroy` command in the Databricks CLI. Enter the following command to revert all changes that were created in this hands-on exercise. You'll need to confirm that you would like to permanently delete all resources:

```
$ databricks bundle destroy
```

So far, we've created a simple workflow and DLT pipeline defined in a source notebook in a target Databricks workspace. We've used a local code editor to author the DAB project and deployed the changes from our local machine. However, in production scenarios, you'll be collaborating with teams within your organization to author data pipelines and other Databricks resources that all work together to generate data products for your organization.

In the next section, we'll look at how we expand upon this simple exercise and work with team members to deploy Databricks resources such as workflows, notebooks, or DLT pipelines using automation tools.

Hands-on exercise – simplifying cross-team collaboration with GitHub Actions

Often, you'll be working across a team of data engineers working to deploy Databricks assets such as DLT pipelines, all-purpose clusters, or workflows, to name a few. In these scenarios, you'll likely be using a version control system such as GitHub, Bitbucket, or Azure DevOps to collaborate with members of a team.

DABs can be easily incorporated into your CI/CD pipelines. Let's look at how we can use GitHub Actions to automatically deploy changes made to our main branch of the code repository and automatically deploy the resource changes to our production Databricks workspace.

GitHub Actions is a feature in GitHub that allows users to implement a CI/CD workflow directly from a GitHub repository, making it simple to declare a workflow of actions to perform based on some triggering event, such as merging a feature branch into a master branch. Together with DABs, we can implement a robust, fully automated CI/CD pipeline that deploys changes that have been made to our Databricks code base. This enables our teams to be more agile, deploying changes as soon as they are available, allowing them to speed up the iterative development life cycle and quickly test changes.

Setting up the environment

In this hands-on exercise, we'll be creating a GitHub Action to automatically deploy changes to our Databricks workspace as soon as a branch is merged in our GitHub repository. Let's return to the example from earlier in this chapter. If you haven't already done so, you can clone the example from this chapter's GitHub repository: `https://github.com/PacktPublishing/Building-Modern-Data-Applications-Using-Databricks-Lakehouse/tree/main/chapter09`.

First, let's create a new private folder in the root of our repository – that is, `.github`. Within this folder, let's create another child folder called `workflows`. This nested directory structure is a special pattern whose presence will be automatically picked up by the GitHub repository and parsed as a GitHub Actions workflow. Within this folder, we'll define our GitHub Actions workflow, which also uses a YAML configuration file to declare a CI/CD workflow. Create a new YAML file called `dab_deployment_workflow.yml` within the `.github/workflows` folder.

Next, we'll open the workflow file in our favorite code editor so that it's easier to manipulate.

Configuring the GitHub Action

Let's begin by adding the basic structure to our GitHub Actions workflow file. Within the YAML file, we'll give the GitHub Actions workflow a user-friendly name, such as `DABs in Action`. Within this file, we'll also specify that whenever an approved pull request is merged into the main branch of our code repository, our CI/CD pipeline should be run. Copy and paste the following contents into the newly created file, `dab_deployment_workflow.yml`:

```
name: "DABs in Action"
on:
  push:
    branches:
        - main
```

Next, let's define a job within our GitHub Actions YAML file that will clone the GitHub repository, download the Databricks CLI, and deploy our DAB to our target Databricks workspace. Add the following job definition to the workflow file:

```
jobs:
  bundle-and-deploy:
    name: "DAB Deployment Job"
    runs-on: ubuntu-latest

    steps:
      - uses: actions/checkout@v3
      - uses: databricks/setup-cli@main
      - run: databricks bundle deploy --target prod
        working-directory: ./dabs
        env:
          DATABRICKS_TOKEN: ${{ secrets.DATABRICKS_SERVICE_PRINCIPAL_
TOKEN }}
```

You'll also notice that we've used the same Databricks CLI `bundle` command to deploy our Databricks resources as we did in the earlier example, using our local installation to deploy resources. Furthermore, under the `working-directory` parameter, we've specified that our DAB configuration file will be found at the root of our GitHub repository under the `dabs` folder. We've also leveraged GitHub Secrets (`https://docs.github.com/en/actions/security-for-github-actions/security-guides/using-secrets-in-github-actions#creating-secrets-for-a-repository`) to securely store the API token for authenticating with our target Databricks workspace, as well as followed the best practice of using a service principal (see the *User-to-machine authentication* section) to automate the deployment of our resources.

You'll recall that service principals are restricted to a subset of API calls and follow the best practice of least privilege, whereas a user account would provide more privileges than are necessary. Furthermore, our users can come and go from our organization, making maintenance activities such as user deprovisioning a headache.

Testing the workflow

Now that we've defined when our CI/CD pipeline should be triggered and the workflow job responsible for deploying our DAB to our target workspace, we can test the GitHub Actions workflow.

Let's add a section to our existing GitHub Actions workflow file that will trigger the `my_first_dab_job` Databricks workflow that we created in the previous example. You'll also notice that, under the `needs` parameter, we declare a dependency on `DAB Deployment Job`, which must be completed before we can execute a run of the Databricks workflow. In other words, we can't test the changes without deploying them first. Add the following job definition below the `bundle-and-deploy` job in the workflow file:

```
run-workflow:
  name: "Test the deployed pipeline workflow"
  runs-on: ubuntu-latest
  needs:
    - bundle-and-deploy
  steps:
    - uses: actions/checkout@v3
    - uses: databricks/setup-cli@main
    - run: databricks bundle run my_first_dab_job
      working-directory: ./dabs
      env:
        DATABRICKS_TOKEN: ${{ secrets.DATABRICKS_SERVICE_PRINCIPAL_
TOKEN }}
```

Save the GitHub Actions workflow file. Now, let's test the changes by opening a new pull request on our GitHub repository and merging the pull request into the main branch of the repository.

First, create a new feature branch using `git`:

```
$ git checkout -b increaseAutoScaling
```

Next, open the DAB configuration file for the Databricks workflow in a code editor. Update the autoscaling size of our job cluster from four worker nodes to five. Save the file and commit the changes to the branch. Finally, push the changes to the remote repository. Using a web browser, navigate to the GitHub repository and create a new pull request in GitHub. Approve the changes and merge the branch into the main branch. Ensure that the GitHub Actions workflow is triggered and that the code changes have been deployed to the target Databricks workspace. You should also see that a new run of the `my_first_dab_job` Databricks workflow has been executed by the GitHub Actions workflow.

Now that we've seen how easy it is to incorporate our DABs into a CI/CD pipeline, let's expand on this example to see how DABs can assist us when we want to deploy different versions of our code base to a Databricks workspace.

Versioning and maintenance

DABs make it simple to deploy changes to different environments iteratively. There may be scenarios where you might want to experiment with different changes and document that those changes come from a particular version of your repository. The top-level `bundle` mapping permits users to specify a repository URL and branch name to annotate different versions of your code base that are deployed to target Databricks workspaces. This is a great way to document that a bundle deployment comes from a particular repository and feature branch. For example, the following code annotates that an asset bundle uses an experimental feature branch as the project source:

```
bundle:
  name: new-feature-dab
  git:
    origin_url: https://github.com/<username>/<repo_name>
    branch: my_experimental_feature_br
```

As another example, DABs make it simple to automate and document regular maintenance activities such as upgrading Databricks runtimes to the latest release. This is a great way to experiment with beta versions of the runtime and test compatibility with existing Databricks workflows. DABs can be used to automate the manual deployment and testing process, and even roll back changes if workflows begin to fail, for example.

Summary

In this chapter, we covered how to automate the deployment of your Databricks resources using DABs. We saw how integral the Databricks CLI was in creating new bundles from preconfigured templates, authenticating the CLI tool with target Databricks workspaces, triggering Databricks workflow runs, and managing the end-to-end bundle life cycle. We also saw how we can quickly iterate on design and testing by using a development mode inside of our DAB configuration file.

In the next chapter, we'll conclude with the skills necessary to monitor your data applications in a production environment. We'll touch on key features in the Databricks Data Intelligence Platform, including alerting, viewing the pipeline event log, and measuring statistical metrics using Lakehouse Monitoring.

10

Monitoring Data Pipelines in Production

In the previous chapters, we learned how to build, configure, and deploy data pipelines using the Databricks Data Intelligence Platform. To round off managing data pipelines for the lakehouse, in this final chapter of the book, we'll dive into the crucial task of monitoring data pipelines in production. We'll learn how to leverage comprehensive monitoring techniques directly from the Databricks Data Intelligence Platform to track pipeline health, pipeline performance, and data quality, to name a few. We will also implement a few real-world examples through hands-on exercises. Lastly, we'll look at the best practices for ensuring that your data pipelines run smoothly, enabling timely issue detection and resolution, and ensuring the delivery of reliable and accurate data for your analytics and business needs.

In this chapter, we're going to cover the following main topics:

- Introduction to data pipeline monitoring
- Pipeline health and performance monitoring
- Data quality monitoring
- Best practices for production failure resolution
- Hands-on exercise – setting up a webhook alert when a job runs longer than expected

Technical requirements

To follow along with the examples provided in this chapter, you'll need Databricks workspace permissions to create and start an all-purpose cluster so that you can import and execute the chapter's accompanying notebooks. It's also recommended that your Databricks user be elevated to a workspace administrator so that you can create and edit alert destinations. All code samples can be downloaded from this chapter's GitHub repository at `https://github.com/PacktPublishing/ Building-Modern-Data-Applications-Using-Databricks-Lakehouse/tree/ main/chapter10`. This chapter will create and run several new notebooks, estimated to consume around 10-15 **Databricks Units** (**DBUs**).

Introduction to data pipeline monitoring

As data teams deploy data pipelines into production environments, being able to detect processing errors, delays, or data quality issues as soon as they happen can make a huge impact on catching and correcting issues before they have a chance to cascade to downstream systems and processes. As such, the environment that data teams build and deploy their pipelines in should be able to monitor them and alert them when problems arise.

Exploring ways to monitor data pipelines

There are several ways that data teams can monitor their data pipelines in production from within the Databricks Data Intelligence Platform. For example, data teams can manually observe updates regarding their data pipeline by doing the following:

- Viewing pipeline status from the **Delta Live Tables** (**DLT**) UI

- Querying pipeline information from the DLT event log

While these manual means provide a way to quickly view the latest status of a data pipeline in an ad hoc manner, it's certainly not a scalable solution, particularly as your data team adds more and more pipelines. Instead, organizations turn to more automated mechanisms. For instance, many organizations choose to leverage the built-in notification system in the Databricks Data Intelligence Platform. Notifications are prevalent in many objects within the platform. For example, data administrators can configure notifications in the following scenarios to alert data teams about a change in status pertaining to a particular Databricks resource:

- DLT pipeline (either on update or on flow)

- Databricks workflow (at the top-most job level)

- Databricks workflow task (finer-grained notification than the preceding option)

While these notifications can be helpful to alert teams about events or status changes during data processing, data teams also need mechanisms for alerting each other about issues in the contents of the data landing into the enterprise lakehouse.

Using DBSQL Alerts to notify data validity

The Databricks Data Intelligence Platform can create alert notifications driven by a query within the DBSQL portion of the platform called **DBSQL Alerts**. DBSQL Alerts can be a useful tool to alert data teams about the data landing in their enterprise lakehouse. DBSQL Alerts operate by specifying a particular query outcome condition that must be met for the data to be considered valid. However, if a particular condition in an Alert is violated, such as an order amount crossing above a certain dollar amount threshold, for example, then the system will trigger a notification to send to an alert destination. The following diagram depicts a DBSQL Alert that notifies recipients via email when there are sales orders exceeding a specific dollar amount – in this case, that's $10,000. In this example, the query is a max aggregation, the triggering condition is when the max aggregation exceeds $10,000, and the alert destination is an email address.

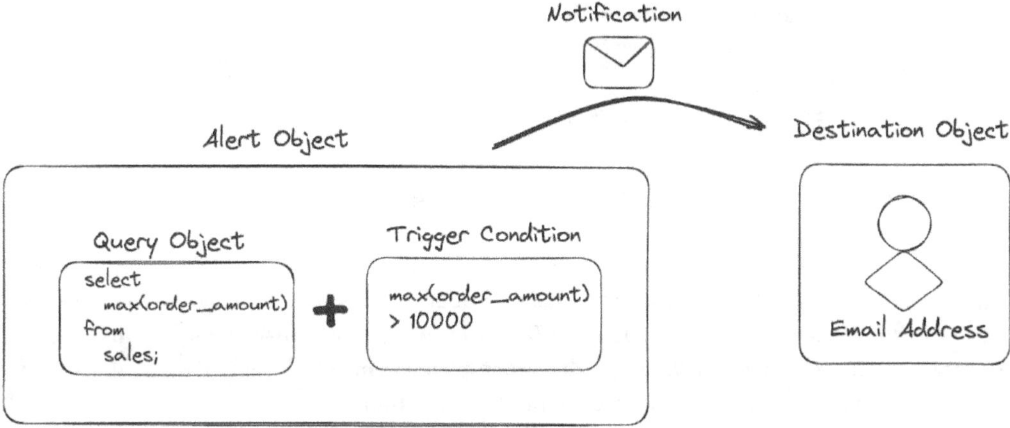

Figure 10.1 – Configuration of a DBSQL Alert notifying recipients via email

Furthermore, DBSQL Alerts can be scheduled to execute on a repeated schedule, for example once every hour. This is an excellent way to automate *data validation* checks on the contents of your datasets using the built-in mechanism from within the Databricks Data Intelligence Platform. The following screenshot is an example of how alerts can be used to schedule a data validation query on a repeated schedule and notify data teams when a particular condition or set of conditions has been violated.

20_percent_deposit_required ☆

UNKNOWN

Last triggered at   None

Query   Max Order Amount ↗

Trigger condition

Value column		Operator	Threshold value
max(order_amount)	First row	>	10000.00

When query result has no rows, set state to OK

Notifications

When alert is triggered

Send notification each time alert is evaluated, until back to normal.

When alert returns back to normal

☑ Send notification

Template   Set to default notification template.

Figure 10.2 – Configuration of an Alert triggering condition

Another mechanism for monitoring data pipelines in production is through workflow notifications. Within the Databricks Data Intelligence Platform, notification messages can be delivered to enterprise messaging platforms, such as Slack or Microsoft Teams, or to incident management systems such as PagerDuty. Later in the chapter, we'll explore how to implement an HTTP webhook-based delivery destination, which is popular in web services architecture environments.

There are two types of notifications that can be sent from within a particular workflow – job status and task status. Job status notifications are high-level statuses about the overall success or failure of a particular workflow. However, you can also configure notifications to be sent to monitoring destinations at the task level, such as if you'd like to monitor when tasks within a workflow are retried.

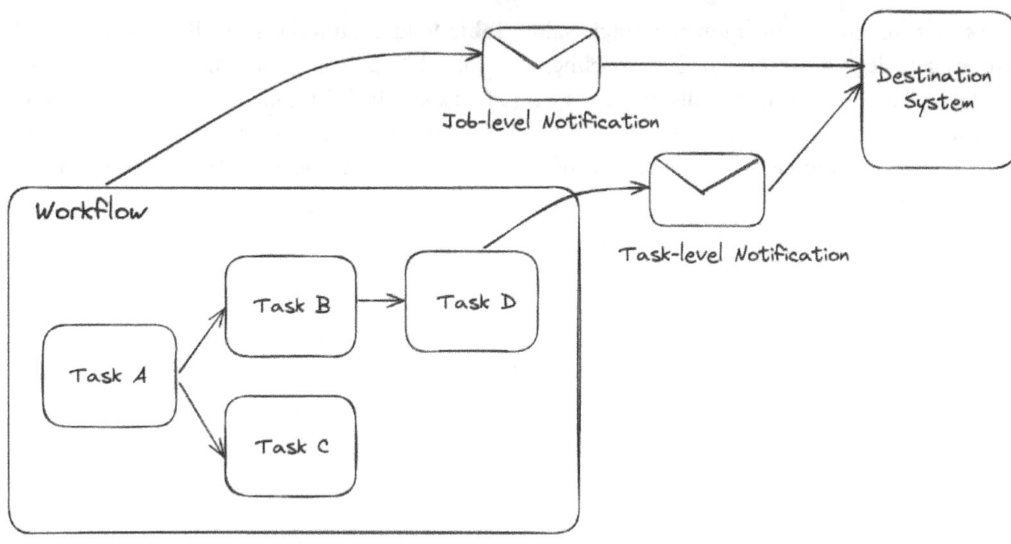

Figure 10.3 – Configuring job- and task-level notifications

While alert notifications are a great way to automate the notification of team members when problems arise, data teams also need to monitor the health of data pipelines in a periodic and ad hoc manner. We will discuss this in the next section.

Pipeline health and performance monitoring

The Databricks Data Intelligence Platform provides a location for data teams to query the status of data pipelines called the event log. The event log contains a history of all events that pertain to a particular DLT pipeline. In particular, the event log will contain an event feed with a list of event objects with recorded metadata about the following:

- What type of event occurred

- A unique identifier of the event

- Timestamps of when the event occurred

- A high-level description of the event

- Fine-grained details about the event

- An event-level indication (`INFO`, `WARN`, `ERROR`, or `METRICS`)

- The origin source of the event

Unlike scalar functions, which return a single value, **Table Valued Functions** (**TVFs**) are functions that return a table as the result. For DLT pipelines that publish to a catalog and schema within Unity Catalog, the Databricks Data Intelligence Platform offers a special TVF called `event_log()` to query comprehensive information regarding a given DLT pipeline. The `event_log()` function can take one of two arguments as input: a fully qualified table name of a pipeline dataset or a pipeline ID as an argument.

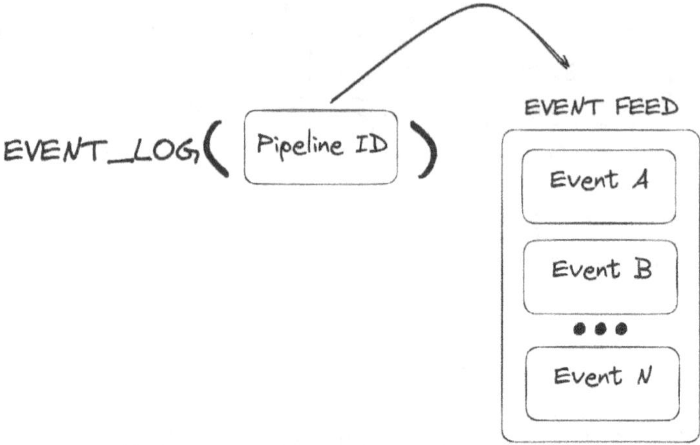

Figure 10.4 – The event_log() TVF returns a list of events that occurred

The `event_log()` function will retrieve information about a given DLT pipeline, including the following:

- Outcomes of data quality checks (expectations)
- Auditing information
- Pipeline update status
- Data lineage information

A common approach to make it easier for data stewards to query events for a particular DLT pipeline is to register a view alongside the datasets for a particular pipeline. This allows users to conveniently reference the event log results in subsequent queries. The following SQL **Data Definition Language** (**DDL**) statement will create a view that retrieves the event log for a DLT pipeline with the `my_dlt_pipeline_id` ID:

```
CREATE VIEW my_pipeline_event_log_vw AS
SELECT
  *
FROM
  event_log('<my_dlt_pipeline_id>');
```

Sometimes, the event log for a particular pipeline can grow too large, making it difficult for data stewards to quickly summarize the latest status updates. Instead, data teams can narrow the event log feed even further to a particular dataset within a DLT pipeline. For example, data teams can create a view on top of a specific dataset to capture all the events using the `table()` function and provide a fully-qualified table name as an argument to the function. The following SQL DDL statement will create a view that retrieves the event log for a dataset called `my_gold_table`:

```
CREATE VIEW my_gold_table_event_log_vw AS
SELECT
  *
FROM
  event_log(table(my_catalog.my_schema.my_gold_table));
```

The `event_log()` TVF function provides data teams with great visibility into the actions performed on a particular DLT pipeline and dataset making it easy to implement end-to-end observability and auditability.

> **Important note**
>
> Presently, if a DLT pipeline is configured to publish output datasets to Unity Catalog, then only the owner of a particular DLT pipeline can query the views. To share access to the event logs, the pipeline owner must save a copy of the event log feed to another table within Unity Catalog and grant access to other users or groups.

Let's look at how we might leverage the `event_log()` function to query the data quality events for a particular DLT pipeline.

Hands-on exercise – querying data quality events for a dataset

> **Important note**
>
> For the following exercise, you will need to use a shared, all-purpose cluster or a Databricks SQL warehouse to query the event log. Furthermore, the event log is only available to query DLT pipelines that have been configured to store datasets in Unity Catalog. The event log will not be found for DLT pipelines that have been configured to store datasets in the legacy Hive Metastore.

Data quality metrics are stored in the event log as a serialized JSON string. We'll need to parse the JSON string into a different data structure so that we can easily query data quality events from the event log. Let's use the `from_json()` SQL function to parse the serialized JSON string for our data quality expectations. We'll need to specify a schema as an argument to instruct Spark how to parse the JSON string into a deserialized data structure – specifically, an array of structs that contain information about the expectation name, dataset name, number of passing records, and number of failing records. Lastly, we'll use the `explode()` SQL function to transform the array of expectation structs into a new row for each expectation.

We can leverage the previously defined views to monitor the ongoing data quality of the datasets within our DLT pipeline. Let's create another view pertaining to the data quality of our DLT pipeline:

```sql
CREATE OR REPLACE TEMPORARY VIEW taxi_trip_pipeline_data_quality_vw AS
SELECT
  timestamp,
  event_type,
  message,
  data_quality.dataset,
  data_quality.name AS expectation_name,
  data_quality.passed_records AS num_passed_records,
  data_quality.failed_records AS num_failed_records
FROM
  (
    SELECT
      event_type,
      message,
      timestamp,
      explode(
        from_json(
          details :flow_progress.data_quality.expectations,
          "ARRAY<
            STRUCT<
              name: STRING,
              dataset: STRING,
              passed_records: INT,
              failed_records: INT
            >
          >"
        )
      ) AS data_quality
    FROM
      my_table_event_log_vw
  );
```

Several common questions that are posed by data teams include: "How many records were processed?", "How many records failed data quality validation?", or "What was the percentage of passing records versus failing records?". Let's take the previous example a step further and summarize the high-level data quality metrics per dataset in our pipeline. Let's count the total number of rows having an expectation applied, as well as the percentage of passing records versus failing records for each of the datasets in our DLT pipeline:

```
SELECT
  timestamp,
  dataset,
  sum(num_passed_records + num_failed_records)
    AS total_expectations_evaluated,
  avg(
    num_passed_records /
    (num_passed_records + num_failed_records)
  ) * 100 AS avg_pass_rate,
  avg(
    num_failed_records /
    (num_passed_records + num_failed_records)
  ) * 100 AS avg_fail_rate
FROM
  taxi_trip_pipeline_data_quality_vw
GROUP BY
  timestamp,
  dataset;
```

We get the following output:

	event_type	message	dataset	expectation_name	num_passed_records	num_failed_records
1	flow_progress	Completed a streaming update of 'raw_taxi_trip_data'.	raw_taxi_trip_data	valid_trip_distance	500000	0
2	flow_progress	Completed a streaming update of 'raw_taxi_trip_data'.	raw_taxi_trip_data	valid_trip_amount	500000	0
3	flow_progress	Flow 'taxi_trip_silver' has COMPLETED.	taxi_trip_silver	valid_fare_amount_usd	10000	0
4	flow_progress	Flow 'taxi_trip_silver' has COMPLETED.	taxi_trip_silver	valid_trip_distance_km	10000	0
5	flow_progress	Flow 'taxi_trip_silver' has COMPLETED.	taxi_trip_silver	valid_taxes_amount_usd	10000	0
6	flow_progress	Flow 'taxi_trip_silver' has COMPLETED.	taxi_trip_silver	valid_trip_distance_miles	10000	0

6 rows | 1.83 seconds runtime

Figure 10.5 – Events captured in the DLT event log

As you can see, the `event_log()` function makes it simple for data teams to query comprehensive information regarding a given DLT pipeline. Not only can data teams query the status of a pipeline update but they can also query the status of the quality data landing into their lakehouse. Still, data teams need a way to automate the notification of failing data quality checks at runtime, as is the scenario when the data accuracy of downstream reports is critical to the business. Let's look closer at this in the following section.

Data quality monitoring

Ongoing monitoring of the data quality of datasets within your lakehouse is critical for the success of business-critical data applications deployed to production. Take, for example, the impact that a sudden ingestion of null values on a joined column might have on downstream reports that rely on joining together upstream datasets. Suddenly, **business intelligence** (**BI**) reports might refresh, but the data may appear stale or outdated. By automatically detecting data quality issues as soon as they arise, your data team can be alerted of potential issues and take immediate action to intervene and correct possible data corruption or even data loss.

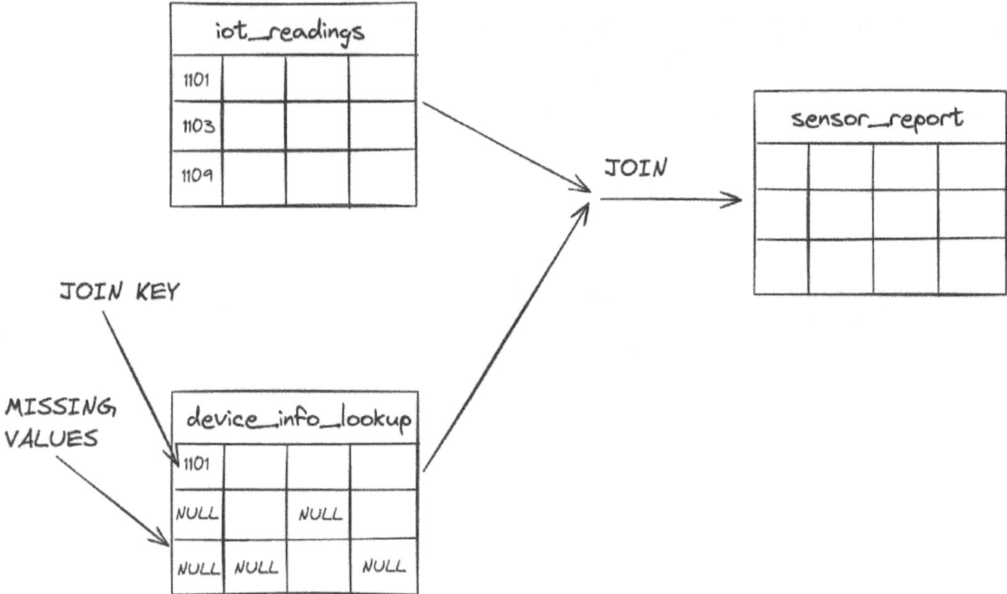

Figure 10.6 – Detecting issues early is important to ensure the quality of downstream processes

Introducing Lakehouse Monitoring

Lakehouse Monitoring, a recent feature of the Databricks Data Intelligence Platform, gives data teams the ability to track and monitor the data quality of data and other assets in the lakehouse. Data teams can automatically measure the statistical distribution of data across columns, number of null values, minimum, maximum, median column values, and other statistical properties. With Lakehouse Monitoring, data teams can automatically detect major problems in datasets such as data skews or missing values, and alert team members of issues so that they can take appropriate action.

Lakehouse Monitoring is most useful when used to monitor the data quality of Delta tables, views, materialized views, and streaming tables. It can even be used in **Machine Learning** (**ML**) pipelines, measuring the statistical summaries of datasets and triggering alert notifications as soon as data drift is detected. Furthermore, Lakehouse Monitoring can be customized to be fine- or coarse-grained in the monitoring metrics.

Lakehouse Monitoring begins with the creation of a monitor object, which is then attached to a data asset such as a Delta table in your lakehouse. Behind the scenes, the monitor object will create two additional tables inside your lakehouse to capture statistical measures of the corresponding Delta table or other data assets.

The monitoring tables are then used to power a Dashboard, which can be used by data teams and other stakeholders to get a view into the real-time data insights of the quality of your data in the lakehouse.

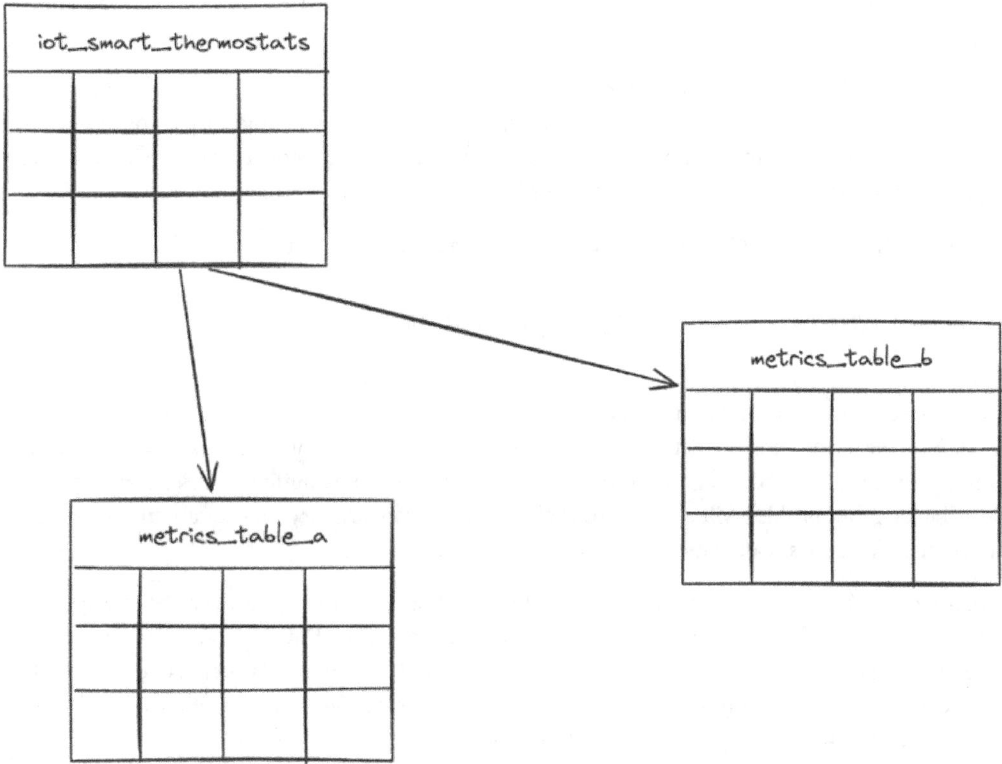

Figure 10.7 – A lakehouse monitor will create two metrics tables for the monitored data asset

A lakehouse monitor can be configured to measure different aspects of a data asset, which is also referred to as a profile type. There are three *monitor profile types* that can be created:

- **Snapshot**: This is a generic, yet robust monitor. It's useful to monitor data quality and other metrics of a table.

- **Time series**: It's useful for time series datasets. It's used to monitor the data quality over time period windows.

- **Inference**: It's useful to compare the quality of an ML model inference versus the input over a window of time periods.

In this chapter, we'll only be covering the time series and snapshot types. Discussing inference is out of the scope of this book, but you are encouraged to explore how Lakehouse Monitoring can be helpful for ML use cases (`https://docs.databricks.com/en/lakehouse-monitoring/fairness-bias.html`).

Monitors can also be created that compare the statistical metrics of a table versus a baseline table. This can be useful in scenarios such as comparing the relative humidity of smart thermostat devices for this week as compared to last week, or comparing the number of recorded sales in a particular dataset for a monthly sales report versus last month's report, for example.

Let's look at a practical example of using a lakehouse monitor in a lakehouse.

Hands-on exercise – creating a lakehouse monitor

In this hands-on exercise, we're going to create a lakehouse monitor for measuring the data quality of a target Delta table. Although our Delta table does contain timestamp information, we'll choose a *snapshot profile* to monitor the data quality of a target Delta table in our lakehouse. Recall that the snapshot profile is a generic lakehouse monitor that also proves to be quite versatile, as mentioned earlier. The snapshot profiler will allow us to measure standard summary metrics about our dataset or insert custom business calculations around the data quality.

Like many resources in the Databricks Data Intelligence Platform, there are a variety of ways that you can create a new lakehouse monitor. For example, you can use the Databricks UI, the Databricks REST API, the Databricks CLI (covered in *Chapter 9*), or automation tools such as Terraform, to name a few. Perhaps the simplest mechanism for creating a new monitor is through the UI. In this hands-on exercise, we're going to use the Databricks UI to create the lakehouse monitor. This is a great way to get started experimenting with Lakehouse Monitoring and with different data quality metrics to measure your datasets. However, it's recommended in production scenarios to migrate your lakehouse monitors to an automated build tool such as **Databricks Asset Bundles (DABs)** (covered in *Chapter 9*) or Terraform (covered in *Chapter 8*).

If you haven't done so already, you can clone the accompanying code resources for this chapter at `https://github.com/PacktPublishing/Building-Modern-Data-Applications-Using-Databricks-Lakehouse/tree/main/chapter10`.

The first step is to generate a target Delta table, which we would like to monitor the data quality. Clone or import the data generator notebook or create a new notebook with the following code generator source code.

In the first cell of the notebook, we'll leverage the `%pip` magic command to download and install the `dbldatagen` Python library, which is used to generate sample data:

```
%pip install dbldatagen==0.4.0
```

Next, we'll define a helper function for generating a synthetic dataset containing smart thermostat readings over time:

```python
import dbldatagen as dg
from pyspark.sql.types import IntegerType, FloatType, TimestampType


def generate_smart_thermostat_readings():
    """Generates synthetics thermostat readings"""
    ds = (
        dg.DataGenerator(
            spark,
            name="smart_thermostat_dataset",
            rows=10000,
            partitions=4)
        .withColumn("device_id", IntegerType(),
                    minValue=1000000, maxValue=2000000)
        .withColumn("temperature", FloatType(),
                    minValue=10.0, maxValue=1000.0)
        .withColumn("humidity", FloatType(),
                    minValue=0.1, maxValue=1000.0)
        .withColumn("battery_level", FloatType(),
                    minValue=-50.0, maxValue=150.0)
        .withColumn("reading_ts", TimestampType(), random=False)
    )
    return ds.build()


# Generate the data using dbldatagen
df = generate_smart_thermostat_readings()
df.display()
```

Finally, we'll save the newly created dataset as a Delta table in Unity Catalog:

```
(df.write
    .format("delta")
    .mode("overwrite")
    .saveAsTable(FULLY_QUALIFIED_TABLE_NAME))
```

Now that our Delta table has been created in our lakehouse, let's use the UI in the Catalog Explorer to create a new monitor.

From the left-side navigation bar, click on the Catalog Explorer icon. Next, navigate to the catalog created for this chapter by expanding the list of catalogs or using the **Search** field to filter the results. Click on the schema that was created for this chapter. Finally, click on the Delta table that was created earlier by our data generator notebook. Click on the data quality tab that is appropriately titled **Quality**.

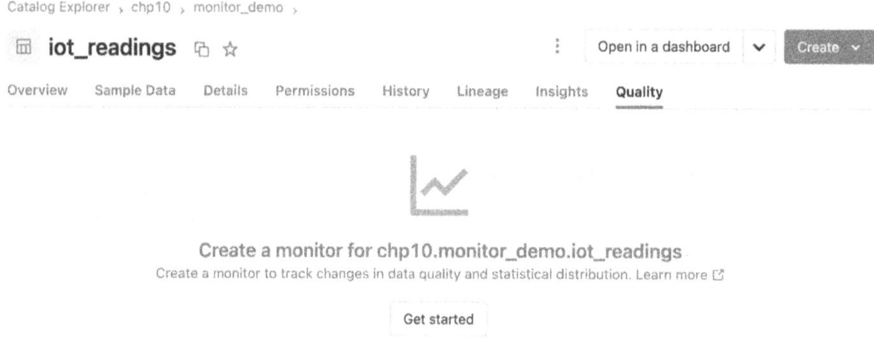

Figure 10.8 – A new monitor can be created directly from the Databricks UI

Next, click on the **Get started** button to begin creating a new monitor. A pop-up dialog will open, prompting you to select the profile type for the monitor, as well as advanced configuration options such as the schedule, notification delivery, and workspace directory for storing the generated dashboard.

Click the dropdown for the profile type and select the option for generating a snapshot profile.

Next, click on the **Advanced Options** section to expand the dialog form. The UI will allow users to capture dataset metrics, either manually or by defining a cron schedule for executing the metrics calculations on a repeated schedule. You'll notice that the dialog provides the flexibility to define the schedule using a traditional cron syntax, or by selecting the date and time drop-down menus in the dialog form. For this hands-on exercise, we'll choose the former option and refresh the monitoring metrics manually through the click of a button.

Optionally, you can choose to have notifications about the success or failure of monitoring metrics calculations sent via email to a list of email recipients. You can add up to five email addresses for notifications to be delivered to. Ensure that your user email address is listed in the **Notifications** section and that the checkbox is checked to receive a notification for failures during the metrics collection.

If you recall from earlier, a lakehouse monitor will create two metrics tables. We'll need to provide a location in Unity Catalog to store these metrics tables. Under the **Metrics** section, add the catalog and schema name created for this chapter's hands-on exercise. For example, enter `chp10.monitor_demo`.

The last item that we need to specify is a workspace location for storing the generated dashboard for our lakehouse monitor. By default, the generated assets will be stored under the user's home directory, for example, `/Users/<user_email_address>/databricks_lakehouse_monitoring`. For this hands-on exercise, we'll accept the default location.

We're ready to create our monitor! Click the **Create** button to create the lakehouse monitor for our Delta table.

Since we haven't configured a schedule for our lakehouse monitor, we'll need to manually execute a metrics collection. Back in the Catalog Explorer, under the **Quality** tab of our Delta table, click on the **Refresh metrics** button to manually trigger a metrics collection.

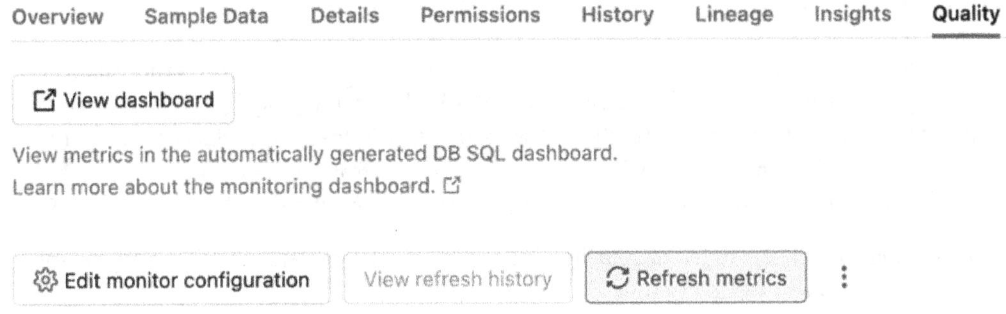

Figure 10.9 – Monitoring metrics can be manually triggered from the Catalog Explorer UI

An update of the table metrics will be triggered to execute and will take up to a few minutes to complete. Once the update has completed, click the **View dashboard** button to view the metrics captured. Congratulations! You've created your first lakehouse monitor and you're well on your way to implementing robust and automated data quality observability for your data team.

Now that we have an idea of how to alert our team members when production issues arise, let's turn our attention to a few approaches to resolve failures in production deployments.

Best practices for production failure resolution

The DLT framework was designed with failure resolution in mind. For example, DLT will automatically respond to three types of common pipeline failures:

- Databricks Runtime regressions (covered in *Chapter 2*)
- Update processing failures
- Data transaction failure

Let's look at update failures and data transaction failures in greater detail.

Handling pipeline update failures

The DLT framework was designed with robust error handling in mind. During a pipeline update, the framework will attempt to apply the most recent updates to tables defined in the dataflow graph. If a processing error occurs, the framework will classify the error as either a retriable error or a non-retriable error. A retriable error means that the framework has classified the runtime error as likely an issue caused by the current set of conditions. For example, a system error would not be considered a retriable error, since it relates to the runtime environment that execution retries will not solve. However, a network timeout would be a retriable error, since it could be impacted by the temporary set of network environment conditions. By default, the DLT framework retries a pipeline update twice if it detects a *retriable* error.

Recovering from table transaction failure

Due to the nature of the Delta Lake transaction log, changes to a dataset are atomic, meaning that they can only happen if a table transaction (such as a **Data Manipulation Language** (**DML**) statement) is committed to the transaction log. As a result, if a transaction fails in the middle of its execution, then the entire transaction is abandoned, thereby preventing the dataset from entering a non-deterministic state requiring data teams to intervene and manually reverse the data changes.

Now that we understand how to handle pipeline failures in production, let's cement the topics from this chapter through a real-world example.

Hands-on exercise – setting up a webhook alert when a job runs longer than expected

In this hands-on exercise, we'll be creating a custom HTTP webhook that will notify an HTTP endpoint about the timeout status of a scheduled job in Databricks.

A webhook alert is a notification mechanism in the Databricks Data Intelligence Platform that enables data teams to monitor their data pipeline by automatically publishing the outcome of a particular job execution run. For example, you can receive notifications about the successful run, execution state, and run failures.

> **Why are we using a workflow rather than a DLT pipeline directly?**
>
> In practice, a DLT pipeline will often be just one of many dependencies in a complete data product. Databricks workflows are a popular orchestration tool that can prepare dependencies, run one or more DLT pipelines, and execute downstream tasks as well. In this exercise, we'll be configuring notifications from a Databricks workflow, as opposed to notifications directly from a DLT pipeline, to simulate a typical production scenario.

Let's start by navigating to your Databricks workspace and logging into your workspace. Next, let's create a new workflow. We'll start by navigating to the Workflow UI by clicking on the workflows icon from the workspace navigation bar on the left-hand side. Give the workflow a meaningful name, such as `Production Monitoring Demo`.

If you haven't done so already, you can download the sample notebooks for this chapter's exercise at `https://github.com/PacktPublishing/Building-Modern-Data-Applications-Using-Databricks-Lakehouse/tree/main/chapter10`. We'll be using the IoT device data generator notebook, titled `04a-IoT Device Data Generator.py`, and the IoT Device DLT pipeline definition notebook, which is titled `04b-IoT Device Data Pipeline.py`.

In the Workflow UI, create a new workflow with two tasks. The first task will prepare an input dataset using the `04a-IoT Device Data Generator.py` notebook; the second task will execute a DLT pipeline that reads the generated data using the `04b-IoT Device Data Pipeline.py` notebook.

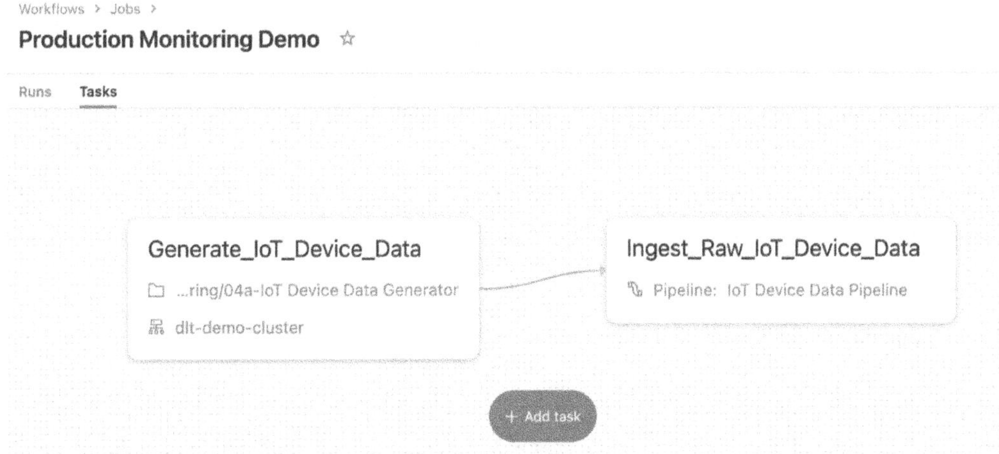

Figure 10.10 – The workflow will generate IoT device data and execute a DLT pipeline update

Now that our workflow has been created, let's imagine, for example, that our pipeline is taking longer than expected to execute. Wouldn't it be helpful to be notified if there are potential processing delays, so that your data team can investigate immediately or prevent a long-running job from running up a large cloud bill due to a processing mishap?

Fortunately, the Databricks Data Intelligence Platform makes it simple to configure this type of notification. Let's create a timeout threshold for our workflow. This will automatically notify our HTTP webhook endpoint that our workflow is taking longer than expected to execute. Once our workflow has exceeded this timeout threshold, the current execution run is stopped, and the run is marked as *failed*. We would like to be notified of this type of failure scenario.

From the Workflow UI, click on the newly created workflow, **Production Monitoring Demo**, to reveal the details. Under the **Job notifications** section, click on the **Add metric thresholds** button to add a new run duration threshold. Let's add a maximum duration of 120 minutes to the maximum threshold. Click the **Save** button. Next, click on the + **Add notification** button to add a new notification. Expand the **Destination** drop-down menu to reveal the choices and select + **Add new system destination**. A new browser tab will open, presenting the workspace administration settings for your Databricks workspace. Under the **Notifications** section, click on the **Manage** button. Click the **Add destination** button. Select **Webhook** for the destination type, provide a meaningful name for the destination, enter the endpoint URL for which the notifications should be sent, and enter the username and password information if your endpoint uses basic HTTP authentication. Click the **Create** button to create the Webhook destination.

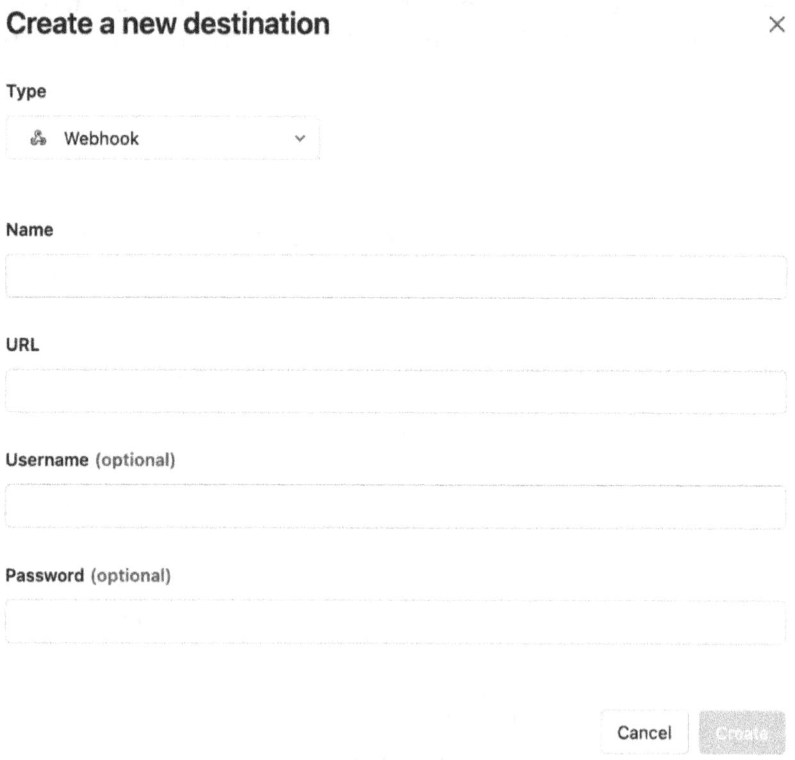

Figure 10.11 – Creating a new Webhook destination

Finally, click the **Save** button to finalize the metric threshold notification.

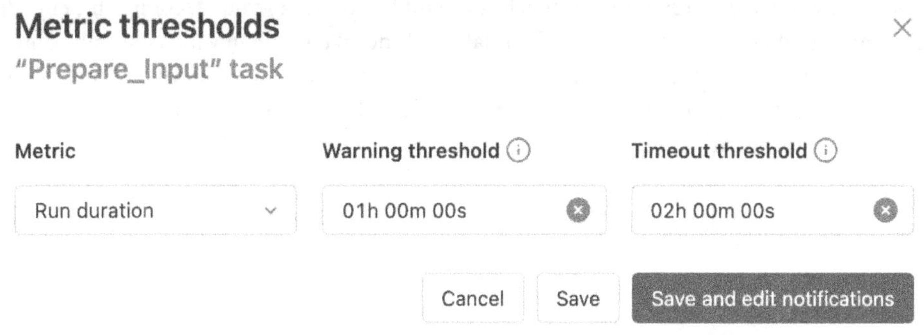

Figure 10.12 – Execution duration thresholds can be set on a workflow's tasks

Now that we've established a run duration threshold, whenever our workflow runs for longer than 120 minutes, our workflow will be stopped and a notification message with a status message of **Timed Out** will be sent to our HTTP webhook destination.

Congratulations! You've now automated the monitoring of your data pipelines in production, allowing your team to be automatically notified whenever failure conditions arise. This means that your teams can step in and correct data processing issues as soon as they happen and minimize potential downtime.

Summary

In this chapter, we covered several techniques for implementing pipeline and data quality observability so that data teams can react as soon as problems arise and thwart major downstream disruptions. One of the major keys to becoming a successful data team is being able to react to issues quickly. We saw how alert notifications are built into many aspects of the Databricks Data Intelligence Platform and how we can configure different types of alert destinations to send notifications when conditions are not met.

We covered monitoring capabilities built into the Databricks platform, such as the pipeline event log that makes it easy for pipeline owners to query the data pipeline's health, auditability, and performance, as well as data quality, in real time. We also saw how Lakehouse Monitoring is a robust and versatile feature that allows data teams to automatically monitor the statistical metrics of datasets and notify team members when thresholds have been crossed. We also covered techniques to evaluate data quality throughout the pipeline, preventing downstream errors and inaccuracies.

Lastly, we concluded the chapter with a real-world exercise for automatically alerting data teams in the event of a real and all-too-common problem – when a scheduled job runs for longer than expected.

Congratulations on reaching the end of this book! Thank you for taking this journey with me through each chapter. We've covered a lot of topics, but you should feel proud of your accomplishments thus far. By now, you should have a well-rounded foundation of the lakehouse on which you can continue to build. In fact, I hope that this book has filled you with inspiration to continue your lakehouse journey and to build modern data applications that do great things. I wish you the best of luck and encourage you to keep learning!

Index

packtpub.com

Subscribe to our online digital library for full access to over 7,000 books and videos, as well as industry leading tools to help you plan your personal development and advance your career. For more information, please visit our website.

Why subscribe?

- Spend less time learning and more time coding with practical eBooks and Videos from over 4,000 industry professionals
- Improve your learning with Skill Plans built especially for you
- Get a free eBook or video every month
- Fully searchable for easy access to vital information
- Copy and paste, print, and bookmark content

Did you know that Packt offers eBook versions of every book published, with PDF and ePub files available? You can upgrade to the eBook version at packtpub.com and as a print book customer, you are entitled to a discount on the eBook copy. Get in touch with us at customercare@packtpub.com for more details.

At www.packtpub.com, you can also read a collection of free technical articles, sign up for a range of free newsletters, and receive exclusive discounts and offers on Packt books and eBooks.

Other Books You May Enjoy

If you enjoyed this book, you may be interested in these other books by Packt:

Databricks Certified Associate Developer for Apache Spark Using Python

Saba Shah

ISBN: 978-1-80461-978-0

- Create and manipulate SQL queries in Spark
- Build complex Spark functions using Spark UDFs
- Architect big data apps with Spark fundamentals for optimal design
- Apply techniques to manipulate and optimize big data applications
- Build real-time or near-real-time applications using Spark Streaming
- Work with Apache Spark for machine learning applications

Machine Learning Security Principles

John Paul Mueller

ISBN: 978-1-80461-885-1

- Explore methods to detect and prevent illegal access to your system
- Implement detection techniques when access does occur
- Employ machine learning techniques to determine motivations
- Mitigate hacker access once security is breached
- Perform statistical measurement and behavior analysis
- Repair damage to your data and applications
- Use ethical data collection methods to reduce security risks

Packt is searching for authors like you

If you're interested in becoming an author for Packt, please visit authors.packtpub.com and apply today. We have worked with thousands of developers and tech professionals, just like you, to help them share their insight with the global tech community. You can make a general application, apply for a specific hot topic that we are recruiting an author for, or submit your own idea.

Share Your Thoughts

Now you've finished *Building Modern Data Applications Using Databricks Lakehouse*, we'd love to hear your thoughts! Scan the QR code below to go straight to the Amazon review page for this book and share your feedback or leave a review on the site that you purchased it from.

https://packt.link/r/1-801-07323-6

Your review is important to us and the tech community and will help us make sure we're delivering excellent quality content.

Download a free PDF copy of this book

Thanks for purchasing this book!

Do you like to read on the go but are unable to carry your print books everywhere?

Is your eBook purchase not compatible with the device of your choice?

Don't worry, now with every Packt book you get a DRM-free PDF version of that book at no cost.

Read anywhere, any place, on any device. Search, copy, and paste code from your favorite technical books directly into your application.

The perks don't stop there, you can get exclusive access to discounts, newsletters, and great free content in your inbox daily

Follow these simple steps to get the benefits:

1. Scan the QR code or visit the link below

https://packt.link/free-ebook/978-1-80107-323-3

2. Submit your proof of purchase
3. That's it! We'll send your free PDF and other benefits to your email directly

www.ingramcontent.com/pod-product-compliance
Lightning Source LLC
Chambersburg PA
CBHW080326030726
47593CB00010B/2899